W9-CBU-425

UNIVERSITY LIBRARIES
THE UNIVERSITY OF TEXAS
PRAESIDIUM
DISCIPLINA
CIVITATIS
AT BROWNSVILLE

THE FIGHT IS ON IN
T E X A S

THE FIGHT IS ON IN TEXAS

A History of African American Churches of Christ in the Lone Star State, 1865-2000

EDWARD J. ROBINSON

Abilene, Texas

The Fight is on in Texas

A History of African American Churches of Christ in the Lone Star State, 1865–2000

ISBN 978-0-89112-532-7 (cloth)
ISBN 978-0-89112-533-4 (paper)

Library of Congress Control Number: 2007942386

Printed in the United States of America

Cover design by Rick Gibson
Interior text design by Sandy Armstrong

For information contact:
Abilene Christian University Press
1648 Campus Court
Abilene, Texas 79601

1-877-816-4455 toll free
www.abilenechristianuniversitypress.com

To

Phyllis (Holt) Davis
and
Gus Farmer,

Christian scholars and mentors

And to the memory of:

G. P. Holt
(1923–2001)
and
Nokomis Yeldell
(1929–2007),

men of God who preached what they believed
and believed what they preached

CONTENTS

Preface 9

Prologue 11
The Fight Is on in Texas

Part I: From Disciples of Christ to Churches of Christ

Chapter 1 19
The Mother Church:
The Antioch Church of Christ in Midway, Texas

Chapter 2 27
"Texas Is a Hard Field":
Forgotten Trailblazers in African American Churches of Christ

Chapter 3 39
"A Natural Born Killer":
K. C. Thomas and the Rise of African American
Churches of Christ in Dallas

Part II: The Legacy of Marshall Keeble in Texas

Chapter 4 51
The Keeble Invasion:
Marshall Keeble's Evangelistic Endeavors in the Lone Star State

Chapter 5 67
"Nothing Can Overcome the Word of God":
Luke Miller and the Rise of African American
Churches of Christ in East Texas

Chapter 6 79
Out on the Firing Line:
L. H. Alexander, F. A. Livingston, and the Rise of African American
Churches of Christ in West Texas

Part III: The Legacy of G. P. Bowser in Texas

Chapter 7 89
Standing on Apostolic Ground: G. P. Bowser, the *Christian Echo*,
and the Division between African American Churches of Christ and
Disciples of Christ in Texas

Chapter 8 105
"A Fighter from the Heart": J. S. Winston and the Quest for Leadership in African American Churches of Christ in Texas

Chapter 9 119
"Just Want to Be the White Man's Brother": R. N. Hogan and the Race Problem in Churches of Christ

Part IV: The Education of Black Disciples of Christ and Black Churches of Christ in Texas

Chapter 10 137
The Booker T. Washington of Texas:
J. N. Ervin and the Jarvis Christian Institute Experience

Chapter 11 155
"A Young Moses Arose":
Jack Evans and the Legacy of Southwestern Christian College

Epilogue 173
"Hard-Fighting Soldiers":
African American Churches of Christ in Texas in the Twenty-First Century

Appendix I 177

Appendix II 179

Bibliography 209

Index 215

PREFACE

I grew up in the Border Street (now Seminary Heights) Church of Christ in Jacksonville, Texas. Luke Miller, a disciple of Marshall Keeble, established this congregation in 1940. Thus in some ways, I am a spiritual great grandson of Marshall Keeble.

In 1985 I enrolled in Southwestern Christian College (SWCC) in Terrell, Texas, where the following year I received the G. P. Bowser Preaching Award. At that time, I had no idea who Bowser was or how significant he was in the history of African American Churches of Christ. My matriculation at SWCC made me a spiritual descendant of Bowser. I happily and readily acknowledge my indirect connection to the Keeble–Bowser spiritual lineage.

In this book, I seek to tell their stories in the Texas context. As readers will discover, however, the story of African American Churches of Christ in Texas is more complex and much larger than Bowser and Keeble. Scores of devoted white and black men and women contributed to the rise of African American Churches of Christ in the Lone Star State. Consequently in sharing this fascinating story, I am simultaneously telling my own story.

While writing this book, I acquired many debts. Dr. Ervin Seamster, dynamic preacher for the Light of the World Church of Christ in Dallas, introduced me to Waydell Nixon, who subsequently turned me on to the history of the oldest African American Church of Christ in Texas—the Antioch Church of Christ in Midway. Mr. Nixon proved to be a living encyclopedia as he answered my questions about the origins of many black churches in Texas.

After much pestering and prodding, several congregations in Texas sent me historical sketches of their churches, including the Tudor Street Church of Christ in Paris, the Seminary Heights Church of Christ in Jacksonville, the North Tenth and Treadaway Church of Christ in Abilene, the Bryan Church of Christ in Bryan, the Eastside Church of Christ in Corsicana, the Cedar Crest Church of Christ in Dallas, the Lawrence and Marder Church of Christ in Dallas, the Marsalis Avenue Church of Christ in Dallas, the Eastland Church of Christ in Fort Worth, the Fifth Ward

Church of Christ in Houston, the East Cotton Street Church of Christ in Longview, the West Side Church of Christ in Marshall, Sterne Avenue Church of Christ in Palestine, Thomas Boulevard Church of Christ in Port Arthur, the Greenville Avenue Church of Christ, the Laurel Street Church of Christ in San Antonio, the Highway 80 Church of Christ in Big Spring, the Grand Avenue Church of Christ in Sherman, the Church of Christ on Martin Luther King Jr. Drive in Sulphur Springs, the North Tenneha Church of Christ in Tyler, and the Hood Street Church of Christ in Waco. These historical sketches contained invaluable information.

Special thanks to John L. Robinson, who read the entire manuscript and offered insightful suggestions, and to Don Haymes, an erudite librarian at Christian Theological Seminary in Indianapolis, Indiana, who helped me to see that an understanding of the theological tension between the Disciples of Christ and the Churches of Christ in Texas was impossible without knowledge of the *Christian Courier*. Special thanks also to my family: Toni, Clarice, Ashley, and Erika. Thanks to Cremmon Alexander, wife of the late L. H. Alexander, for taking time to sit for an interview. I offer commendations to the following people: Leonard Allen, Claude I. Andrews, Valanderous Bell, Doris Benitez, Norvie Cottingham Sr., Choice Dudley, Jack Evans Sr., Ben Foster, Doug Foster, Charles Fulbright Sr., Shelton T. W. Gibbs III, Gary Holloway, Rick Hunter, Betty J. McCalister, Kavian McMilion, Ian Nickerson, Joe Pouncy, Roscoe Rhodes Sr., Ruby Robinson, C. E. Shaw, Jerry Taylor, Nora Taylor, Willie Tucker, Joseph C. Walsh Jr., John C. Whitley, Dorothy Wiseman, and E. D. Wyrick.

I hope this work will spur others to fill in gaps that this book leaves behind by gathering materials to write their own congregational histories. How can we know where we're going if we don't know from whence we have come?

Edward J. Robinson

PROLOGUE

The Fight Is on in Texas

"There are but few loyal brethren out in this part of Texas; so you can see that the fight is on out West."[1] With this remark in 1916, John T. Ramsey, an African American evangelist from Tennessee, reported on his promising evangelistic work in the Lone Star State and reflected the feisty mentality that gripped the hearts and souls of black preachers in Churches of Christ. African American Churches of Christ mirrored this combative disposition in their sermons, writings, debates, and dealings with their religious neighbors who held different theological perspectives. As they waged this war against black Baptists, Methodists, Presbyterians, Catholics, Pentecostals, and others, they contested as well the biblical views and practices of their African American brethren among the Disciples of Christ (Christian Church).

Both Churches of Christ and Disciples of Christ descended from the nineteenth century religious reform effort termed the Restoration Movement. Although founder Alexander Campbell focused on Christian unity, by the early twentieth century the fellowship had divided over such issues as the use of instrumental music in worship and extra-congregational organizations. The theological and sociological tension between black non-instrumental "loyals" and "digressives" in the Restoration Movement lingered deep into the twentieth century.[2] Such black ministers as Marshall Keeble, G. P. Bowser, R. N. Hogan, and J. S. Winston, through their combative and courageous preaching, condemned other religious groups while transforming entire black Disciple congregations into Churches of Christ across Texas. This was "the fight" John T. Ramsey so eagerly joined.

African American Churches of Christ inherited the "fighting style" from their "loyal" white cohorts, especially the Churches of Christ that sprang up in the Lone Star State. One historian has noted that "Nowhere among Churches of Christ did the legalistic tradition more thoroughly join itself to the scolding style than in Texas. This is not to say that . . . Texas was altogether lacking grace-oriented leaders. My point here is simply that the Texas experience contributed to the hard, legalistic side of Churches of Christ in significant ways."[3] The rugged and rough environment, both geographic and social, of the Texas frontier fostered a combative mindset in white Churches of Christ toward other religious groups, and these reciprocated in turn. African American Churches of Christ in the state, often under the tutelage of white brethren, similarly imbibed and zealously advanced a contentious disposition when dealing with black denominations. The ingesting of the writings of white journals, such as the *Gospel Advocate* and the *Firm Foundation*, as well as their own periodicals, the *Christian Echo* and the *Christian Counselor*, prompted African American Christians to attack constantly and mercilessly those whom they deemed steeped in religious error.

While a few historians have written important histories of white Disciples of Christ and Churches of Christ in Texas, none has undertaken the task of chronicling the emergence of black Churches of Christ in the Lone Star State.[4] This work seeks to fill this void. It contends that the arduous labor of key black evangelists, aided by the unflagging generosity of white Christians, empowered the rise of African American Churches of Christ in Texas. Vesta Rea Melton, a black Christian woman in Houston, captures the essence of this current study in her 1949 report on the origins of an African American Church of Christ in Conroe, just north of Houston. Melton commented that "Through the help of God Almighty and the aid of the white disciples there, our courageous minister, Bro. Walter Weathers was permitted to lend them approximately 5 weeks of his precious time. During that time, 26 precious souls were baptized and 3 restored."[5] What held true for the black congregation in Conroe stood similarly true for other churches across Texas, as three factors contributed to the rise of African American Churches of Christ: divine assistance, the beneficence of white Christians, and the bold and untiring efforts of black preachers.

This study further argues that even though whites in Churches of Christ genuinely cared about the spiritual plight of their black neighbors, they scrupulously and rigidly adhered to the Jim Crow mandates requiring that they keep blacks out of their white congregations. As early as 1878, for example, white members of the Church of Christ in McKinney adamantly rejected a black Christian who sought membership in their congregation. Segregation thrived in Christian communities just as it did in the broader society. One scholar has argued that "long before the little signs—'White Only' and 'Colored'—appeared in the public utilities they had appeared in the church."[6] Some white leaders and members of Churches of Christ in Texas apparently esteemed the social customs of Jim Crow higher than the spiritual teachings of Jesus Christ.

This racism scarcely lessened during the advance of the twentieth century. By mid-century, while black ministers such as J. S. Winston regularly appealed to white believers to help launch a secondary school to train African American preachers, others such as R. N. Hogan accused Anglo Christians of supporting the predominantly black Southwestern Christian College in Terrell, Texas, to keep black students out of their own white schools. Fiery and racially sensitive preachers like Hogan fought what they perceived as the erroneous practices of black religionists while passionately and unabashedly contesting the views of racist whites in Churches of Christ.

A number of reasons warrant a study detailing the emergence of African American Churches of Christ in Texas. The 235 congregations in Texas count 28,216 members, more black adherents of Churches of Christ than in any other state in the Union. In addition Terrell remains the home of Southwestern Christian College, the only accredited college controlled by African Americans in Churches of Christ. This struggling yet significant institution, established in 1949, has produced many notable church leaders who themselves have contributed to the growth and development of Churches of Christ in Texas and the wider world. In another important context, the *Christian Echo*, a journal founded by G. P. Bowser in 1902, published reports during the 1940s and 1950s that open windows into the life of black Churches of Christ in Texas. Beyond this, two of the most influential black preachers in the history of Churches of Christ, Bowser and Marshall Keeble, left indelible marks and complex legacies in the Lone Star State. Thus when David Lipscomb observed in 1884 that "a Tennessean may always feel at home in Texas,"[7] he unwittingly presaged the evangelistic success that Bowser and Keeble, both from Tennessee, would enjoy in the Lone Star State.

Finally, blacks in Churches of Christ and their counterparts in the related Disciples of Christ had an ambiguous, tenuous, and often contentious relationship. Many black preachers, who later emerged as prominent leaders in Texas Churches of Christ, received academic and ministerial training at Jarvis Christian College, an all-black school in Hawkins, Texas, established by white Disciples of Christ in 1913. Paradoxically, many African American preachers in Churches of Christ, barred from the white schools of their own fellowship, received a cordial welcome from their black "digressive" brethren whom they constantly assailed. An analysis of the growth of black Churches of Christ in Texas must address these pivotal aspects of the black religious experience.

Any work on black Churches of Christ in Texas, however, faces important challenges. Because African American Churches of Christ, like their white counterparts, have insisted that they are merely New Testament Christians, they have often shrugged off any indebtedness to Barton W. Stone and Alexander Campbell.[8] This ignoring of their spiritual roots has influenced blacks in Churches of Christ to be poor record-keepers, operating from a sense of timelessness, feeling little obligation to locate themselves through record keeping. Few among them have compiled histories of their congregations, rendering it impossible to reproduce a historical sketch of all black Churches of Christ in Texas. Adding to this problem, the anti-institutional, congregational autonomy of African American Churches of Christ means that there exists no fellowship-wide collection of primary or secondary sources; with no central, denominational headquarters, Churches of Christ are deficient in record-gathering, archival capability. A study of African American Churches of Christ in Texas is further complicated by lack of a complete run of the *Christian Echo*. Despite these frustrating limitations, scattered but sufficient primary and secondary sources exist to undergird a credible work on this vibrant and complex religious group.

For purposes of clarity, this book is organized into four parts. The first division offers a historical overview of the oldest African American Church of Christ in Texas and assesses the pioneering work of four forgotten black preachers who toiled in the Lone Star State in the early twentieth century. The second examines the evangelistic labors of Marshall Keeble and a few of his spiritual sons, Luke Miller, L. H. Alexander, and F. A. Livingston, while part three explores the theology of G. P. Bowser and the educational and evangelistic work of two of his most influential protégés, J. S. Winston and R. N. Hogan, who contributed invaluably to the growth and expansion of black Churches of Christ in Texas. The final part illumines the interconnected educational pursuits among the black Disciples of Christ and black Churches of Christ.

This work responds also to the words of Abigail Adams to her husband, John Adams: "remember the ladies."[9] The research depends heavily on the records left by devoted, diligent, yet largely invisible women in African American Churches of Christ who faithfully and zealously contributed reports concerning the congregations they attended. More than reporters, however, these black sisters won souls, cooked meals, hosted gatherings, encouraged others, and served as agents for the *Christian Echo.* Their faithful testimonies, left behind in the pages of G. P. Bowser's paper, offer brief, yet unique glimpses into the inner workings of African American Churches of Christ in Texas.

A mixture of secondary and primary sources, such as the *Firm Foundation*, *Gospel Advocate*, and especially the *Christian Echo*, furnish the foundation of this work. The protagonists are the unsung black men and women whom white Christians supported morally and monetarily so that they might plant and stabilize black congregations across the state. This book seeks to help lift the veil of obscurity from the lives of these African American Christians who joined John T. Ramsey's "fight . . . out West" and who helped make black Churches of Christ in Texas what they are today.

PART I

From Disciples of Christ to Churches of Christ

Chapter 1

THE MOTHER CHURCH

The Antioch Church of Christ in Midway, Texas

And the disciples were called Christians first in Antioch.

—Acts 11:26

The Antioch Church of Christ in Midway, Texas, holds the distinction of being the oldest African American Church of Christ in the Lone Star State.[1] Founded in 1865 on a plantation in Madison County, the Antioch congregation took its name from a biblical city, reflecting its intent to imitate the teachings and practices of New Testament Christians. The larger religious community to which the Antioch congregation belonged was known variously as the Stone–Campbell Movement or the Restoration Movement. It emerged and flourished in the early nineteenth century on the North American frontier. Spearheaded by two zealous ministers, Barton W. Stone and Alexander Campbell, the Restoration Movement sought to unite all Christians on the teachings of the Bible alone.[2] From its inception, black slaves attached themselves to this religious reform movement, and they too endeavored to adhere rigidly to what they perceived to be the "pure gospel."[3] This principle clearly drove those African American Christians who founded the oldest black Church of Christ in Texas.

Origins of the Antioch Church of Christ

The origins of the Antioch Church of Christ remain somewhat nebulous, yet any clarification of the congregation's obscure history must begin with Patrick H. Hayes and his son Hugh L. Hayes. A native of Ireland, Patrick H. Hayes made his way to the United States and eventually to Texas in the 1830s. The 1850 census for Leon County (just north of Madison County), Texas, describes Hayes's family as consisting of his wife, Amanda, and four children: Malissa, James, Hugh, and Mary.[4] The Slave Schedule for the same year marked Hayes as owning thirty-two slaves.[5] A decade later Hayes, who had taken up residence in Madison County, owned just twenty slaves,[6] suggesting that he sold some of them, some absconded, some died, or a combination thereof. Regardless of the slaves' fate, Hayes remained a wealthy man, so much so that fifteen years after the end of slavery, he retained real estate property valued at $53,450 and a personal estate worth $66,800.[7]

Hugh L. Hayes, Patrick's second son, was born in 1848, and after the Civil War he attended Washington and Lee University under President Robert E. Lee. Hugh returned to Texas after falling in love with and marrying Susan Margaret Goree and assumed oversight of a seven thousand-acre estate, the Seven Oaks Plantation near Midway. Susan's father, Dr. Langston James Goree Sr., owned an eight hundred-acre plantation in Survey of Madison County. Dr. Goree, a practitioner of botanic medicine, immigrated from the Southeast in 1840.[8]

The several good works on slavery and Reconstruction in Texas fail to mention the Hayes plantation,[9] leaving us with no clear view into the inner workings of slave life in Madison County, Texas. However, the testimony of black bondsmen who lived in or near Midway offers us a glimpse into slave life in Southeast Texas, although the tenability of such testimony may be questioned. Soul Williams, who came to Texas from Mississippi, later reported living in comfortable slave quarters, working under bearable conditions, and eating plenty of food. "My master had a good home and he always had good quarters for his slaves. Our quarters were long and in one corner we had one post that was a rail for our bed, covered with sheep skin or cow hide with straw throwed over that for us to sleep on. I never did any work until I was freed. I'se always stayed around the house and drove my master where he wanted to go or saddled his horse for him. No sir, I never did have any money. Sometime the master would give me five or ten cents and I would spend that for candy."

Williams noted that he and other slaves in nearby Leon County had plenty of food to eat."We had beef, pork and plenty good old grated corn bread. I cooked in [an] old time skillet and we fried bacon on an old flat iron or platter, they are called now. The negroes that had families were issued grub, they cooked at home on the rock fireplace. Yessir, boss, our master catch big old fat coon or possum and have old mammy to cook them with potatoes around they."[10] Like Williams, Charles Sandles, a native of Tennessee who came to Texas in 1865, testified that his owner, Tom Lynch, fed his slaves plentifully. He further noted that his owner refused to teach his slaves to read or write, but he always made them go to church. "Maser read the Bible to us every Sunday morning and taught us to always tell the truth no matter who it hurt as he was an awfully religious man."[11]

What was true for Charles Sandles's owner seemed to hold true for Hugh L. Hayes. According to F. F. Carson, a native of Madison County and noteworthy black evangelist in Churches of Christ, Hayes was affiliated with the Stone–Campbell Movement, and he helped establish the Antioch Church of Christ in Midway. Hayes owned Carson's paternal great grandfather, Anthony Carson, also a member of Churches of Christ. "During the days of slavery my great grandfather, Ant[h]ony Carson, worked for the Hugh Hayes family (white), who were members of the church of Christ. After my great grandfather was freed Brother Hayes established the Antioch church of Christ."[12] That Hayes helped launch the first black Church of Christ in the Lone Star State suggests his commitment to the principles of the Stone–Campbell Movement as well as his realization that after the abolition of slavery African Americans wanted to control their own destinies and their own institutions.

The Gift of the Antioch Church of Christ

Mack Allen Bailey

The Antioch Church of Christ not only enjoys the distinction of being the oldest black congregation among Churches of Christ in Texas, but it has also produced a number of black ministers. These men traversed the Lone Star State and other parts of the country and world, making impressive contributions to the growth and expansion of this Christian body. Among the first black preachers emerging from the Hayes plantation was Mack Allen Bailey (1869–1943), whose father, Jeffery Bailey, was owned by Patrick and Hugh Hayes. At age nineteen, Mack married Addie Wheaton; their union produced eleven children. Bi-vocational, Mack both preached and farmed. As a minister, he regularly walked or rode a horse to spread the gospel. Through his preaching efforts, he planted a Church of Christ in Riverside, Texas. As a successful farmer, he accumulated 120 acres of land, and this prosperity enabled him to send three of his children, Patsy, Pearly, and Daniel, to predominantly black schools in Texas. Daniel attended Jarvis Christian College in Hawkins and Mary Allen College in Crockett, finally earning a BS degree from Paul Quinn College in Waco and teaching for over thirty years in public schools in Madison and Tarrant counties.[13]

Jessie Warrick

One of Mack Allen Bailey's converts was Jessie Warrick. After his conversion to Churches of Christ and his marriage to Bula Richard in 1922, Warrick helped establish congregations in Coleman, Brownwood, and Fort Stockton, Texas. In the early 1940s, he relocated to California and founded Churches of Christ in Richmond and Stockton.[14]

William M. Childress

William M. Childress (1877–1927), another descendant of Hayes plantation slaves, was born to Jim and Fannie Neal Childress. After entering the ministry at an early age, Chlidress soon became one of the pioneer black preachers in Churches of Christ, helping start and stabilize fledgling congregations in Dallas, Houston, Palestine, Jacksonville, Lyons, and Jasper. One chronicler of his life noted: "As he traveled about, he would knock on doors of people's homes and as soon [as] he would tell them that he was a Church of Christ preacher, they would shut the door in his face." This statement reveals the antipathy some people held toward members of the Stone–Campbell Movement. Childress passed away on August 12, 1927 after preaching in Jasper.[15]

F. F. Carson

Francis Frank Carson (1909–1987), one of the most influential preachers to rise from the Antioch congregation, was born in Midway. He converted to Churches of Christ at age fourteen under the passionate evangelistic ministry of William M. Childress. In 1926 Carson enrolled in Jarvis Christian College and completed his high school work and a year of college courses. Four years later Carson, after studying at the all-black school in East Texas, concluded that the Disciples of Christ and Churches of Christ were one group. "I got on the wrong side of the fence, thinking that the Christian Church and church of Christ were the same," Carson wrote in hindsight, "but when I went home, yes, when I went home—you know the rest." After matriculating from the black school in East Texas, Carson returned to rural Midway before relocating to urban Dallas. There he discovered substantial differences between the Disciples of Christ and the Churches of Christ, and thus aligned himself with the latter group. While living and working in Dallas, Carson says he "found the North Dallas Church of Christ and was restored by Brother K. C. Thomas. There I received the inspiration to preach."[16]

Upon entering the preaching field, Carson ministered for a few years in Atoka, Oklahoma, and Wichita, Kansas. In the early 1940s, he began preaching in Ennis, Texas, before moving to Richmond, California, where he accomplished his most impressive and lasting work. While ministering to the Southside Church of Christ in Richmond, he erected an elaborate church building and appointed elders and deacons. While building up the Southside Church of Christ, Carson found time to establish a new congregation in Vallejo and help stabilize churches in Linden, Oakland, Madera, and Sacramento, California. Additionally, he and his Southside flock in Richmond sponsored a Nigerian student, Isong Ibokete, through Pepperdine College and supported missionary Tom Tune in Hong Kong as well as a preacher in Korea. Carson also traveled to Nigeria to evangelize there.[17]

J. S. Winston, who first met Carson in Dallas in 1938, developed a cordial and enduring relationship with the evangelist from Midway. Winston never forgot the kindness Carson showed him when his wife, Mizetta, became seriously ill and eventually passed away in 1986.[18] "During the serious illness of my late wife, without my asking, he sent to me $1,000.00," Winston wrote of Carson, "and later encouraged the Church [in Richmond] to send me financial assistance. F. F. Carson, was a kind and generous man, he not only helped me and my family, but he was considerate of everyone. He truly was my dear brother and true friend."[19] The preacher from an ordinary Southeast Texas community accomplished extraordinary things, profoundly impacting the lives of many people around the globe.

The Nixon–Baccus Family

Other Midway natives apart from F. F. Carson also furthered the expansion efforts of black Churches of Christ. The Nixon family had ties to the Antioch Church of Christ. Edward Nixon and his wife, Giley Childress Nixon, were parents of Declara Nixon Bailey, Edna Nixon Baccus, Hollins, Kermit, and Walter Nixon. Kermit, after soldiering in World War II, preached several years in Gladewater, Texas. Walter T. Nixon, born in Midway in 1910, ministered to congregations in Madisonville and Lovelady, Texas. One of his sons, Waydell, preached several years for the Cedar Crest Church of Christ in Dallas, before assuming the pulpit of a black flock in Ennis, Texas.[20] Edna Nixon Bailey, after relocating from Midway to Dallas, helped strengthen the oldest black Church of Christ there. She and her husband had seven children—six daughters, all of whom became educators, and one son, Carl C. Baccus, who went on to a stellar preaching career in southern California. Through his lively and fiery preaching and the melodious singing of Finos Graves, James Ashurst, and Willie Norwood, the Southside Church of Christ in Los Angeles grew from a small offshoot of the Figueroa congregation in 1956 to a membership of 1,800 over a forty-year period.[21]

German McGilbra

German McGilbra (1909–1972), yet another black preacher, emanated from the Antioch congregation. After his education in the Madison County public schools and in the Nashville Christian Institute, a Nashville, Tennessee, school for black youth in Churches of Christ, McGilbra married Ola Nash. In the early 1940s, McGilbra established what is now the Dallas West Church of Christ, a congregation that continues to thrive.[22]

These examples underscore the extraordinary role played by the small and obscure Antioch Church of Christ in Midway, Texas, in the origins, growth, and expansion of African American Churches of Christ not only in the Lone Star State, but also in other parts of the nation and the world. The Antioch Church of Christ not only holds its distinction as the oldest independent black church in Texas, but it also deserves credit and recognition for producing numerous preachers[23] who exerted exceptional influence far beyond the small hamlets of central Texas. The history of African American Churches of Christ in Texas, in a significant sense, began "first in Antioch."

From Disciples of Christ to Churches of Christ

Additionally, from 1865 to 1920, scores of blacks in the Stone–Campbell Movement in Texas slowly transitioned from pro-instrumental and pro-missionary Disciples of Christ or Christian Churches to anti-instrumental and anti-missionary Churches of Christ. It remains unclear who served as the principal leaders of this spiritual and theological transition. According to Declara Nixon Bailey, a member of the Antioch Church of Christ, I. Q. Cooper came to Midway, Texas, in 1904 and "began teaching them that the Christian Church was wrong and that the Church of Christ was the only church." Cooper, although a well-versed Bible teacher, did not practice what he taught; he married a woman in Midway when he already had a wife. Bailey reported that Cooper's first wife sued him. Cooper, attempting to fight his case without a lawyer, lost and was sent to prison in Huntsville. The day he was released, according to Bailey, "he walked out the prison door and dropped dead."[24]

It is also likely that Austin McGary, a white Church of Christ leader, was partly responsible for widening the gap between the Disciples of Christ and Churches of Christ. Born in Huntsville in 1846, McGary grew up in a Methodist Church and was educated in the McKenzie Institute in Clarksville. In 1862, he joined the Huntsville "Grays" and served in the Civil War along the Texas–Louisiana coasts. After the war, McGary returned to Madison County and worked as a sheriff. An opponent of the Ku Klux Klan at Willis, he served as a conveying agent for the Texas state penitentiary. In the early 1880s, McGary, after encouragement from his sister J. W. Gillespie, turned to religion and received baptism at the hands of Harry Hamilton. In 1884 McGary established the *Firm Foundation*, a journal that argued that people who had not been baptized "for the remission of sins" should be re-baptized.[25] While McGary's periodical exerted considerable influence on the theological formation of black Churches of Christ in Texas, the *Gospel Advocate*, a Tennessee periodical, proved to have the greatest impact on white and black Churches of Christ in the Lone Star State. Forgotten black pathfinders such as John T. Ramsey brought the latter journal from Tennessee to Texas and shaped the minds of black Christians who identified with Churches of Christ.

Any understanding of the origins of black Churches of Christ in Texas, however, must begin with the Antioch Church of Christ in Midway. From this congregation emerged many dedicated men and women who planted, strengthened, and stabilized churches not only in the Lone Star State but well beyond. The Antioch congregation nurtured such young men as F. F. Carson who, after matriculating at Jarvis Christian College, ministered effectively in California and Africa.

Chapter 2

"TEXAS IS A HARD FIELD"

Forgotten Trailblazers in African American Churches of Christ

Texas is a great field,
but it has not been taught.

—Samuel Robert Cassius (1928)

When black ministerial trailblazers crossed over into the Lone Star State in the early twentieth century, they entered a land marked by a harsh legacy of physical brutality, political inequity, racial discrimination, social injustice, and mob-enforced white supremacy. Such a perilous environment forced caution upon black trailblazers who navigated the treacherous waters of Jim Crow Texas. In 1881, a local rancher shot and killed a black soldier in San Angelo, heightening racial animosity in the West Texas town.[1] Twelve years later some fifteen thousand white spectators in Paris, Texas, watched the burning of Henry Smith, a black resident accused of raping and murdering a five-year old white girl. In 1906, after the Army posted three black infantry companies to Brownsville, Texas, Lon Evans claimed that a black soldier tried to rape her. Evans's husband passed on the information to Maj. Charles Penrose, warning that his men would be murdered in the streets unless the culprit was handed over to civil authorities, and Major Penrose quickly revoked all passes and confined his soldiers to the military post.[2]

At midnight, ten to twenty night-riders went on a ten-minute shooting fray, firing several rounds of ammunition into public buildings and private homes in downtown Brownsville, killing a Hispanic bartender and wounding a police officer whose arm had to be amputated. Mayor

Frederick J. Combe immediately accused black soldiers of shooting up the town. Accepting these accusations without investigation, the Army's inspector general recommended that all three companies be discharged without honor. Pres. Theodore Roosevelt endorsed the decision and ignited a national uproar as irate blacks and impartial whites denounced the verdict. The Brownsville Incident left a bitter and lasting legacy in Texas, as white officers questioned the character and capability of black soldiers, and black civilians distrusted the U. S. Army's ability to guarantee racial and social justice for all soldiers.[3]

In 1915, five thousand furious white residents of Temple stormed the courthouse, seized Will Stanley, and dragged him to the public square where they burned him to death. Stanley allegedly beat to death a Mr. and Mrs. Grimes and three of their six children. The following year, a mentally-challenged black teenager, Jessie Washington, was lynched in Waco for raping a white woman, Lucy Fryer. After Washington's charred corpse was displayed publicly for several days, a horseman lassoed and dragged it through Waco's streets until the skull broke away from the rest of the body.[4]

In 1917 the city of Houston counted a population of 130,000 people, 30,000 of them African Americans. Like many of cities in the Jim Crow South, Houston was rigidly segregated and blatantly anti-black. Its city council purchased one hundred acres of land for public parks, but designated none for African Americans. Houston's blacks participated in general elections only if they paid the required state poll tax of $1.50 each year. In this racially charged milieu, Houston's white citizens viewed black soldiers of the Twenty-Fourth Infantry as a threat to racial harmony and taunted them, precipitating a race riot that resulted in the deaths of seventeen whites. The U. S. Army, after a farce trial, hanged black soldiers.[5]

Adding fuel to the fires of racist violence, the second Ku Klux Klan sprang to virulent life in 1920. Unlike the first Klan of Reconstruction, which was essentially anti-black, the second Klan, born in Stone Mountain, Georgia, in 1915, added Jews and Catholics to the hate list. Since, however, neither Jews nor Catholics could be identified by skin color, blacks still bore the brunt of the Klan's violence. Comprised of whites from all backgrounds, including ministers, politicians, and businessmen, the second Klan labored beneath the banner of "100 percent Americanism," posing as a "law and order" organization. While the reborn KKK whipped and tarred and feathered white abortionists, bootleggers, child molesters, gamblers, pimps, wayward wives and husbands, it directed most of its vituperation toward blacks. In the early 1920s, among its other atrocities, the Klan whipped and burned the letters "KKK" into the forehead of a black Dallas bellboy for flirting with a white woman, and hooded whites in Houston castrated a black dentist for associating with white women.[6]

Political inequity accompanied racial violence in the Lone Star State. In 1923 the Texas State Legislature passed a law excluding African Americans from the Democratic Party primary and ordering election officials to toss out their votes. The next year Dr. Lawrence A. Nixon, a black dentist in El Paso, attempted to cast his ballot but was denied. From 1900 to 1940, black Texans, in the words of one scholar, were "outsiders."[7] African American preachers in Churches of Christ, acutely aware of such racial hostility, recognized that their safety depended on their compliance with the statutes of segregation, written and unwritten. No small wonder then that Marshall Keeble, the most effective black preacher in Churches of Christ, refused to baptize white men or, especially, women when evangelizing in the Jim Crow South. After six white women responded to Keeble's preaching in Chattanooga, Tennessee, he noted that "I always have some of the white brethren to take their confession."[8] Keeble continued the precautions he practiced in the Volunteer State when he went farther west. Black ministers, whether Keeble or his lesser known colleagues, who entered the state of Texas in the early twentieth century dared not contest the social, racial, and political injustices that permeated the state. Lynch law ensured their compliance. So they came to advance the "pure gospel," not challenge the cultural status quo. This chapter explores the evangelistic endeavors of three of these forgotten black trailblazers.

John T. Ramsey

Tennessee native John T. Ramsey, among the first permanent black evangelists to labor in Texas, first entered the state in 1913. He later claimed to have been the first black preacher in Churches of Christ at Mount Calm in South Texas. Even though inclement weather caused him to abort his gospel meeting there, Ramsey confidently believed his sermons would yield future results. "On the day I left Mount Calm for Dallas, some Baptist people came to see me off. They asked: 'If we become members of the church of Christ, will you visit us monthly?'"[9] Ramsey carefully crafted his preaching to lead Baptists, Methodists, and Pentecostals out of their traditions into Churches of Christ.

While evangelizing among black Texans in the Mount Calm community, Ramsey thanked white believers W. H. Nelson and J. E. Goodloe for their support and generosity. "Brother Nelson asked that I come to Mount Calm and hold a meeting for the colored people, and said that they would do all they could for me and the people." Afterward Ramsey could "cheerfully say that the meeting was abundantly supported by the white church." White Christians' support of black evangelists empowered the rise of African American Churches of Christ in Texas. This pattern of white-to-black philanthropy, always situated carefully within Jim Crow parameters, originated in Texas during Ramsey's tenure there. Ramsey himself asked: "Why not all the white churches take up a work of that kind? Help the poor colored people; it is your duty."[10]

Ramsey, however, devoted most of his time gathering black believers in the city of Dallas. In 1916 Ramsey described his struggles as a black preacher in the Lone Star State. "I have been just as busy as I used to be in Tennessee and Kentucky. I did not have time to write much; I had to work, and work hard." Ramsey lamented that there were only a "few loyal brethren out in this part of Texas; so you can see that the fight is on out West." During the course of the previous year, Ramsey reported preaching 103 sermons and baptizing forty-six people, eighteen of whom joined a congregation in Dallas. "Most of my work was in destitute places," Ramsey wrote. "But all that know me and of my work know that I preach daily, except when I am going from place to place."[11]

While toiling as an itinerant preacher in Texas, Ramsey fluctuated between emotions of optimism and pessimism. On the one hand, Ramsey's spirit lifted when the *Gospel Advocate* arrived at his house. "I rejoice when the day comes for my *Gospel Advocate*. I am never too busy to read it." Established in 1855 by Tolbert Fanning and David Lipscomb, the Nashville periodical extended its impact far beyond Tennessee; it simultaneously kept Ramsey "up with all my brethren and their work" and informed readers of Ramsey's activities in Texas. On the other hand, Ramsey sorrowed that some white believers in Dallas showed virtually no concern over the spiritual plight of African Americans. "Texas is a hard field in which to work among my people," Ramsey wrote, "and the white brethren in this city seem to care very little for the colored people. Not one cent has been given to me from the Dallas brethren for this work, and this is a shame." Ramsey firmly believed that white Churches of Christ possessed the financial and numerical capacity to finance his mission work in Texas. "Five or ten dollars monthly would be a great help in this hard struggle. Will some good brother or sister or church help me to raise this amount each month? This is a small sum for so many strong churches of Christ."[12]

In 1917 Ramsey, after spending four years in Dallas, announced plans to sink permanent roots there. "I have fully decided to make Dallas my home. Notwithstanding this, all who know me fully know that I will go where duty demands, regardless of personal preference." He revealed further that from his Dallas base he would include visits to Missouri, Ohio, Arkansas, Mississippi, Alabama, and Illinois in his preaching efforts. Ramsey doubtlessly planned these excursions to preach and to solicit support for his evangelistic work in Texas.[13] Later that year Ramsey again depicted challenges he faced in Dallas. Even though he successfully gathered thirty-five or more saints, he noted that they had scattered, concluding that since his flock had "no meetinghouse in which to worship, many went to other places, and for that it has been a little hard on me to do all that I wanted to do or could do. However, we have a little band yet who are willing to live as the Book directs; and if I had the help that is needed, it would only be a matter of time till we would have a great church among my people in this wicked city."[14]

A visit from T. B. Larimore, a venerable white minister from Tennessee, boosted Ramsey and Churches of Christ in Dallas. "Since Brother and Sister Larimore's visit to our city," Ramsey wrote, "I have been made to realize the need of greater work in Dallas. Their visit made us all better." White members of the Pearl and Bryan Church of Christ convened "a meeting with the other congregations of the city and have decided to take up the needs of my work among my people. This is due to Brother and Sister Larimore's visit to Dallas." The Larimores endorsed Ramsey's work and character when he preached in Tennessee, and "These words caused the brethren to decide at once." Emboldened and encouraged by the renewed interest of white leaders in Dallas, Ramsey announced that "I feel that it will be only as short time now until we shall have a meetinghouse of our own; we hope to take Dallas for Christ."[15] Ramsey, like other black preachers in Churches of Christ, understood that without white support, the prognosis for black evangelism appeared bleak.

In 1918 Ramsey joined the brotherhood of Churches of Christ in lamenting the death of David Lipscomb. Ramsey particularly singled out the impact Lipscomb and his periodical, the *Gospel Advocate*, had on his life. "I have been a reader of *Gospel Advocate* for about fifteen years, and I am safe in saying that it has made me to-day what I am—the writings from such men as D. Lipscomb, T. B. Larimore, E. A. Elam, E. G.

Sewell, A. B. Lipscomb, J. C. McQuiddy, M. C. Kurfees, H. Leo Boles, F. W. Smith, and other great men whom I shall not mention for lack of space." Ramsey's testimony demonstrates the influence white editors of the *Gospel Advocate* had in shaping the theology of African American Churches of Christ. "I can truly say," added Ramsey, "that the *Gospel Advocate* is the best and safest paper among the brotherhood to-day, and we cannot do without it." Such endorsements corroborate Stephen D. Eckstein Jr.'s observation that "the *Gospel Advocate* exerted the greatest influence in molding church opinion in the Lone Star State against the missionary society and organ."[16] The *Gospel Advocate* familiarized black Churches of Christ with the two theological factors that distinguished them from the Disciples of Christ.

In March of 1918 Ramsey expressed more excitement and enthusiasm about remaining in the Dallas area. With a membership of almost twenty in his congregation, he hoped to secure a "good, comfortable house" in which to worship. Ramsey further noted that Dallas, with a population of 2,500 black residents, was a "splendid place to live." The citywide meeting conducted by T. B. Larimore and a small monetary contribution from the Larimores gave Ramsey "a greater desire to continue the work in Dallas." But Ramsey made it clear he did not plan to remain permanently in the city. "I only want to stay in Dallas long enough to put the work in order as it should be."[17]

The next year John A. Howland, minister for the Spring Street Church of Christ, invited Ramsey to preach in a protracted meeting in Murfreesboro, Tennessee. Ramsey's messages generated baptisms daily, including an eighty-two-year-old man. Howland praised Ramsey as one who "knows just how to preach the word in the way that all can understand. He does not fail to declare the whole counsel of God, but he preaches it in the spirit of meekness." Howland made clear his intent to keep Ramsey permanently in Tennessee. "It is being reported that there will be a chance to get Brother Ramsey back to Tennessee to stay. Should this be true, I am sure that the faithful churches in Tennessee will take hold with Brother Ramsey and work as never before."[18]

By 1920, however, Ramsey had relocated from Dallas to Beaumont, Texas. While evangelizing there, Ramsey held an eight-day meeting for the Mitchell Chapel Church of Christ, baptized six people, and restored one to a faithful life. Among those baptized was John Mitchell, an eighty-five-year-old man and the first black resident to settle the area. Ramsey added that Mitchell "gave the lot, many years ago, on which the meetinghouse now stands. I found a loyal band of Christians here, and they are willing to do all they can to help make Texas what it should be."[19] In May of 1920 Ramsey reported preaching the gospel in Beaumont "to a people that never heard it before. I am glad to be engaged in such a work." He expressed his "heartiest thanks" to a Brother Forrest and the white congregation of that city for their support. Writing during the aftermath of World War I, Ramsey affirmed that the gospel was the solution to world peace. "The world seems to be upset since the great world war. We are trying to make peace with all nations, but this can only be done by preaching the gospel to them." In order to advance the Word of God among all nations, Ramsey pleaded with his supporters to help him purchase a $300 tent. "We have but few houses in this part of the country (Southeast Texas), and for that reason a tent is badly needed. . . . I can do a great work in this part of the State with a tent."[20]

Details of Ramsey's departure from the state of Texas and of his death remain unclear. Plainly, however, Ramsey stands among the first black pioneer preachers to labor consistently in Texas. Yet while Ramsey failed to leave behind a viable black congregation, he did plant some of the first seeds for African American Churches of Christ in the state. Ramsey's evangelistic activity presaged the struggles black evangelists would encounter when toiling in Texas, foreshadowed African American preachers' reliance on white benevolence, and revealed that white journalists played a key role for the theological formation of black Churches of Christ in Texas. More significantly, Ramsey brought to Texas the theological perspective of the *Gospel Advocate*, which helped transform black Disciples of Christ into black Churches of Christ.

Samuel Robert Cassius

But Ramsey was not the only black preacher to labor in the Lone Star State in the early twentieth century. Samuel Robert Cassius, a former slave from Virginia, converted to the Stone–Campbell Movement in 1883 and soon after began his preaching career. Cassius entered the Oklahoma Territory in 1891, serving as an evangelist, farmer, educator, politician, author, and "race man." Altogether Cassius spent thirty-one years in Oklahoma, the so-called black man's "paradise." Cassius refused to be a stationary preacher, however, traveling widely through North America and Canada.[21]

Cassius sojourned at times in the state of Texas. In the summer of 1915, the Oklahoma evangelist informed *Gospel Advocate* readers that he

Samuel Robert Cassius (1853-1931), a former slave from Virginia, converted to the Stone-Campbell Movement in the 1880s and emerged as a reputable black leader in Churches of Christ in the 1890s. Cassius did evangelistic work in Texas as early as 1915.

(Courtesy of Disciples of Christ Historical Society, Nashville, Tennessee)

entered the Lone Star State after a "small, young, struggling congregation" in Bryan, Ohio, sent him money to cover his expenses. Upon arriving in the Texas capital, he found a large black population but no African American Church of Christ. "Texas is the largest State in the Union, and Austin, its capital, has the largest dark-skinned population of any city in the Southwest. Every kind of religion and every kind of vice known to man's imagination is here, but there is no church of Christ among my people, either 'digressive' or 'loyal.'" Cassius planned to remain in Austin for three weeks to plant a congregation, yet he confessed that his success there depended largely on the support of white leaders, G. H. P. Showalter and S. A. Enochs. "I feel sure that I have in Brother Showalter, of the *Firm Foundation*, a strong-supporter and an able friend," Cassius wrote, "as I believe I have, also, in the church of Christ in this city (I mean the white brethren). I have found in Brother S. A. Enochs, although he is a white man and a poor man, a true yokefellow of my people. It is through him that I am here in this work, and it is to vindicate his judgment that I am going to give the very best effort of my life."[22] White leaders entrusted African American evangelists with the preaching of the "pure gospel" to their black neighbors, even as black preachers such as Cassius relied on white Christians to support them.

A few months after his Austin trip, Cassius disclosed that white believers in Bryan, Ohio, again enabled him to visit Texas by sending him a $20 check. "My place is out on the forefront of the evangelization of my people," Cassius testified, "therefore I have resolved to face my duty as I see it in God's word." Driven by this sense of divine obligation and empowered by a spirit of white generosity, Cassius vowed to continue his work in the Texas capital city, "if the brethren in Austin will do as they have agreed and provide me a place to hold the meeting." He then praised the *Gospel Advocate* for generating interest from white Christians in the North. "It was through the *Gospel Advocate* that the attention of the church at Bryan was attracted toward my work. Thus, step by step, the loyal press of our church is arousing an interest in the greatest work of the twentieth century."[23] Even though Cassius failed to establish a black congregation in Austin, his reports reveal that some white Christians from the North reached across racial and regional lines to assist black evangelists in the South.

Cassius revisited Texas again in 1928 when white minister W. D. Campbell invited him to Fort Worth. "Brethren, I am out here in Texas, where there are a great many colored people and plenty of churches, societies and every known brand of religion in the world. To speak more plainly, I am in Fort Worth, and if there were more gospel preachers like Elder W. D. Campbell, there would be no need to write this letter."[24] Cassius's preaching yielded no visible results, but it "put new life into that little band of colored disciples."[25]

T. H. Merchant

The small group of black Christians Cassius encountered in Fort Worth was likely the little flock T. H. Merchant had gathered a few years earlier. A native of Hope, Arkansas, the black preacher came to Fort Worth at the behest of white Christians there. After a black man, a former Methodist, responded to Horace W. Busby's gospel message, white believers in the Fort Worth area recognized their spiritual obligation to African Americans. "This event," reported Frank L. Cox, "brought to the minds of many disciples of Fort Worth a deeper realization of our responsibility to the colored people of our city. About twenty thousand colored people live here, and the outstanding fact is that there is not a New Testament church among them." Convinced that they had "neglected a people at our very doors," three white congregations—the Polytechnic, Highland Park, and Glenwood Churches of Christ—collaborated in launching "a movement whereby the colored people of this city may hear and accept the gospel." To help them meet this obligation to evangelize African Americans in Fort Worth, the three churches brought in T. H. Merchant, a black evangelist from Longview.[26]

White leaders deemed Merchant a trustworthy and a competent minister. "He is clean and able," said Cox. "His experience as a preacher qualifies him in a special way." Elders of the Glenwood congregations agreed to oversee Merchant's evangelistic activity. "By mutual agreement the elders of Glenwood will supervise the work." After relocating from Longview to Fort Worth in the winter of 1924, Merchant planned to "stay until the cause of Christ is firmly established among the colored people. We expect to stand behind the work in a financial way until it is self-supporting."[27] Cox's report, like those of Cassius, reconfirms the white beneficence in empowering the emergence of African American Churches of Christ in Texas.

A year later Merchant announced to his *Gospel Advocate* audience that when he had arrived in Fort Worth on March 3, 1924, the city had no black Church of Christ, but he succeeded in establishing one. "When I began," announced Merchant, "we had no congregation; now we have a regular place of meeting, with eleven members. Eight of these meet regularly, one is off attending school, and two are inactive because of age, being seventy-one and seventy-two years of age, and one of them having also lost his eyesight." He added that "The church is helping to care for them. They are worthy of all we do for them."[28] The African American congregation Merchant planted in Fort Worth continues as the Allen Avenue Church of Christ.

While focusing his energy and attention on the work in Fort Worth, Merchant also found time to evangelize in the growing city of Houston. "I held a very good meeting in Houston, this being the first time the gospel of Christ was ever preached to the colored people in that great city of over one hundred and sixty thousand souls." Merchant, although reporting no baptisms, felt certain that "some good was done." He gladly reported, "The four white churches of Christ helped mightily in the meeting, and paid me well for my services in preaching the gospel to my race."[29]

After gathering the flock in Fort Worth, Merchant filled the pulpit of a fledgling black congregation in Marshall, Texas, planted by black evangelist G. P. Bowser in 1928. Merchant, assuming oversight of what is now the West Side Church of Christ,[30] continued his evangelistic work in other Texas cities as well as in other southern states. In the mid 1930s, his extensive travels encompassed Quanah[31] and Elrod, Texas, and Jackson, Mississippi.[32] In Haynesville, Louisiana, as he preached among black southerners, Merchant withstood unpleasant weather and competition from a Freewill Baptist meeting to baptize four Baptists and two Methodists, with the aid of white co-religionists.[33] In 1939 Merchant's preaching tour carried him as far as Guthrie, Oklahoma,[34] and three years later he divided his time between congregations in Marshall and Kilgore, Texas.[35] Even though Merchant worked in areas beyond Texas, he made perhaps his greatest contribution to African American Churches of Christ in Texas by stabilizing them.

John T. Ramsey, Samuel Robert Cassius, and T. H. Merchant exemplified the many black seed planters and pathfinders in Texas in the early twentieth century. Their evangelistic work paved the way for other African American evangelists, and to Merchant, particularly, belongs the credit for establishing the first black Church of Christ in one of the state's largest cities, Fort Worth; from this small beginning sprang several black congregations in the city. The emergence of African American Churches of Christ in nearby Dallas, however, stemmed from the efforts of an obscure, yet pivotal black figure named K. C. Thomas, the subject of the next chapter.

Chapter 3

"A Natural Born Killer"

K. C. Thomas and the Rise of African American Churches of Christ in Dallas

A time to kill,
and a time to heal.

—Ecclesiastes 3:3

As T. H. Merchant led in the founding of black Churches of Christ in Fort Worth, K. C. Thomas drove the emergence of African American congregations in Dallas. We know little of Thomas's life before he surfaced in Church of Christ journals in the early 1920s. By 1921 he had taken up residence in Guthrie, Oklahoma, to help Samuel Robert Cassius, a black preacher and resident of that community, to build up a congregation there. Cassius wrote: "Not that Bro. Thomas is not an able preacher, because it is acknowledged that he is one of the most forceful colored preachers in the Southwest, but the trouble is, he is a natural born killer; that he is forever on the offensive. Seemingly his zeal is not according to knowledge. He is like many others of our most able men; they love to show people the way to hell, and get so interested in it that they forget to persuade them to accept God on the terms of the Gospel."[1] Cassius felt that Thomas possessed too belligerent a mindset, practicing a "hard style" as he attacked and condemned denominations that he believed stood in religious error.[2]

Cassius leveled further criticism against Thomas regarding a debate the latter held with William Moore, preacher of the Church of God. This sect, Cassius pointed out, drank water instead of wine for communion, washed feet as a church ordinance, and prayed only the Lord's Prayer

K. C. Thomas preached in Oklahoma before relocating to Dallas, Texas, in the early 1920s. Thomas was the impetus behind the emergence of African American Churches of Christ in the Dallas-Fort Worth Metroplex. *(Photo taken from Lectureship Booklet).*

as found in Matthew 6:9–13. Even though white members of the West Guthrie Church of Christ supported Thomas in his discussion with Moore, Cassius reported, "Neither one of the men understood how to debate, or else they did not know how to handle the subject. The debate closed on the first night, having done more harm than good."[3] If Thomas had few polemical skills, however, he preached with fiery passion and effectiveness.

The Cedar Crest Church of Christ

By the mid 1920s Thomas had relocated from Oklahoma to Dallas where he found seven "loyal" disciples meeting in the home of Dovie

Bagsby. White members of five congregations—the Oak Cliff, Pearl and Bryan, Sears and Summitt, Western Heights, and Sunset Churches of Christ—agreed to give Thomas $100 each month for a year and a half, or "until he had succeeded in making the work self-supporting."[4] As happened so frequently, the indefatigable efforts of a black evangelist combined with the generosity of white Christians to give rise to black Churches of Christ in Dallas.

Armed with material and spiritual support, Thomas worked diligently from 1924 to 1930 enlarging the membership of the Mitchell Street Church of Christ from seven to 153 congregants. The expanding body became "entirely self-supporting" within sixteen months.[5] "It will be remembered," reported W. L. Oliphant, minister of the predominantly white Oak Cliff Church of Christ, "that an agreement was made to pay Brother Thomas' salary for eighteen months, or until the work was self-supporting; well, at the end of sixteen months, Brother Thomas informed us that the congregation could take care of its own expenses." Thomas, recognizing the importance of church leaders apart from a preacher, appointed four elders, Hobart Ross, Arthur Hann, Mack Jones, and O. B. Butler, together with four deacons, J. H. Starks, Shermond Jackson, Dennie Herring, and C. E. Crayton.[6]

Leaders of the five supporting white congregations then helped Thomas and his flock select a church building in the "best section of Oak Cliff's negro resident district." The building, comprising a four hundred-seat auditorium, basement, baptistry, preacher's office, and eight classrooms, cost $7,500. Upon completion $1,650 remained to be paid, and the black congregation paid off the balance. Oliphant concluded, "I wish to say something about the minister, K. C. Thomas—and I am sure that I am expressing the sentiments of all the brethren in Dallas who have had dealings with him. He has the ability to preach and defend the pure gospel. I have heard him in debates with a missionary Baptist, and a 'Pentecostal.' He defended the truth ably, and, in my estimation, defeated these advocates of false doctrines. We have found K. C. Thomas to be clean, reliable and honest. In all our dealings with him, he has shown himself worthy of our confidence. We are anticipating his doing a still greater work among his people."[7]

Unlike Samuel Robert Cassius who criticized Thomas's debating technique but praised his preaching, Oliphant applauded both his polemical and homiletical skills. Possibly Thomas had learned from his Oklahoma experiences and had taken Cassius's critique to heart. Notwithstanding these conflicting reports, Thomas clearly served as a catalyst for the growth of what is now the Cedar Crest congregation, the oldest black Church of Christ in Dallas. When Thomas died in 1938, however, he received little recognition or praise.[8]

But even as K. C. Thomas worked so effectively at Mitchell Street, other evangelists also reached into the black citizenry of Dallas with their message. By 1939 Jack Shields had assumed oversight of the Sparks Street Church of Christ, a congregation which continued to progress after a Luke Miller meeting produced six baptisms and one restoration.[9] The next fall white congregations collaborated and sponsored a two-week meeting with the eminent black evangelist Marshall Keeble, whose preaching engendered four baptisms and two restorations. "Bro. Keeble will never know the good he did in Dallas," reported L. M. Wright. "This was his first time to be with us." Wright, a devoted member of the Mitchell Street Church of Christ, also noted that the local minister Jack Shields "made his confession and says that he intends to stay with the church."[10] This comment referred to a split that had developed in the congregation, leading Shields and five other disaffected members to worship upstairs in the Black and Clark Funeral Home in Dallas.[11] Wright went on to praise white believers for being "faithful and patient with us through all of our struggles."[12]

In the summer of 1941, Keeble returned to Dallas and baptized twelve people. Keeble's meeting made a lasting impression in Dallas, again earning the gratitude of L. M. Wright. "We can still hear the words of Brother Keeble ringing in our ears," reported Wright. Keeble's preaching success was made possible by white Christians in Dallas who "have been so faithful with trying to get the gospel to our people."[13] On November 2, 1941, Russell H. Moore, a native of Wichita, Kansas, and one of Keeble's host of converts, assumed the ministry of Dallas's Ninth Street Church of Christ (formerly the Mitchell Street Church of Christ).[14] During Moore's three-year tenure with this congregation, it continued to make great strides spiritually, numerically, and financially. Disappointment, however, invaded Moore's home on March 25, 1942, when his wife, Alberta J. Moore, died.[15] Six months after his first wife's death, Moore, while preaching in Memphis, married Annie Mae Butler, a native of Conway, Arkansas.[16] On April 18, 1943, Moore relocated to Miami, Florida, taking up the leadership of the Liberty City Church of Christ.[17]

Moore's Dallas church soon acquired the services of C. C. Locke, a native of Mississippi and a disciple of Marshall Keeble, who became Ninth Street's preacher in 1944. The membership expressed delight over the advent of Locke and his wife who "seem to be real Christian people." Locke kept his flock busy with a sewing class on Tuesday, a prayer meeting on Wednesday, and hospital visitations on Thursday. In addition to preaching competently, Locke also proved to be "a songster." Ninth Street members realized the value of Locke's singing ability, "since so many of our singers have moved to other places." L. M. Wright concluded, "Now that we have a regular minister, we can fight Satan the more that the Lord's work can be farthered [sic]."[18] When Locke arrived in Dallas, the congregation had sixty members who contributed $35 each week. Within

This flyer (date unknown) advertises a gospel meeting at the North Tenneha Church of Christ in Tyler, Texas. Russell H. Moore, a convert of Marshall Keeble, collaborated with George Robin.

(Photo courtesy of Choice Dudley and the North Tenneha Church of Christ)

two decades the membership had increased to 615 congregants giving $1,000 weekly, and Locke led his flock into a new building at a new location in 1963. The church became known as the Cedar Crest Church of Christ[19] and thrived under Locke's adroit administration, ardent evangelism, and forceful preaching.[20] He continued serving and leading the Cedar Crest congregation until his death in 1979.[21]

The Lawrence and Marder Church of Christ

After successfully launching what is now the Cedar Crest Church of Christ in 1924, K. C. Thomas helped establish the Thomas Avenue Church of Christ in north Dallas four years later. Three men, Philip Thomas, P. Thomas, and Robert Crawford, helped continue the fledgling congregation after K. C. Thomas's death in 1938.[22] On September 10, 1940, the congregation relocated to south Dallas, becoming Macon Street Church of Christ. Under H. H. Gray's dynamic leadership, the congregation grew and flourished. A young, energetic, and committed minister, Gray understood the significance of trained church leaders, consistently emphasizing, "a church is no stronger than its leaders."[23]

By 1942 the Macon Street congregation had experienced "a steady growth" with a larger membership, increasing monetary offerings, and a vision to erect a new building.[24] On June 14, 1942, several events converged to make that Sunday "the greatest day in the history of the colored work in Dallas. This was made possible by the help of our many white friends." The Macon Street congregation began by airing the first radio broadcast on that day with R. N. Hogan preaching. "The broadcast over KSKY by Brother Hogan and our singers was heard by many of our race here and abroad. Brother L. R. Rand, a well-known gospel preacher from Jefferson, Texas, wrote that tears of joy were shed by many who gathered in his home to hear the program." Next, the women of the Macon congregation, led by Carrie Washington and Eva Starks, prepared a congregational breakfast and dinner in their homes. Then, the "overflowing crowd," which was "unable to even get under the tent" that had been raised, collected $244.71 to help pay off the balance of $328.08 on the church property. H. H. Gray again singled out the support of white Christians in acknowledging, "Many white disciples were present to encourage us." Gray expressed confidence that the balance of $83.37 would be erased, "as some of the other white congregations have promised to send their contributions to Brother Etheridge (white), who is handling this transaction. Brother Etheridge has done a great work with our people. Brother Eugene Smith (white) played a major part in making the Sunday drive a success."[25] In Jim Crow Texas, with its rigid racial separation, blacks and whites in Churches of Christ reached across segregated barriers to erect a house for God.

In addition to the material support from white disciples, other black congregations spiritually encouraged the Macon Street Church of Christ. In the fall of 1942, Russell H. Moore, a preacher for what became the Cedar Crest Church of Christ, held a meeting at the Macon Street congregation. Eva Starks, a member at Macon Street, reported, "We appreciate very much those having attended this meeting from Oak Cliff, East Dallas and other parts of the city."[26] That December members of Macon Street rejoiced because of the "nice seats, new oil stove and new song books just purchased by the congregation. Our lot and house belongs to us now." Bi-racial cooperation and collaboration spurred along the work in south Dallas. "A very interesting meeting was held Sunday evening, November 15, among the white and colored to further solve the problem of the work there." Numerical growth accompanied the material increase at the Macon Street congregation, as Starks reported five additions and exulted that "The outlook for others is very good. The spirit of cooperation is existing."[27]

The following year Starks noted that the Macon Street flock, after a good meeting with R. N. Hogan, was "going forward."[28] Hogan's fiery preaching engendered eighteen responses—seven baptisms, nine restorations, and two who came from the Christian Church. "Brother R. N. Hogan," wrote Starks, "used Isaiah's hammer and broke to pieces the doctrines and commandments of men."[29] But Starks expressed frustration that she and her church family were "not pleased with our worshipping place, we hope to improve conditions soon." Events surrounding World War II presented opportunities to make the envisioned facility improvements a reality since war-driven employment led some African Americans in Dallas to prosper, and Starks urged black Christians to give their financial resources to God's work. "While the war is on and so much money is being made, homes, cars, clothing and food is [*sic*] being prepared for years to come. Let us think, and use our means to the glory of God."[30]

By the fall of 1943 the Macon Street Church of Christ had relocated to the intersection of Lawrence and Marder Streets. "We are glad of our new location and will be so happy when we get a better house to worship in," Starks wrote. She further observed that Mr. and Mrs. E. S. Lockett, former members of Mount Horem Baptist Church, received baptism "for remission of sins." The restorations of Hazel Steven, Dorthy Carter, and Katherin Houston to a faithful life cheered Sparks as she reported that a number of blacks had immigrated to Dallas in the 1940s. K. C. Thomas Jr., Lovette Johnson, Dollie Mae McIntosh, and Imogene McIntyre were "buying, and making Dallas their home."[31] A couple of months later, Starks gave another glowing report. "The Lawrence and Marder St. church of Christ in south Dallas, where H. H. Gray is laboring so faithful, so hard and so earnestly, is growing rapidly." After commenting on other activities in neighboring churches, Starks urged, "Dallas must get up and go. We must be dependable. Let us pray that the work continue[s] to grow."[32]

The Lawrence and Marder Church of Christ early on demonstrated concern for others. Mrs. K. C. Thomas reported that her son, K. C. Thomas Jr., was able to enroll in the Bowser Christian Institute, and she thanked the congregation. "It was through the help of the different brothers and sisters of the Lawrence and Marder St. church of Christ, where H. H. Gray labors, that made it possible at this time."[33] As recipients of generosity from white Christians, the leaders and members of Lawrence and Marder in turn helped others.

In 1944 the Lawrence and Marder Church of Christ began building a new edifice. "We are thankful and happy to announce that our new building is now being erected by Brother Roy Winston from Oklahoma City." Starks announced that the congregation was "working enthusiastically" and looking forward to a "good reception at this new location."[34] She then provided a historical sketch of the congregation, noting that Marshall Keeble recommended H. H. Gray to the south Dallas congregation. When Gray first arrived in 1940, many church members "had quit and others were discouraged." Three years later, Gray secured "an ideal location and had the church building moved to this lot." The congregation paid $1,200 cash to have the church building relocated and remodeled, and Starks added that the "white brethren had sewerage installed at a cost of about $240.00." Because of the contributions of white saints and the unflagging labor of Gray, the Lawrence and Marder congregation flourished. While expanding their own numbers, they sent G. P. Bowser's school in Fort Smith, Arkansas, "a $26.50 donation and a box of food," while sending Keeble's school in Tennessee $34. Starks lauded Gray as "faithful, loyal, level-headed, humble and cooperative. We pray for him and his fine wife long lives, and much success in the Lord's work."[35]

Alvertice Bowdre, Sr. (standing in the middle between two men) led the Hatcher Street Church of Christ in Dallas, Texas, for almost three decades. This congregation is now the Southern Hills Church of Christ and continues to thrive.

(Photo courtesy of Doris Benitez and Nora Taylor)

Starks not only kept black Christians abreast of the happenings at Lawrence and Marder through the *Christian Echo*, but she also helped secure new subscriptions to the black periodical.[36] Starks reported that members of the Lawrence and Marder congregation moved into their new building on February 4, 1945, and they delighted in securing a loudspeaker, which broadcast the worship services throughout the community. Starks also announced that there were "three nice new church buildings in Dallas": the Ninth Street (now Cedar Crest) Church of Christ, the Lawrence and Marder Church of Christ, and the East Dallas Church of Christ.[37] In 1941 white members of the Oak Cliff congregation financed the East Dallas Church of Christ. Three years later, R. B. Thurmond assumed oversight of this thriving congregation, remaining until his death in 1972. After Thurmond's demise, Mac Wright, a young and dynamic minister, began preaching for the congregation.[38]

By the 1940s and 1950s African American Churches of Christ had sprouted up across the city of Dallas. The Hatcher Street Church of Christ, originally an all-white congregation, transitioned to all-black. "As the population began to shift in about 1950 from a predominantly white to a predominantly colored neighborhood with a majority of the white membership moving out to the Kaufman Highway area, it was decided among the brethren to procure a meeting place in closer proximity to their new homes." Like many white southerners who engaged in "white flight" when ethnic minorities began infiltrating a neighborhood, white believers of the Hatcher Street congregation "turned over" their property "to the colored brethren to carry on the work among the new residents." Both white and black Christians used the facilities until 1953 when Alvertice Bowdre Sr. became minister of the all-black Hatcher Street congregation which eventually evolved into what is now the Southern Hills Church of Christ. Within a short time Bowdre, "through the help of the Lord and the support of our fellow Christians both white and colored," enlarged the church's membership from twenty to 113 members.[39]

In various ways the black fellowship of Churches of Christ expanded from such foundations. In 1959 the Cherry Valley Church of Christ sprang up through the efforts of L. M. Johnson.[40] The most numerically successful effort developed when Elbert Moore and twenty members began meeting in the predominantly black Hamilton Park community in northeast Dallas. After three decades of "building to serve," this congregation relocated and became the Greenville Avenue Church of Christ in Richardson, Texas. Under the dynamic preaching, teaching, and shepherding of Shelton T. W. Gibbs III and several committed elders, this congregation has grown into the largest African American Church of Christ in the Lone Star State.[41]

Today's approximately twenty black Churches of Christ in Dallas proper with their six thousand-plus adherents[42] owe their origins to both the beneficence of white believers and the passionate toil of K. C. Thomas. White Christians in Dallas trusted Thomas, believed in his ability to advance the cause in their city, and cast their full support behind his evangelistic endeavor. But the story of African American Churches of Christ in Dallas encompasses more than Thomas's zealous efforts. Marshall Keeble, C. C. Locke, R. N. Hogan, Russell H. Moore, and other black preachers regularly visited Dallas and substantially contributed to the growth of Churches of Christ in the city. Perhaps more importantly, women contributed substantially to the development and expansion of black Churches of Christ as they cooked meals, canvassed neighborhoods, supported their preachers, and gave reports about the Lord's work in their community. Without their tireless efforts, and especially without their writings in the *Christian Echo*, we would be grossly ignorant of the origins of black Churches of Christ in Dallas.

PART II

The Legacy of Marshall Keeble in Texas

Chapter 4

THE KEEBLE INVASION

Marshall Keeble's Evangelistic Endeavors in the Lone Star State

I have never heard nor seen greater power in the pulpit. Sin was condemned, error exposed, and the church and Christ exalted to the heavens, and no man can do this with a greater degree of success than Marshall Keeble.

—Joe H. Morris, 1939

The Great Depression plunged Americans into economic distress and destitution, yet whites in Churches of Christ looked beyond their own deplorable circumstances and worked to alleviate the spiritual plight of African Americans. Driven by a conflicting sense of moral obligation to save the souls of black people and a desire to maintain racially separate congregations, white Churches of Christ in Texas frequently called black evangelists to preach to their black neighbors. The most sought-after black preacher during the Depression era was Marshall Keeble. While John T. Ramsey, Samuel Robert Cassius, T. H. Merchant, and K. C. Thomas were the first black seed planters in Texas, African American Churches of Christ took no vibrant form in the state until the advent of Marshall Keeble.

Born to former slaves in Middle Tennessee in 1878, Keeble grew up in the turbulent milieu of the post–Reconstruction era. White southerners, enraged over the outcome of the Civil War as well as the passage of the Thirteenth, Fourteenth, and Fifteenth Amendments, unleashed a campaign of terror against their black neighbors, stripping them of their civil rights and ushering in the bleakest era of the African American experience. The indifference of white politicians in the North and the racist portrayals of black people by northern white journalists and cartoonists contributed to the downward spiral of African Americans into a state of second-class citizenship.[1] Yet in Marshall Keeble's world, the love of a devout mother and the stability of a diligent father counterbalanced this cruel environment to give him a sense of pride and dignity, which empowered him to navigate the treacherous waters of the Jim Crow South.[2]

Others in addition to his parents guided the youthful Keeble. As a young adult he studied the eventful life of Booker T. Washington. Devouring Washington's *Up from Slavery* "from lid to lid," Keeble discovered ways of getting along with white people and how to garner monetary support from Anglo leaders.[3] Just as the president of the Tuskegee Institute won widespread support from wealthy benefactors such as Andrew Carnagie, John D. Rockefeller, and Julius Rosenwald, Keeble similarly secured moral and material support from A. M. Burton, an affluent white Christian businessman from Nashville. Burton's constant generosity enabled Keeble to traverse the United States and eventually the world preaching the "pure gospel" and planting black congregations.

Samuel W. Womack, Keeble's father-in-law, was doubtlessly his most influential mentor. A former slave from Middle Tennessee, Womack converted to the Disciples of Christ in 1866 and shortly thereafter emerged as a noteworthy preacher in the Volunteer State. After the Stone–Campbell Restoration Movement split into the Disciples of Christ and the Churches of Christ in the early twentieth century, Womack sided with the latter group, which opposed the use of instrumental music in worship and the conduct of evangelism through missionary societies. Womack, himself under the influence of David Lipscomb's *Gospel Advocate* journal, steered Keeble away from the "digressives" to the "loyals." Keeble acknowledged that his father-in-law "first got me to see that I was wrong while working with the 'digressives,' and I came out from them over twenty years ago, and from that day on I tried to make my life like his; and though he is gone, I shall continue to try and imitate the Christian life he has left behind."[4]

If Womack initially led Marshall Keeble away from the Disciples of Christ and into the Churches of Christ, several white preachers contributed to his development as a proclaimer of the "pure gospel." In 1914 John McPherson, a white evangelist, preached a citywide campaign in Nashville and produced twenty-seven baptisms. During the three-week meeting, Keeble, always an eager learner, copied all of McPherson's lessons for use in his coming career. Keeble assembled a set of evangelistic skills from a variety of preachers such as McPherson, making them uniquely his own. Four years later Keeble, using the abilities he had carefully honed, established his first congregation, the Oak Grove Church of Christ in Henderson, Tennessee. N. B. Hardeman, an influential white minister in Churches of Christ, helped secure the Oak Grove school for Keeble's meeting in Henderson. This practical assistance and endorsement encouraged the black evangelist and enabled him to baptize eighty-four people in this campaign as he launched his unprecedented life's work.[5]

Marshall Keeble in Houston

Armed with this cast of Tennessee supporters, Keeble first invaded the state of Texas as an evangelist in 1929, when he went to Houston to evangelize the city's 63,337 African Americans. After reading and hearing

Marshall Keeble hailed from Middle Tennessee, but he left an indelible mark on Churches of Christ everywhere he traveled, especially in the Lone Star State. The date of this photo is unknown.

(Courtesy of the Center for Restoration Studies, Abilene Christian University)

of Keeble's success as an itinerant preacher in the pages of the *Gospel Advocate* and the *Firm Foundation*, Dr. Asa H. Speer, a white leader in Houston, arranged for the evangelist from Nashville to preach there. "I am now at Houston in a tent meeting," reported Keeble. "The outlook is good and we are praying for success. The white churches here called me to labor with my people."[6]

Rain dampened Keeble's three-week meeting, but the hospitality of a few black Christians and the camaraderie of white saints encouraged him. When Keeble arrived in the city, he stayed with a black couple, Lee and Laura Richardson, who "know how to treat a stranger," and this was his invariable practice in the ironbound segregationist culture of the South. He praised Anglo believers in Houston. "All the white churches in Houston supported this meeting in every way they could. Dr. Speer (white) led the song service every night. He is so anxious to see that all people hear the gospel." Christians such as Speer recognized a need for the presence of Churches of Christ among black people as well as white and sought the "pure word of God" for all Texans. Keeble had "never met with greater encouragement at any place. Dr. Speer was so much enthused over my efforts that he gave me his personal check for fifty dollars."[7]

Keeble's efforts yielded eleven baptisms and the nucleus of a fledgling congregation, which is now the Fifth Ward Church of Christ in Houston. White Christians in the city assumed oversight of the small black flock and began to "meet with the colored disciples every Sunday afternoon and teach them, and in this way the wolves are kept off of the sheep." White believers also made arrangements for a black preacher to work with the church on a fulltime basis.[8] T. H. York, a black minister from Detroit, Michigan, became the first regular minister of the Fifth Ward congregation from 1932 to 1934. A committed and altruistic preacher, York often applied his monthly salary of $25 toward the purchase of land situated on the corner of Stonewall and Waco Streets.[9] During York's tenure as minister, Keeble continued his visits. In the spring of 1934, the Nashville preacher, during a three-week meeting in Houston, baptized thirty-two and noted, "The Heights Church, with the aid of others, sponsored this meeting. The white brethren stood by us as we held up Christ."[10] He also praised T. H. York as a "pleasure to work with."[11]

York returned to Detroit in 1934; he was succeeded by Sutton Johnson who ministered to the Fifth Ward congregation until 1940. O. L. Aker, a Keeble convert from Alabama, succeeded Johnson for one year. Then in 1941, the Fifth Ward Church of Christ soared to new heights with the arrival of R. N. Hogan, whose congregation in southern California, the Figueroa Church of Christ, granted him a two-year leave of absence to work in Houston. Through Hogan's indefatigable labor, the Fifth Ward congregation grew large enough to support itself, no longer needing assistance from the all-white Heights Church of Christ.

During the same year Hogan and Samuel L. Cebrun collaborated with white Christians in Huntsville to plant a Church of Christ for African Americans. Hogan's report in the Fifth Ward church bulletin indicates the racist mentality of white believers in Huntsville who erected a separate church building when there was "only one member (Colored) of the Church of Christ in the entire town." The "Weekly Bulletin" explained, "The reason to build the building was to knock out the excuse that the Colored people did not have a place to worship."[12] Some white Christians in Texas, eager to see their black neighbors baptized into their fellowship, did not want them worshiping in their church building.Their spirit of white supremacy accompanied their spirit of bi-racial cooperation.

After Hogan returned to Southern California in 1943, he was succeeded by Paul Settles Sr. from 1944 to 1950, followed by Jesse T. Burson. From 1958 to 1965, A. E. Derrick served as minister; from 1965 to 1972, John C. Whitley assumed leadership of Fifth Ward. From 1972 until the early twenty-first century, Thomas Foster served as minister, developing the Fifth Ward congregation into one of the largest black Churches of Christ.[13]

In addition to being the oldest black Church of Christ in Houston, the Fifth Ward congregation has possessed a passionate evangelistic spirit. Appreciating their own origins as the children of mission-minded Christians, leaders and members of the Fifth Ward Church of Christ have consistently and unselfishly worked to launch other congregations in Houston, in Texas, and beyond.[14]

Marshall Keeble in Paris

The Fifth Ward church, which Marshall Keeble established in 1929, inaugurated his impressive work in the Lone Star State where he planted several more black congregations in the 1930s. In one instance in 1932, white leaders of the Lamar Avenue Church of Christ in Paris invited Keeble and his song leader, Luke Miller, to preach to African Americans. The Nashville evangelist transformed a local dance hall into a Christian center as he converted ninety-two African Americans and established what is now the Tudor Street Church of Christ. R. L. Colley, minister of the Lamar Avenue congregation, reported that the Keeble–Miller campaign encountered "much opposition" which "only served to increase the interest." Colley explained:

> He [Keeble] held an open invitation to any one to show that he was teaching error, from the beginning to the close of the meeting; three made an effort to take him down, but all in vain. The First Christian preacher here tried him one night, but he had business out of town. A Baptist preacher tried him, and Keeble made him deny his doctrine, many of his members fell out with him and obeyed the gospel as a result. A high powered "Holiness" was imported from San Antonio, to handle the unruly condition, but he failed before he ever mounted the pulpit; his ability was less than the others that tried to put him out. M. Keeble is a power with the gospel sword; he is humble and knows his place and keeps it at all times. He refuses to be flattered by nice things said about his ability. He is cool and deliberate at all times. He was never confused, even when they would rise up in the audience and call his hand; he always had a correct reply the very moment his hand was called.[15]

Colley's testimony reveals white Christians' deep appreciation for the black evangelist's preaching skill and his ability to refute what he perceived to be false teaching and their admiration for his composure, humility, and willingness to "keep his place" at all times. White saints in East Texas cast their full support behind a black minister who complied with the codes of Jesus Christ and Jim Crow.

Immediately after the establishment of the Tudor Street congregation, white leaders in Paris shaped plans to sustain the newly gathered flock. "Expecting the colored church of Christ in Paris to be by far the largest church of the colored people in a short time," Colley and other white leaders asked Luke Miller, a Keeble convert and song leader from Alabama, to relocate from Valdosta, Georgia, to their northeast Texas community. "I am now laboring with the colored church established by Brother Keeble here," wrote Miller. "The white church called me. They are encouraging me very much. R. L. Colley, their minister, is as fine a man as I have ever met."[16] The following year white saints in Paris encouraged the newly planted congregation by pouring their resources into a building program. "The work here was established by the white church here. They helped us to build a nice meeting house and have helped with my support for the year. I have never seen better Christians."[17] In 1937 Keeble returned to Paris for an evangelistic meeting. Even though his preaching yielded "no additions," he remarked, "the church was greatly edified, and many white brethren came from miles around to encourage us."[18]

In the early 1940s, Columbus Grimsley, a native of Florida, came to Paris to minister to the Tudor Street Church of Christ. Grimsley helped stabilize the black congregation, as he enlarged the church's membership, increased its building fund, purchased additional property, and rebuilt the preacher's home.[19] One sister commended Grimsley's efforts, noting, "We are being strengthened very much by his teaching."[20] Grimsley himself reported that the Paris congregation was "one of the greatest Churches in the Brotherhood." He added that by 1946 the congregation had developed "singers, ministers, and teachers."[21]

The next year Grimsley left Texas and began preaching for the West Simpson Church of Christ in Tucson, Arizona. During his seven-year tenure in Paris, however, Grimsley reported baptizing eighty-five people, restoring several more, and building a $4,000 church parsonage[22]; he also rebuilt the church building destroyed by fire in 1947, installed new pews, and established a "fine congregation" in Hugo, Oklahoma.[23]

Marshall Keeble in Port Arthur

In May 1935 O. C. Lambert and white believers in Port Arthur invited Marshall Keeble to preach the "pure gospel" there. Keeble's meeting produced forty-one baptisms, leaving behind a new congregation (now the Thomas Boulevard Church of Christ). As he ordinarily did, the Nashville evangelist credited local white Christians for their moral and material aid. "Brother O. C. Lambert (white) made all arrangements for the meetings, and not a thing was overlooked. He is one of the hardest workers I ever saw."[24]

The next month Luke Miller, one of Keeble's most effective protégés, relocated to Port Arthur to fortify the infant congregation. "I was called here by the Sixth church of Christ (white)," Miller wrote. "They have also supported me in the work. They are great Christian people and have helped and encouraged the work among us in every way. Brother O. C. Lambert is their minister. I have never met at more godly man, nor a better teacher of God's word. He is known and respected by the people of Port Arthur, because he fights for what he believes." Miller, too, was a fighter, and his diligent evangelism soon increased the newly founded congregation from forty-one to eighty-eight members.[25]

By the spring of 1937 Miller and his congregation had moved into a new building with seating for four hundred. "The Sixth Street church (white) established this work," Miller wrote, "supporting me and thus allowing the colored church to put their money into a building fund. We were able to pay for almost all the material as it was placed on the ground. Brethren A. J. Brutton and Clide Smith (both white) also donated their part of the carpentry and electrical work."[26] In the fall of the same year, Marshall Keeble revisited Port Arthur and lauded the white believers there for their assistance in the form of money, time, and labor. "Luke Miller is doing a great work," reported Keeble, "but he could not do it if the white church was not standing behind the work. They mean to see that the work is self-sustaining before they turn them loose for the wolves to eat them up, thank God."[27]

Marshall Keeble in Waco

Nineteen years after the horrific lynching of Jesse Washington, a handicapped black man accused of raping a white woman in Waco, Marshall Keeble preached in that city for three weeks, resulting in twenty-six baptisms, and established what is now the Hood Street Church of Christ.[28] White Christians attended the Keeble meeting in large numbers as "Interest grew each night, and the two white churches there cooperated in sponsoring this meeting. Brother W. D. Bills did everything in his power to assist and encourage us. It was an inspiration to be in the midst of such people. The two white churches have gone together and called a colored man here to labor with this new church."[29]

They chose O. L. Aker, a one-time Methodist minister, to nurture the newly planted Waco congregation. After serving the young flock for several weeks, Aker acknowledged the potential for growth as well as the generosity of white believers there. "This is a splendid mission, and there are some fine people here; a fine Christian spirit has been shone me since coming here. The white church, with the cooperation of the colored church of Christ, stormed wife and me with a surprise of an assortment of groceries. It was highly appreciated by us. I must say the white church is awfully nice in looking after the comfort of wife and me."[30] Aker's testimony, like that of many others, reveals how whites and blacks in Churches of Christ collaborated to establish and sustain separate congregations in the Jim Crow era.

In 1936 Aker again praised white members of both Columbus Avenue Church of Christ and the East Waco Church of Christ. "These churches," explained Aker, "were instrumental in having me come here to nurse these babes, for which I am thankful and happy. These white brethren are real Christians. They see that I am paid for my labor with my people; they have been nice and kind to me in every way. Since coming to Waco, this little mission has doubled in number. Most of the members are loyal Christians in every way." Like his spiritual father Marshall Keeble, Aker credited the assistance of white believers with his evangelistic success. "The white brethren here have made it possible for me to accomplish what I have; and I have not labored with any better than they, for they have the spirit of Christ."[31]

Aker's report offers insight into race relations between whites and blacks in Texas Churches of Christ during an era of unending racial segregation. White saints in Waco selected and nourished new Christians by giving monetary support to their black minister who nurtured them spiritually. White believers in Texas, insisted Aker, were "real Christians," "nice," "kind," and "loyal." They were sincere and genuine in their dealings with African Americans because they possessed, in Aker's words, "the spirit of Christ." Despite their sincerity and integrity in reaching out to their black neighbors, white Christians in Texas arranged philanthropies in the context of unchallenged segregation as products of and participants in a southern racist culture. This pervasive anti-black system stigmatized blacks as biologically inferior to whites, brooked no defiance of the social order of the New South, and proscribed any racial integration at the congregational level.

Marshall Keeble in Tyler

On September 8, 1935, Marshall Keeble closed a successful gospel meeting in Tyler with fifty-five baptisms and twelve restorations from the Christian Church. He reported, "The white church here called us to labor here. Brother Harvey Scott labors here. He did all in his power to make the meeting a success."[32] The efforts of Keeble and Scott resulted in what is now the North Tenneha Church of Christ in Tyler. Elmo W. Anderson, a native of Henderson and a graduate of Jarvis Christian College, became the first located preacher for the newly planted congregation in Tyler. "My coming to Tyler," noted Anderson, "has been made possible through the white church of which Brother Harvey Scott is the minister."[33] White Christians in Tyler helped plant North Tenneha, then sustained the young, struggling congregation. "The work here in Tyler is doing fine," reported Anderson in 1936.[34] Apart from monetary support, white Christians strengthened black congregations through spiritual guidance, contributing to the theological formation of African American Churches of Christ throughout Texas.

The year 1936 proved pivotal for the new black church in Tyler. In February Anderson reported that a young lady became a member of North Tenneha, after being "convinced through Brother Harvey Scott's radio sermons on Sunday morning"[35]; in the same month, Joel Thompson reported that the Tyler congregation enjoyed "continuous growth" under Anderson's leadership with twenty-two additions. "Thirteen came from the Christian church, and nine have been baptized."[36] During his one-year tenure Anderson reported sixty additions and increased the church's membership to well over 100. He again lauded the white Christians for their assistance. "A great number of these additions have been made possible through the radio work of Brother Harvey Scott, minister of the church of Christ (white)."[37]

Marshall Keeble in Lubbock

Marshall Keeble's evangelistic labors extended well beyond East Texas. In the summer of 1932, he preached nineteen days in Lubbock before crowds of over three thousand people, most of whom were white listeners. John T. Smith, a white leader from Denver, Colorado, reported that Keeble presented the gospel with "great power" and in the "simplest manner." Even though African Americans failed to attend Keeble's meeting in "great numbers," sixty-three of those who did attend received baptism and formed what is now the Twentieth and Birch Church of Christ. "We now have a congregation of about seventy members," Smith wrote, "and they are the happiest band I have ever seen. The white brethren will take the oversight."[38]

Marshall Keeble in Mexia

Three summers later white Christians in Mexia sponsored a Keeble meeting for African Americans. Delbert M. Gatlin, a resident of nearby Teague, attended this meeting and reported: "Brother Keeble is giving them the straight gospel without any addition or subtraction. I consider

Brother Keeble one of the best drawing cards in the brotherhood, as people will go to hear him that would not go to hear one of our white brethren, and there is not a man in the field that can preach the gospel any plainer or more convincingly than he can." Keeble's influence as an evangelist extended well beyond Tennessee and other southeastern states, the locus of his work. The black evangelist from Tennessee mesmerized Texans, white and black, with his simple, practical, and forceful preaching. White Christians in Texas expected Keeble not only to bless their black neighbors, but also to rejuvenate and revitalize their own white congregations. "We are hoping that great good will be done in Mexia," Gatlin expressed, "not only with the colored people, but with the white people also."[39]

Marshall Keeble in Stephenville and Wichita Falls

In the spring of 1936, Keeble spent several days in Stephenville preaching before audiences mostly composed of white people. Of the twenty-five black people who attended the meeting, only two responded to his messages.[40] While Marshall Keeble enjoyed limited evangelistic success in Stephenville, he found more tangible results in Wichita Falls. In the fall of 1936, white leaders of both the Polk Street and the Austin Street Churches of Christ in that city invited Keeble to preach the Word. Keeble's visit yielded twenty-two baptisms, which comprised a new congregation, the Welch Street Church of Christ.[41] Keeble then sent F. A. Livingston, one of his spiritual sons from Florida, to guide the newly planted church. Livingston reported the next year, "About a year ago I was recommended to the work here by Brother Keeble. The white brethren have stood behind the work 100%. We started off with about twenty members and the number has grown to about fifty. . . . We thank God for men with the missionary spirit."[42]

Marshall Keeble in Greenville

After planting the Welch Street church in Wichita Falls, Keeble spent two weeks in the spring of 1937 in Greenville, where his preaching yielded seventeen baptisms—sixteen African Americans and one white person. This congregation later changed its name to the Eastside Church of Christ.[43] From Greenville, Keeble moved on to Huntsville and baptized two people and restored one. As in other Texas cities, the

A. M. Burton (1879-1966) generously supported Marshall Keeble during his preaching campaigns in Texas and beyond. Significantly, these two men collaborated during a racially segregated era to plant congregations across the United States.

Marshall Keeble (1878-1968) left behind several black congregations in the Lone Star State. He often mentored young students at the Nashville Christian Institute. Here Keeble is surrounded by Robert Woods and Fred Gray (front row) and Hassen Reed and Robert McBride (back row).

Keeble campaign in Huntsville was "a mission meeting supported by the white church. Ted Norton, minister of the white church, encouraged us much."[44] Yet at times even the dynamic combination of Keeble's preaching and white support failed. White Christians sponsored a Keeble meeting in Overton, where inclement weather kept crowds small; only two responded and no black congregation took root.[45]

Marshall Keeble Tours Texas

In the fall of 1939, Keeble toured several Texas cities where he had earlier established congregations. In each locale Keeble singled out the support that white Christians constantly provided for these emerging black churches. In Houston he noted that white saints "completed a nice place of worship for the colored church," and white Christians in Port Arthur were "standing by" the church he had planted four years earlier.[46] In the years following, Keeble returned to Port Arthur and his preaching brought ten baptisms and one restoration. He praised the all-white Sixth Street Church of Christ for "greatly assisting" in the development of the black congregation.[47]

Marshall Keeble in Dallas

Marshall Keeble established no congregation in the city of Dallas, but his presence and preaching there indelibly impacted the churches already there. In the fall of 1940, Keeble noted that "all of the white churches in Dallas" cooperated to bring him there, where his ministerial efforts gained thirteen baptisms and one restoration.[48] Impressed by the interest of white saints in Dallas, Keeble reported, "The meeting was greatly encouraged by all of the white churches, who are supporting three colored preachers in this field. Thousands are hearing the pure gospel, and there is a bright future for the colored work in Dallas. Thousands of colored people are brought to Christ every year by the efforts of the white churches."[49]

Later that year Keeble spent fourteen days in Wellington and immersed seventeen people. He then noted, "The white church supported the meeting," before adding, "I was in Texas ten weeks, and there were fifty baptisms."[50] The following year Keeble revisited Wellington and announced four baptisms and two restorations. "That church was established by the white church last year," Keeble wrote, "and I was surprised to find it in the new building. It also has a home for the preacher. The white church made this possible. It is supporting the colored preacher."[51]

Marshall Keeble in Pecos

In the 1950s, Keeble again toured Texas, but not simply as an evangelist. In the summer of 1951, a combined fundraising tour and evangelistic effort carried him to Pecos. He took with him three students from the Nashville Christian Institute, a Christian school in Tennessee for which he sought support. "I carry these boys with me that brethren may see what Christian education means to colored boys when given an opportunity," he wrote.[52] Keeble's three-week joint campaign ended with six baptisms and the establishment of a new congregation. The Nashville evangelist noted that white Christians in Pecos not only sponsored the meeting, but they also "promised to build them a meetinghouse within forty-five days, if the Lord wills. This is a very ripe field for the gospel." He added, "The people were carried away with the little boys' preaching every night and the one that led the singing was praised by all who heard him. The white brethren gave all of the boys new suits and they fixed me up nicely. We all left there happy and greatly encouraged."[53] When Keeble returned to Pecos two months later, he was astonished to see that the white Christians there had already erected a $10,000 building for the black church.[54]

Marshall Keeble's Texas Tour in the 1950s

In 1954 Keeble, as president of the Nashville Christian Institute, traversed the Lone Star State soliciting funds for his K–12 school in Tennessee by showcasing some of his talented students. While in Texas Keeble visited the black congregation in Port Arthur, which he had established two decades earlier. He noted, "This church now numbers over four hundred and they have been for some time self-supporting. They recently remodeled their building and it is beautiful." From Port Arthur Keeble went to Texas City and preached there three weeks. "The church in Texas City (white) financed this meeting and attended in large numbers." From Texas City Keeble moved to Houston for a two-week meeting, ending with four baptisms and six restorations. Keeble again singled out the faithful support of white Christians in Houston who "invited me to hold this meeting financed by them." He added, "Sometimes there were over fifteen hundred present and at times there were more white people than colored people present. The white brethren bought over two hundred pounds of meat to be barbecued so we could have a dinner on the ground on the Lord's day. Such demonstrations as this will convince the world that the spirit of Christ prevails in the church of Christ." While in Houston, Keeble also preached at the all-black Fifth Ward church, which had just completed $40,000 in physical improvements.[55]

Marshall Keeble's evangelistic meetings in Texas drew countless numbers of white and black listeners—at times attracting more Anglos than African Americans. While the black evangelist from Nashville inaugurated many African American Churches of Christ in Texas, he also contributed to the rise of Anglo congregations there as well—a striking, perhaps unique, achievement in an era embittered by vicious segregation. Keeble, a black preacher whose race consigned him to inherent inferiority, could somehow persuade whites to entrust him with their souls' eternal destiny. This powerful and practical preacher profoundly affected the lives of both white and black Texans. Yet despite his gifts and power, he could not have accomplished what he did without the generous monetary support of zealous and devout white Christians across the South. Even though racism tainted and vitiated the philanthropy of these white saints, that racism could not negate what this remarkable black preacher and his sincere white supporters accomplished in Texas.

Chapter 5

"NOTHING CAN OVERCOME THE WORD OF GOD"

Luke Miller and the Rise of African American Churches of Christ in East Texas

*But the word of God continued
to increase and spread.*

—Acts 12:24

Luke Miller is doing a great work in Texas.

—Marshall Keeble, 1940

Born in 1904 in Alabama, Luke Miller grew up in the Jim Crow Deep South and emerged as a significant catalyst behind the development of African American Churches of Christ in East Texas. While much of Miller's early years remain unknown, his life forever changed in 1920 when Marshall Keeble came to Decatur, Alabama. Keeble, the premier black evangelist in Churches of Christ, entered Decatur by invitation of white Christians to evangelize African Americans. Recalling his conversion experience, Miller stated, "I obeyed the gospel in Decatur, Alabama. The white church there called Brother M. Keeble to preach to the colored people." Impressed by the bi-racial cooperation in Jim Crow Alabama, Miller and other curious black spectators flocked to Keeble's protracted meeting. "Many white people came out to encourage the meeting and to help him [Keeble] put over the job. We had never seen so many white people at a colored meeting, so that drew many colored people out to see why the white people were there." Miller testified that Decatur's black community "came to see, but after they got there, they heard the truth. I was in that number that were baptized. The white Christians' presence at a meeting always draws my people to come out and hear the word of God, and become Christians."[1]

Shortly after his conversion, Miller began assisting his spiritual father, Marshall Keeble, as a song leader. Accompanying Keeble on his evangelistic tours, Miller learned how to conduct protracted meetings himself. By the late 1920s Miller had smoothly transitioned from song leader to fulltime evangelist. In 1927 G. F. Gibbs, a white leader for Churches of Christ in South Carolina, solicited the services of Miller, who traveled to preach in Greenville for his first effort as a fledgling evangelist.[2]

Luke Miller in Florida

Two years later Keeble invaded Florida and planted black congregations in Lakeland, Tampa, and St. Petersburg. After establishing these churches, Keeble commissioned Miller to divide his time equally among the three. White Christians in Florida happily endorsed Miller's work. "He is very bright and apparently very humble," P. G. Millen, a white leader in Florida, reported, "and he has the boldness and courage to denounce sin in 'high places,' and that is what it takes to show sectarianism that they are wrong." Millen added, "'Sugar-coating' the gospel will never do it. I would to God that we had more Keebles and Millers."[3] White Floridians' approval of Keeble and Miller came because of their preaching skill, but regardless of any ability or devotion, their exemplification of the time-honored values of the "old darkey" or the "old Negro" predicated all words of endorsement. In short, they won the hearts of white Christians across the South because of their work and because they refused to challenge the racial status quo of the segregated South.[4]

The year following Miller's foray into Florida, P. G. Millen again noted his enduring contribution. "Much of the good that has been done for the three congregations since Brother Keeble's meetings the early part of this year can justly be attributed to Brother Luke Miller, of Decatur, Ala. He is a noble proclaimer of the pure gospel to his people and is worthy of a very much better support than he is now getting. . . . " Millen called Miller a "worthy man of God" and urged fellow white believers to give him more monetary support.[5]

Keeble similarly commended Miller's evangelistic work in Florida. "Brother Luke Miller, the colored preacher that I converted about ten

Luke Miller (1904-1962) was unquestionably Marshall Keeble's most effective preaching son. Miller's evangelistic labors produced several thriving black congregations in the Lone Star State.
(Photo taken from Luke Miller's Sermons*).*

years ago at Decatur, Ala., is working with this congregation [in St. Petersburg], also at Tampa and Lakeland. He is doing a great work, which is greatly appreciated by both white and colored people." Over a seven-month period, Miller baptized forty-six people. "His wife," Keeble added, "is a wonderful helpmate in the work."[6] Regrettably, virtually nothing is known about Miller's wife, even though Keeble spoke well of her.

In the spring of 1930, Keeble planted a black Church of Christ in Plant City, Florida, by baptizing thirty-five "precious souls." Miller assumed leadership of this newly gathered flock. White Christians in Plant City immediately planned "to buy a nice, large store building for them to worship in," as well as "a home for Brother Miller, the young colored preacher." Whites in Churches of Christ, in compliance with segregation's dictates, erected separate church buildings to keep African Americans out of their churches. Certainly cognizant of this contradiction, Keeble worked within it and highlighted Miller's impact on Florida churches, stating, "Brother Miller's work in this section is making a wonderful impression on both the white and colored brethren."[7]

In May of 1930 Keeble closed a meeting in Lakeland, Florida, with twenty-five baptisms. He again accentuated the important work of Miller, noting, "Brother Miller is the young evangelist working in this State. The white brethren are much impressed with his humble, meek, and Christlike disposition."[8] In segregation's distinctive dialect, that Miller was "meek and humble" meant that he could gain the trust of whites across the South, and they in turn made it possible for him to work as a potent church planter in Texas. In 1931 Miller reported that he had baptized ninety-five persons and received ten from the Christian Church during the previous year in Florida. He also found time to assist his spiritual father, Marshall Keeble, during a protracted meeting in Atlanta, Georgia.[9] Keeble reported that Miller led the singing exceptionally well.[10]

Luke Miller in Paris

In the fall of 1932, Miller left his Florida work and took up residence in Paris, Texas, to serve the Tudor Street Church of Christ. Marshall Keeble had established the congregation earlier that summer with approximately one hundred baptisms. On May 13, 1933, Miller reported that the black congregation in Paris had moved into a new building and added new members. "Through the blessing of God and the assistance of the white church, we were able to hold our first service in our new meetinghouse May 7. We thank God for such friends. There have been fifty-five additions here this year."[11] Like most black preachers in Churches of Christ, Miller, while ministering in one place, continued to evangelize other areas. In 1933, while working with black saints in Paris, Miller responded to a call from white Christians in Holdenville, Oklahoma. After preaching there three weeks, Miller baptized forty, including two Baptist preachers and one Pentecostal clergyman. Miller especially credited white believers for their assistance. The Holdenville meeting, announced Miller, "was sponsored by the white church. They greatly encouraged me in every way. Brother Thomas, who preaches for the white church, is a wonderful man and did much to encourage the meeting."[12]

Luke Miller in Corsicana

Miller, however, accomplished his most impressive evangelistic work in the Lone Star State. In the summer of 1933, white Christians invited Miller to Corsicana where he baptized 218 people, received five from the Christian Church, and planted what is now the Eastside Church of Christ with 225 members.[13] In the spring of 1934, Miller fell critically ill while conducting an evangelistic campaign under the auspices of G. H. P. Showalter and other white Christians. Marshall Keeble reported that Miller's song leader, Brother Morehead, "had a heart attack in Brother Miller's car. Brother Miller was shocked so badly he has been in bed ever since and the doctors are doubting his recovery. His mother, a widow woman, had to send a doctor after him at Paris, Texas, and carry him to Decatur, Alabama, where he lives." Keeble then appealed to Christians across the country to come to Miller's aid financially. "This young man is loved by all who know him. He has always been meek and humble. Brethren right at this time anything that we can do for him will help him greatly. Let us all pray for him."[14]

Luke Miller in Port Arthur

The Lord evidently answered the prayers, for by the summer of 1935 Miller had recovered enough to oversee a newly planted church in Port Arthur, which Keeble had established a short time earlier. Aware of Miller's health problems, the white saints there did not expect him "to do much work . . . but they wanted to help me to continue to improve in health. I am thankful for such friends, also for the prayers and letters of friends during my illness." Miller received more than prayers and get-well cards; white believers in Port Arthur gave him their money and provided the black congregation with enough resources to move into a new building seating four hundred.[15]

Luke Miller in Beaumont

While working in Port Arthur, Miller regained physical strength and began preaching in other areas in East Texas. In the summer of 1937, he conducted a meeting in Beaumont where white members of the South Park Church of Christ "called" him. O. C. Reynolds, South Park's minister, assisted Miller during the preaching campaign. Miller reported, "The meeting resulted in twelve obeying the gospel. W. S. Nichols, a prominent lawyer, will teach a Bible class each Friday night." White Christians in Texas not only underwrote black preachers such as Miller with financial aid, they also proffered spiritual guidance to fledgling black believers. African Americans endeavored to help themselves as well, as Miller arranged for one of his own protégés to assist the recently established church in Beaumont. "One of the preachers that developed in the Port Arthur congregation will preach for them each Sunday."[16]

Luke Miller in Orange

From Beaumont, Miller moved on to Orange, Texas, where he preached for four months "in the heart of the colored section, with sectarian churches and beer parlors all around." Miller's potent and practical preaching yielded seventeen baptisms, including a Methodist preacher and a Baptist deacon. With these conversions, a new black Church of Christ sprang up in Orange. W. G. Bass, a white leader in the area, commended Miller, stating, "Too much cannot be said for Brother Miller and the good he has done at Orange. He is a wonderful preacher, and he lives what he preaches."[17]

Like his spiritual father, Marshall Keeble, Miller firmly believed that the "pure gospel" transformed people not only for the "hereafter" but also for the "here and now." He rehearsed his personal experiences in Orange to illustrate his point. "While I was in Orange, Texas, in a meeting, the Chief of Police came to the meeting every night. One night after I had preached he came into the building, asking: 'Where is the preacher?' Well, I don't have to tell you I had cold chills for awhile, but I soon got up nerve enough to say: 'Here am I.' He came close and said: 'I have been hearing you preach and if everybody obeyed that gospel, it would make our job easy.' He had watched the effects of the first meeting and said many people that used to be in police court are now living good lives and are good citizens."[18] Here Miller echoed a conviction shared by Keeble, who argued that the gospel not only saved souls eternally but also made people better temporally.[19]

While serving black Christians in Port Arthur, Miller continued responding to calls from white congregations across the South. In the spring of 1938, Marshall Keeble conducted a "good meeting" with twenty-seven baptisms in Port Arthur, and Miller considered that "His preaching was better than ever. Many white people attended from nearby churches as well as the local churches, and they encouraged us very much." After the Keeble meeting, Miller evangelized in Lake Charles, Louisiana, and baptized twenty-one people. "I was called there by the young white church started there by two young preachers, Brethren Badget and Marsh, of Port Arthur. The Sixth Street Church of Christ helped to support me in this mission meeting." Miller then revisited Holdenville, Oklahoma, having been "called by the white church there for my third meeting for the colored people."[20]

Luke Miller in Greenville

While Miller enjoyed considerable ministerial success outside of Texas, he accomplished his most lasting evangelistic work in the Lone Star State. In the summer of 1938, Miller preached two weeks in Greenville to a congregation established by Keeble a year earlier. Building on this foundation, Miller baptized twenty-three. Like his spiritual mentor, Miller was always careful to praise white congregations. "I thank God for the great work that the white churches are doing among my people, and I am also thankful for being called to do what little I can to hold up Christ to my people."[21]

Luke Miller in Bryan

From Greenville, Miller, at the request of F. B. Shepherd and other white Christians, traveled to Bryan and established a congregation there with thirty conversions. In the summer of 1939, Miller returned to Bryan and reaped more results. Shepherd, the chief organizer of Miller's campaigns, lauded the black evangelist, who "just closed a meeting for his race under the direction of the white church here. This is the second meeting of the kind in which the brother has been with us. His work this year was superb, and many whites, besides the colored, heard him and were convinced of the truth of his preaching." After Miller collaborated with Shepherd and other white saints to plant the church in Bryan, Lonnie Smith, a dynamic song leader and Keeble convert from Florida, became its minister. "We are all rejoicing over this splendid meeting," added Shepherd. "Lonnie Smith will continue with this group under the oversight of the white congregation."[22]

Encouraged and inspired by his experiences in Bryan, Shepherd urged other white Christians to reach out to their black neighbors. "The work of colored Luke Miller also contributed much to our success. Two things can be accomplished by a white church supporting negro work: A colored church can be established, and many whites will hear the gospel who would not otherwise hear it from a white preacher. Once interested they can be persuaded to obey the truth when the white man follows."[23] In an era of deeply felt racial animosity, some whites such as Shepherd could swallow their racist sentiment and understand that concern for the spiritual plight of African Americans had mutual benefits as whites led blacks into the Churches of Christ and blacks simultaneously swayed whites to obey the "pure gospel."

But of course to imagine that only the concern of white Christians drove the impetus behind the rise of black Churches of Christ in Texas is to miss the important contributions African Americans themselves made to the emergence of their own congregations. While the racist economic structure of the era severely restricted blacks' fiscal latitude, African Americans in Texas used whatever resources they could muster to reach their own people with God's Word. Charlie Spiller, a zealous black man who converted to the Churches of Christ under the preaching of William Owens in Memphis, moved to East Texas in the late 1930s. While working at the Chevrolet auto dealership in Sulphur Springs, Spiller was disappointed to find no black congregation in the town, so he began searching for a way of changing this situation. Spiller "did not stop until he got with the white brethren at Sulphur Springs, and told them that his people must hear the pure Gospel, and the whites having confidence in him told him to look out for a Gospel preacher, and he sent for Bro. Luke Miller and he came to this little town and baptized 32 and a fine congregation is here now." The date of the founding of the Ardis Street (now the Martin Luther King) Church of Christ remains unclear. But certainly passionate black Christians such as Spiller helped stir interest in the spiritual plight of fellow African Americans. Armed with desire, black Christians rarely possessed the resources to pursue their passion.[24]

Luke Miller in Jacksonville and Cameron

Concern for the souls of black people brought Miller to Jacksonville, Texas, in the summer of 1941. His meeting produced seventy-two baptisms and established what is now the Seminary Heights Church of Christ. Immediately after the founding of this congregation, Brother Veasy, a preacher from Atlanta, Georgia, ministered one year and baptized thirty more people. John Henry Clay followed with a one-year tenure, which engendered fifteen additions. By 1944 Thomas W. Wright, a former Baptist minister who converted to the Churches of Christ, had assumed leadership of the young Jacksonville congregation.[25]

The summer of 1946 found Miller in Cameron where he established a black congregation with twenty-nine baptisms. Jack Southern, a white minister in Cameron, reported, "The colored section of the town has been turned upside down. They had never heard anything like this. We had the meeting in the open air, and there were at least four hundred of the Negro race present every night. They are interested, and it is our duty now to keep them that way. We need a building and a preacher just as soon as possible. The white church here is willing to do all it can, but there is a limit to what it can do because [it is] few in number."[26] While not all white churches in Texas had the numerical and financial strength to support fledgling black congregations, even smaller white churches lent their limited resources to evangelistic efforts.

Luke Miller in Lufkin and Weslaco

By the 1950s Miller had relocated his base to Lufkin, Texas, where he worked for a year. "The past twelve months I have been working in this section, called and supported by the white church of Lufkin. I thank God for this great church and all white churches for the work they are doing to spread the gospel among my people." Miller reported that in 1950 he had established two congregations, helped erect two new church buildings, and produced over two hundred converts.[27]

The next year a Miller meeting in Weslaco, just a few miles from Mexico, resulted in eleven black, and many more white, converts. "Many

A group of Christians standing outside their building in Brownwood, Texas.
(Photo courtesy of Doris Benitez and Nora Taylor)

came out of curiosity and learned the truth and were baptized," Miller reported. "I am thankful to the white church there for calling me and encouraging me so wonderfully." Miller particularly praised Jack Mackey and Bill Reeves who "encouraged and helped me much, as did all the churches and preachers of the Rio Grande Valley."[28]

Luke Miller and the Debating Tradition

Although a highly effective evangelist, Miller was more than a preacher. Like his spiritual father, Miller mastered the art of argumentation and debate, having inherited the debating tradition from white cohorts in Churches of Christ. In 1952 Miller, now working with a fledgling black congregation in Mount Pleasant, traveled to Florence, South Carolina, to debate S. C. Johnson, an apostle for the Church of the Lord Jesus Christ of the Apostolic Faith, Inc. The two men discussed two topics—the Godhead and instrumental music in worship. Louise Whitaker, a member of the West Adair Street Church of Christ in Valdosta, Georgia, reported that when Bishop Johnson arrived he "wanted to call off the debate. He went through with it and was miserably defeated." Johnson, according to Whitaker, insisted that God, Christ, and the Holy Spirit were "one person," and he "claimed to have been baptized by the Holy Spirit as were the apostles, but neither he nor his members were able to find the Scriptures that he wanted. He refused to meet Brother Miller again."[29]

But Miller did debate Johnson again, this time in Miami, Florida. "The churches in Miami called me and supported me," wrote Miller. "Again the truth prevailed. The Bishop was soundly defeated and he and the audience knew it. One of the moderators was baptized after the debate. Nothing can overcome the word of God."[30] A third debate between Miller and Johnson took place in September of 1952. Churches of Christ in Miami "combined" their financial resources to send Miller to Philadelphia, Pennsylvania, to debate Johnson. The discussion was held in Johnson's church building, a former John Wanamaker facility, with over two thousand people in attendance the first night. W. Ray Duncan, a white believer from Miami accompanied Miller to the debate. Johnson, according to Duncan, refused to adhere to the rules and regulations. Miller waited almost two hours before Johnson declined to debate. The second night Johnson engaged Miller for an hour before the Pentecostal preacher again closed the debate. Johnson also used his radio program to launch "vicious" attacks against the Churches of Christ. The station manager warned Johnson to cease his rude "tactics" immediately "or else be put off the air."[31]

After his three debates with Johnson, Miller returned to Miami then continued his evangelistic work in Texas, Alabama, and Louisiana in the late 1950s.[32] In 1954 Marshall Keeble toured the state of Texas to raise funds for the Nashville Christian Institute. When reporting on his tour, Keeble mentioned the contribution of Miller to the development of African American Churches of Christ in Texas. "Luke Miller," wrote Keeble, "spent over fifteen years with this church [in Port Arthur] and he is loved by all of the members, white and colored, for his great work."[33]

Miller's efforts ended on February 1, 1962, when he died of a heart attack in Bradenton, Florida.[34] After his conversion to Churches of Christ in 1920, Miller soon emerged as one of the most beloved and effective black evangelists in the history of Churches of Christ. A convert and protégé of Marshall Keeble, Miller accomplished some of his most impressive work in the Lone Star State, baptizing some ten thousand people and establishing several congregations in Texas in the 1930s and 1940s, the era of the Great Depression and Jim Crow. Even though many white Christians felt the weight of the Depression, they looked beyond their own dismal circumstances, found the material resources, and called African American evangelists such as Luke Miller to evangelize their black neighbors. Through this bi-racial outreach and collaboration, white believers reached out to their black neighbors even as they adhered scrupulously to the customs of segregation.

Chapter 6

OUT ON THE FIRING LINE

L. H. Alexander, F. A. Livingston, and the Rise of African American Churches of Christ in West Texas

This will let the brotherhood know
we are still on the firing line.

—Sopha Pink, 1941

If Luke Miller was the catalyst for the rise of African American Churches of Christ in East Texas, L. H. Alexander and F. A. Livingston served similarly in the state's western regions. Like Miller, Alexander came under the influence and tutelage of Marshall Keeble. Born on March 30, 1912, in Murfreesboro, Tennessee, Lucius H. Alexander was the son of William and Matilda Alexander. After the death of his father, ten-year-old Lucius, his mother, and four siblings moved to Nashville. Matilda Alexander, a devout and loyal Methodist, instructed her family in the way of the Lord. Beyond this, very little is known of Lucius's family background.[1]

The Evangelistic Work of Lucius H. Alexander

In 1926 Lucius, age fourteen, became a member of the Church of Christ in Nashville through the preaching of Marshall Keeble. Three years later young Lucius, encouraged by both white and black leaders, committed himself to preaching the "pure gospel." Recalling his personal experiences, Alexander wrote, "I was helped and encouraged by F. B. Srygley and E. G. Collins, of the Gospel Advocate, and by M. Keeble. During my four years of evangelistic work between four hundred and eight hundred were instructed in the truth." Within a ten-year span Alexander reported that he had planted two congregations, one in Savage, Mississippi, and the other in Bandana, Kentucky. He considered 1936 "my most successful year" as an evangelist, baptizing one hundred people and engaging in six religious debates.[2]

Two other events marked 1936 for Alexander. On October 18 Alexander married Cremmon Campbell, a beautiful young woman from Pensacola, Florida, the daughter of W. C. and Edna Campbell. Marshall Keeble had baptized both parents in 1933 during a meeting in Pensacola. Young Cremmon later received baptism at the hands of Richard Taylor. Shortly after their marriage Lucius and Cremmon Alexander, at the recommendation of Marshall Keeble, moved to Lubbock, Texas, in 1936 during the throes of the Great Depression. In order to help make ends meet in Depression West Texas and in order to help her husband fulfill his divine calling, Cremmon Alexander recalled picking cotton, making dresses from croker sacks, and cutting yards for white Christians to get food. When asked whether she had enjoyed being a preacher's wife, Alexander replied: "I did, but it was hard."[3]

Lucius and his wife stayed with the fledgling black church in Lubbock for a year, working with the congregation, now the Twentieth and Birch Church of Christ, planted by Marshall Keeble in 1932. From Lubbock the Alexanders moved to Abilene where they worked with what is now the North Tenth and Treadaway Church of Christ. During Alexander's seven-year tenure, the Abilene congregation experienced spiritual and numerical growth. The reports of Lewis Diggs and Sopha Pink, faithful members of the Treadaway congregation, portrayed Alexander busy teaching classes, conducting funerals, baptizing lost souls, and preaching both in Abilene and widely beyond.[4]

From Abilene the Alexander clan moved to Denver, Colorado, to resolve a church schism. After a one-year stint in Denver they returned to Texas, settling in Midland in 1944. When Alexander arrived, he found six members meeting in a congregation established by Luke Miller four years earlier. White members of the North A and Tennessee Church of Christ had invited Miller to Midland, where he preached fourteen days and baptized twelve people. J. F. Cofield had served as the church's first minister.[5] Rose Lee Butler, of Midland's Lee Street Church of Christ, lauded Alexander as "our faithful minister, and he is doing a splendid work." She added, "He came to Midland in 1944 and found only six members. The work has grown to over one hundred members and we have built one of

L. H. Alexander (1912-1994) preached for many years in Lubbock, Abilene, and Midland, Texas, and established the annual West Texas Lectureship in Midland, Texas, in 1959. Here Alexander (seated second from the left) is shown with preachers from Texas and beyond.
(Photo taken from Lectureship Booklet)

the nicest brick buildings in the state." The edifice included an auditorium accommodating three hundred people, supported by three classrooms and a preacher's office, and valued at $35,000.[6]

But Alexander's influence reached beyond the city of Midland. While devoting most of his energies to building up the Lee Street congregation, Alexander also found time to plant churches in other West Texas towns. In 1938 Alexander founded a church in Spur, and later organized black congregations in Odessa, Kermit, and Spur. In 1954 he planted a black congregation in Monahans, and two years later he gathered an African American flock in Synder.[7]

In addition to church planting in West Texas, Alexander also mentored several young men who themselves worked as ministers, contributing to the growth and development of black Churches of Christ across the country. Alvin A. Thomas and Jefferson R. Caruthers Sr., two of his most influential protégés, received teaching and training from Alexander.

Thomas ministered several years to the Twentieth and Birch Church of Christ in Lubbock and received invitations from white Christians in Texas to evangelize their black neighbors. He explained, "I was called to Dickens, Texas by the white church there to conduct a meeting for my people at Croton." The meeting continued for ten nights and nine were baptized.[8] Jim Crow practice, of course, mandated the maintaining of separate congregations for these new black Christians.

Like his mentor L. H. Alexander, Thomas broadened his evangelistic reach beyond West Texas. In the spring of 1951, white Christians in McGehee, Arkansas, invited Thomas to preach among their black neighbors. "We have just closed a meeting in McGehee, Ark.," reported Thomas, "sponsored by the white brethren. May God bless them in their effort to spread the gospel. Twenty precious souls were baptized." Thomas left behind a new black congregation of thirty-three people.[9]

Jefferson R. Caruthers, born and reared in Midland, became a member of the Lee Street Church of Christ at an early age. At Alexander's urging, Caruthers began preaching and moved east to Tennessee where he enrolled in the Nashville Christian Institute. While a student there Caruthers traveled with Marshall Keeble on preaching excursions. He then moved to California, finishing high school there before joining the U.S. Air Force. After a brief stint in the military and after living many years in California, Caruthers returned to Texas to serve congregations in Paris and Lubbock. The peripatetic Caruthers then spent several productive years ministering to the Westside Church of Christ in Rockford, Illinois, before relocating to help a newly established congregation in Star City, Arkansas.[10]

In addition to working as a church planter and mentor, L. H. Alexander was also a newspaper editor and author. From 1956 to 1960 Alexander edited the *Southwestern Christian Advocate*, a newspaper that kept Christians in the Southwest abreast of happenings in African American Churches of Christ. The paper, even though short-lived, enjoyed a circulation of approximately five thousand subscribers. Additionally, Alexander in 1985 published a book entitled, *What Did the Apostles Bind?*, and he also contributed articles to the *Christian Counselor*, the *Christian Echo*, and the *Gospel Advocate*.[11]

L. H. Alexander's most enduring legacy, however, may well have been the creation of the Annual West Texas Lectureship. Designed to provide "strength in the gospel, and to uplift Christians and bring them closer to CHRIST," the West Texas Lectureship, launched in 1959, takes place each

April. It attracts hundreds of Christians, mostly African Americans, from across West Texas and neighboring western states, including New Mexico, Arizona, Colorado, and California. Alexander died on May 12, 1994, in Midland, but his legacy still touches the lives of black westerners.[12]

The Evangelistic Work of Fleming A. Livingston

The story of African American Churches of Christ in West Texas, however, reaches beyond the career of L. H. Alexander. Fleming A. Livingston, a native of South Carolina, converted to Churches of Christ in Florida under the preaching of Marshall Keeble. Even though little is known about Livingston's background, he clearly contributed significantly to the emergence of black Churches of Christ in West Texas. Livingston worked as a preacher in Lawton, Oklahoma, for several years. From his base in Oklahoma, Livingston came by the invitation of white Christians to Vernon, Texas, to evangelize African Americans in that Texas town. In the summer of 1935, Livingston's protracted meeting engendered twenty-six baptisms and established a black Church of Christ in Vernon. R. L. Colley, a white leader in Vernon, reported, "Brother Livingston is a great gospel preacher, and will take care of the truth among his race anywhere." While preaching in Vernon, Livingston also debated a Pentecostal minister who "tried to establish his prayer theory with him in debate, but made a poor 'out.' Several made the confession the same night of the debate."[13] Like his spiritual father, Keeble, Livingston embraced the debating tradition begun by Alexander Campbell in the early nineteenth century.[14] Indeed, religious discussions in public often piqued the interest of both white and black listeners who, after being attracted to the protracted meeting, became members of the Churches of Christ.

On September 16, 1936, Livingston relocated to nearby Wichita Falls and assumed leadership of a black congregation planted by Marshall Keeble a month earlier. Livingston, while working in Wichita Falls, also evangelized Lubbock, Corsicana, and Vernon, as well as Bradenton, Florida. Livingston credited white Christians, especially in Wichita Falls, for his success in these cities. "I could not have done the little good accomplished in the above meetings," Livingston wrote, "but for the white disciples in Wichita Falls, where I am laboring with my race. The Tenth and Austin Street and Polk Street congregations have stood behind me fully."[15]

By 1941 the membership of the black Welch Street Church of Christ in Wichita Falls had increased to seventy-two people, and in January of that year Livingston led his flock into a "new building" costing $1,056.81. "The colored church paid $50 on the lot and $50 on the building." The Tenth and Austin Church of Christ and the Buchanan Street Church of Christ, however, funded the balance. At the dedicatory services, black preachers F. A. Livingston, E. W. Anderson, and S. T. W. Gibbs Sr. delivered messages; at the afternoon service, white ministers Robert C. Jones and J. R. Waldrum "made short talks." Jones concluded, "With this nice, new house in a good location, we believe this church is in a position to do great things for Christ among the colored people of Wichita Falls."[16]

Livingston had moved on to Fort Worth by 1950 to serve the Stop Six Church of Christ.[17] In 1951 Carrie C. Ferrell, a member of the Stop Six congregation, praised Livingston for his work with the young people, and she commended his wife for her service to the ladies Bible class. Ferrell particularly thanked white believers for their interest in the Stop Six congregation, stating, "We are grateful for the help from the white disciples and their interest in Brother Livingston."[18] Sister Ferrell understood the importance of black Christians receiving financial assistance from white benefactors.

Throughout the 1950s, Livingston, from his post in Fort Worth, preached across the Lone Star State. Like Keeble, Livingston consistently expressed appreciation to white believers for their support of his preaching campaigns. After preaching in Haskell, Livingston acknowledged, "The white church in Haskell sponsored this work"; while evangelizing African Americans in Knox City, Livingston averred, "I thank God for what the white churches of Christ are doing to send the gospel to my race." After baptizing four people in Burkburnett, Livingston acknowledged that his evangelistic work was "sponsored by the white church in that city."[19] In 1952 Livingston returned to Haskell and baptized three people, including two deacons from the Baptist Church. "The white disciples there," declared Livingston, "have done much to establish the church."[20] The following year, Livingston, after preaching in Electra and Haskell, thanked God "for the fine way in which the white churches of Christ are helping the colored brethren." After advancing the "pure gospel" in Chillicothe and Plainview, Livingston again applauded "the white disciples" for "encouraging and helping me to preach Christ to my race." Livingston, upon planting a black congregation in Oakwood, rejoiced "for the way white Christians are getting behind the work among the colored brethren."[21]

A fundamental reason for such black–white cooperation lay in the shared theology of exclusivism. In 1953 Livingston wrote an article in the *Gospel Advocate* entitled "Don't 'Thumb' Your Way" which reflected the shared theology that pervaded African American Churches of Christ in Texas. Comparing religious seekers to hitch-hikers, Livingston denounced people who sought "to 'thumb' their way to heaven instead of purchasing a ticket." Livingston especially rebuked religionists who accepted the dogma of Baptists, Methodists, and other groups indiscriminately. Such people, Livingston insisted, "'thumb' down any church coming their way. They do not care what model it is—Methodist, Baptist, Presbyterian, Adventist—anything will do."[22] In Livingston's mind, obeying the "pure gospel" entailed one's hearing God's Word, believing it, repenting of one's sins, confessing Christ publicly, and being immersed. These

Fleming A. Livingston, a native of South Carolina, was taught, baptized, and trained by Marshall Keeble. Shown with his wife (above), Livingston left a significant legacy among African American Churches of Christ as a preacher and debater.

five steps, which became an integral part of the theological platform of African American Churches of Christ, had become the standard "plan of salvation" in the Stone–Campbell tradition beginning with Walter Scott about 1827.[23]

On October 11, 1953, Livingston continued his ministerial work in Fort Worth, preaching and restoring seven at the Stop Six Church of Christ.[24] The following March he preached at the Lake Como church in the same city, baptizing seven people and restoring five more. With such results, Livingston quickly exclaimed, "God's word hasn't lost any of its power!"[25] At the end of the 1950s, Livingston moved back to Vernon where the congregation "accomplished more within the last ten months than they had within fifteen years." He then announced plans to evangelize in Columbus, Ohio, and Lawton, Oklahoma.[26] In 1960 Livingston reported that his black congregation in Vernon was "small in number but strong in the faith." While laboring with the congregation there, he also worked to gather a new flock in Crowell, Texas. Livingston again commended white Christians for contributing to these mission works.[27]

F. A. Livingston died in Seattle, Washington, in 1969 after a long life of fulltime evangelism. He shared with Luke Miller and L. H. Alexander the tutelage of Marshall Keeble, and like fellow easterners Miller and Alexander, Livingston arrived in Texas in the 1930s to assume oversight of a new congregation established by his spiritual father. Livingston nurtured several black congregations in the Lone Star State, but his contribution remains virtually unrecognized. Of equal note these three spiritual sons espoused with Keeble a doctrinal position of theological exclusivism, that is, they held that all people beyond the fellowship of Churches of Christ could not claim to be true followers of Jesus. This sectarian perspective not only placed them at odds with, and isolated them from, other religious groups, but it also affected their view of the social issues of their day. Together with many of their white comrades in Churches of Christ, African Americans such as Keeble, Miller, Alexander, and Livingston focused their efforts on improving the spiritual condition of black people, but chose to virtually ignore their social plight. Having determined to dedicate their lives to matters of eternal consequences, they left aside affairs of temporal concern. So in an era of remarkable social upheaval, their sermons and writings largely exhibited no interest in the burgeoning civil rights movement of their day.[28] But through their chosen task, L. H. Alexander and F. A. Livingston played seminal roles in reshaping the religious structure of the Lone Star state.

PART III

The Legacy of G. P. Bowser in Texas

Chapter 7

Standing on Apostolic Ground

G. P. Bowser, the *Christian Echo*, and the Division between African American Churches of Christ and Disciples of Christ in Texas

The school and the Christian Echo,
taught and edited, respectively, by Brother
Bowser, should receive the aid and encouragement
of all, regardless of color... He has only one arm,
and is unable to work or to baptize; but he can set type,
and can preach orally and through the Echo.

—M. F. Womack, 1909

The year 1902 proved pivotal for African Americans in the Stone–Campbell Movement. In that year George Philip Bowser launched in Tennessee the *Christian Echo*, a journal designed to encourage, instruct, and unite blacks in Churches of Christ. Of all the periodicals started by "loyal" African American leaders, only Bowser's journal remains in publication. Bowser's journalistic endeavor helped draw a line of demarcation between black Churches of Christ and black Disciples of Christ. If David Lipscomb and his *Gospel Advocate* distanced whites in Churches of Christ from their white "digressive" brethren, Bowser and his *Christian Echo* helped maintain a broadening wedge between African American Churches of Christ and their black Disciple brethren, underscoring the importance of religious journalism in a movement that rejected any denominational infrastructure.[1]

G. P. Bowser's Journey into Churches of Christ

G. P. Bowser underwent a long and tedious pilgrimage from Methodism to the Churches of Christ. Born in Maury County, Tennessee, in 1874, Bowser grew up in the uncertain and unstable decade of the 1870s. The Panic of 1873, the Hamburg Massacre in South Carolina on July 4, 1876, the withdrawal of federal troops from the South in 1877, and the westward migration of forty thousand "Exodusters" from Mississippi, Alabama, Louisiana, and Tennessee—all scarred the world of young Bowser with terror, violence, and instability.[2] But Bowser, exhibiting what one writer has called "undying dedication,"[3] united with the African Methodist Episcopal Church, received a license to preach in that denomination, and studied biblical and classical languages at Walden University in Nashville. Bowser understood early in life that the path to black independence and upward mobility lay in knowledge.

In 1897 Bowser's theological journey took him from Methodism to the Gay Street Christian Church in Nashville. "Recognizing that the teaching of the Methodist Church is, in many respects, erroneous," Bowser wrote, "I decided to unite with the body of people known as 'Christian.' I am greatly indebted to Brother Samuel Davis for instruction in the way of the Lord."[4] Samuel Davis, a black minister in Tennessee, led Bowser out of the AME Church into the Christian Church or Disciples of Christ, but the black preachers Alexander Campbell and Samuel W. Womack then persuaded him to leave the Christian Church and align himself with Churches of Christ. When later explaining his conversion experience, Bowser remarked, "Being determined to follow Christ according to the plan laid down by the apostles in the book of God, and to follow nothing else, I was still in a state of dissatisfaction. The organ was used; the Christian Womans' Board of Missions, the Young People's Society of Christian Endeavor, the Buds of Hope, and the Stags flourished in our denomination; festivals and such life were resorted to, by the congregation of which I was a member, for the purpose of raising money."[5] Like white "loyals" in Churches of Christ, Bowser came to believe that all evangelistic work and all fundraising efforts must be accomplished through the local church, not an allied organization. J. P. Lowrey, a white leader in Florida Churches of Christ, put Bowser's position most succinctly by asserting, "The church of the Lord Jesus Christ is the only institution on earth through which God has ordained that lost souls should be reached and saved."[6]

After leaving the Gay and Lea Christian Churches, Bowser joined with Alexander Campbell and Samuel W. Womack, two black preachers and co-founders of the Jackson Street Church of Christ in Nashville, who took their stand on "apostolic grounds." Bowser soon emerged as an influential evangelist, educator, and editor among black Christians in Middle Tennessee.[7] In the winter of 1902, a group of African American preachers in Churches of Christ announced plans to publish a periodical for "the teaching of pure New Testament Christianity in the interest of the church of Christ in the United States." The preachers, desiring to stay "more in touch with one another," wanted the periodical to appear first as a monthly and later as a weekly, but the paper, tentatively called *The Minister's Bulletin*, evidently never materialized.[8] Bowser, however, picked up the failed project and created the *Christian Echo*, a journal designed to encourage, instruct, and unite blacks in Churches of Christ.

Perhaps more significantly, Bowser's founding of the *Christian Echo* reflected his desire for black autonomy as well as his interest in uplifting African Americans. Bowser articulated his concern for the social plight of black people in his answer to Henry Robinson who asked whether a Christian should raise money for the National Association for the Advancement of Colored People (NAACP) "to help get a worldly man out of trouble." Bowser replied, "The NAACP is the greatest organization in the world in helping to see the Negro gets justice before the court. If it be in the mind of members of the Church of Christ that justice was not meted out to the murderer, it is up to them to contribute."[9] Significantly, Bowser issued this statement in the pages of the *Christian Echo*, but did not attempt its publication in the columns of the *Gospel Advocate* or *Firm Foundation*. To make such a statement in a white-controlled paper would have been deemed an affront, as Anglos in Churches of Christ tended to draw back from political activity in general, and rarely evinced any concern for the civil rights of blacks. While Bowser's supreme desire focused on evangelizing the souls of black folk and to illuminating their minds, he also understood the importance of social justice for African Americans.

Through the columns of his periodical, Bowser sought to lead blacks in Churches of Christ away from the Disciples of Christ when the rupture in the Stone–Campbell Movement developed in the late nineteenth and early twentieth centuries. In 1915 William M. Davis, a member of the Church of Christ in Turner, Arkansas, wrote to the *Christian Echo* that his congregation was in "bad condition," and he singled out R. C. Harris who "tore off from us on account of quarterlies." Harris, a leader of the church in Turner, evidently believed that using published Sunday school material ("quarterlies") for Bible study was scripturally wrong, so he began "a meeting in his home." Davis further reported that some members in Turner were in "favor of using a digressive preacher" from the Christian Church.[10] In response, Bowser advised, "I do not encourage the use of digressive preachers; better [to] be alone than in error." He also chided Harris for causing a disturbance in Turner, asserting: "There is no more harm to use quarterlies than it would be for one to comment on the Scriptures in preaching. This Brother Harris and all other preachers do."[11] Bowser's response and counsel reflect the growing estrangement between blacks in both the Churches of Christ and the Christian Churches across the movement.

Throughout the 1920s, however, both white and black preachers in Churches of Christ continued to interact with members of the Disciples of Christ in spite of their theological differences. In 1921 W. C. Graves and white members of the West End Church of Christ in Birmingham, Alabama, invited Marshall Keeble to their city to preach to African Americans. Keeble's meeting produced sixty-two responses, fifteen of whom came from the Disciples of Christ. "While in this meeting," he reported, "I also used God's word and brought fifteen 'digressives' to the conclusion to take a stand with us and worship God according to the Scriptures."[12] Keeble's statement indicates that in his view those who worshiped with musical instruments had deviated from God's Word.

White members in both groups of the divided Restoration Movement similarly continued to clash over the use of instrumental music in worship and evangelism through missionary societies. In 1922 T. P. Burt, a white minister of the Church of Christ in Farwell, Texas, informed *Gospel Advocate* readers that his flock was "moving along very nicely," after taking up the use of a building abandoned by members of the Christian Churches. "Our digressive brethren have a house of worship here, which they are not using, having been put out of business last summer during our protracted meeting, when a number of them abandoned the doctrines of men and are now worshiping with the loyal brethren without addition or subtraction."[13] Many black churches mirrored such experiences; in 1925 Marshall Keeble, while preaching in Paducah, Kentucky, reported that the "digressive brethren are permitting us to use their meetinghouse, and they are attending."[14] In 1927 Keeble's seven-day meeting in Louisville, Kentucky, yielded "three baptisms, all from sects, and seven came from the 'digressives.'"[15] In the same year in Tampa, Florida,

Keeble "preached in the digressives' meetinghouse two nights until the tent came." The black evangelist's campaign ended with ninety-nine baptisms, and he noted, "seven came from the 'digressives' and took their stand with the loyal church of Christ."[16] In 1929 G. P. Bowser, after preaching for several weeks in California, reported, "Twelve were baptized in this meeting; four took membership from the Christian Church and two from the Church of the Living God."[17]

In the 1930s, blacks in Churches of Christ continued to welcome brothers and sisters from the Christian Churches into their non-instrumental fellowship without rebaptism. In a 1934 instance, R. L. Colley, a white minister for the Church of Christ in Vernon, Texas, reported a "good day with the church here," gladly announcing two baptisms and four persons who "came from the Christian Church."[18] Later that year, Amos Lincoln Cassius, a son of Samuel Robert Cassius, reported that his "mission meeting" in Phoenix, Arizona, led to the establishment of a congregation in that city. He noted, "Twelve members of the Christian Church promised to attend services."[19] In 1937 Amos furnished a historical sketch of the Phoenix congregation he planted three years earlier, pointing out that several meetings had been conducted by Marshall Keeble, R. N. Hogan, and himself. The trio collaborated to strengthen and stabilize the fledgling flock, and Cassius added, "during the meetings in Phoenix nearly every active member of the Christian Church came to the church of Christ, some demanding baptism."[20]

After helping to establish a congregation in Hobbs, New Mexico, Cassius again gave a short history of what has become known as the Roxanna Church of Christ. He observed, "one other member was located and began to work, two came from the Christian Church and two were baptized." L. W. Sparks, a member of the Christian Church and a visiting schoolteacher from Corsicana, Texas, attended the protracted meeting, and she "questioned the difference between the Christian Church and the church of Christ and publicly announced that she would unite and work with the church of Christ in Corsicana when she returned home."[21]

In the summer of 1938, James L. Lovell, a white editor and avid supporter of black evangelists, reported that R. N. Hogan had baptized three hundred people that year, planted new congregations in Los Angeles, California, Sherman, Texas, and Oklahoma City, Oklahoma, and persuaded numerous people to leave the Christian Church.[22] Later that year, Amos Lincoln Cassius, while preaching in Clearview, Oklahoma, persuaded "Bro. Mayberry and his entire congregation of the Christian

Church" to come "to Christ."[23] Cassius's report indicates a certain ambivalence concerning the status of members of the Christian Churches: he required that they reject the practices of the Christian Church, but he allowed that they were already "in Christ" and need not be re-baptized. By the fall of 1938, E. W. Anderson, a preacher from Texas, had relocated to Denver, Colorado, to work with the Ogden Street Church of Christ. Anderson reported having produced "eight additions since I moved here—seven baptized and one from the Christian Church."[24]

The next year F. B. Shepherd, a white leader among Texas Churches of Christ, was so encouraged by the successful outreach to African Americans in Bryan that he urged other congregations to "sponsor a meeting for the colored." The consequent summer meeting, he reported, "closed with nineteen immersed and several others persuaded to leave the Christian Church and come back home."[25]

The Bowser-Rouse Exchange

Others did not imagine that the practices of the Christian Church diverged from biblical norms. Thomas K. Rouse, a Tennessee native and former member of black Churches of Christ, relocated to Detroit, Michigan, and there aligned himself with the Christian Churches in 1938. Over a twelve-month period, Rouse and his old friend G. P. Bowser carried on a series of exchanges in the *Christian Echo*. In their first discussion, Rouse referred to the use of instrumental music in worship as "simply silly" and "far too valueless to be seriously concerned about." Bowser agreed that instrumental music was indeed "simple," but he added that it was "a simple addition to God's expressed way of making music in the worship."[26]

Rouse insisted that the Lord never commanded that there be no instrumental music in worship. God's son "came to earth and had many things to say for the guidance and salvation of man, and yet He made no such statement. Jesus left His apostles to carry on the spiritual work which he began but they also failed to make any such statement." Bowser retorted that to worship with instruments of music was tantamount to putting "water and lamb chops on the communion table." He added, "the very chapter and verse where Christ and His apostles commanded mechanical instruments of music of worship I will find lamb chops and water in the Lord's supper. The Bible is indeed the revealed will of God to man, and that is just the reason we dare not use the music in the worship. God did not reveal it in the New Testament as His will." In concert with many of his white comrades and contemporaries, Bowser founded his opposition to using musical instruments in worship on the basis of scriptural silence.[27]

In their second exchange, Rouse related the story of a Church of Christ minister who said, "God commanded me to sing, and gave me vocal organs with which to do it, so I don't need a man made instrument to assist me in doing what God commanded." A few days later Rouse met the preacher and asked him to explain the statement. The minister consented and told Rouse, "Give me your Bible and I will show you my reasons for so saying." Then Rouse explained: "He took it, then reached into his coat pocket and got his glasses and started to put them on, when I said, No! No! I object to those spectacles, because God commanded you to read His word and gave you optical organs with which to do so, and you don't need any manmade instrument to assist you in doing God's commands. He laughed, gave me back my Bible and changed the topic of conversation; like Haman of old, he was hanged on his own gallows."[28] Bowser, in reply, differentiated between general commands and specific mandates, explaining: "When a command is given without specifying the how, we are privileged to use our judgment in carrying it out. The command is to 'Go and preach' as the 'how' is not expressed, one may ride, walk or sail." Bowser jested that "I know T. K. [Rouse] well and no instrument is necessary to aid his singing as he and I are lacking in tune. I ask T. K. to look in the Bible looking glass and he will behold himself hanging on the gallows of skepticism for lack of Divine authority for the use of instrumental music in worship."[29]

In the third dialogue, Rouse cited a story from the life of renowned evangelist Billy Sunday to argue that since instruments are in heaven there should be no prohibition against using them in worship on earth. A church member, after complaining that the orchestra in a Billy Sunday preaching service seemed to resemble a circus, asked, "Could we not get along without that instrumental music?" Sunday replied: "Well brother, if you will read your Bible you'll find there is instrumental music in heaven, and God put it there, also in his worship on earth, also you know there is music in the air and God placed it there but there is one place where God did not place any instrumental music (and Mr. Sunday promptly named the often-heard four-letter word) so if you are trying to get away from instrumental music there is where you will have to go."[30] Bowser then referred to Revelation 4:5, 12:3, 14:1–5 to show that many passages in John's Apocalypse must not be taken literally. The 144,000 mentioned in

Revelation, noted Bowser, excluded both Billy Sunday and Rouse. "Mr. Sunday and T. K. with others hold that God put it in the worship on earth, but they will not give us one Bible text from the New Testament to prove it. Bill Sunday might have been a well-read man, but he never did read where God, Christ or any apostle ever authorized instrumental music in church worship."[31]

Rouse then recalled that he discussed the instrumental music topic with a Church of Christ member who said, "Well, I don't see any harm in instrumental music. I don't know why my people fight it." Bowser replied, "Every loyal disciple of Christ fights it because it came from Rome and not from God."[32] From Bowser's perspective, the Roman Catholic Church, not Christ, introduced instrumental music into Christian worship.

Rouse then cited Pres. Franklin D. Roosevelt, who described a "4-inch tail that wags the 96-inch dog." Rouse used the quotation to suggest that Bowser and other members of Churches of Christ were advocates of "religious autocracy." In response, Bowser elevated the writings of John W. McGarvey, a prominent white leader and Bible expositor in the Stone–Campbell Movement, above the wit of President Franklin, asserting, "You quote Mr. Roosevelt, but he has never seen the gospel truth. Surely you would recognize J. W. McGarvey as a 'prudent thinker'" who said, "It appears to me to be the unquestionable duty of all writers and speakers to combine all their power and influence against the introduction of another organ. It is a departure from apostolic practice." Bowser also cited the white reformer, Alexander Campbell, who said, "I presume to all spiritually-minded Christians such aids would be as a cow-bell in a concert." Bowser vowed to return to the Disciples of Christ if Rouse and his cohorts could "find one text with divine authority for the existence of the Christian Church with its innovations."[33]

In the fourth discussion, Rouse delineated a series of contradictions among members of Churches of Christ who argued, "I don't go for this instrumental music stuff because I don't find where the New Testament recommends it." Rouse pointed out that the New Testament did not "recommend" using books, purchasing and erecting church buildings, or setting specific hours for worship, yet Churches of Christ engaged in these practices. He pointed to the New Testament's recommendation of "kissing as a form of greeting," noting that members of the Churches of Christ extended a handshake instead. "I could go on indefinitely pointing out things you do without New Testament recommendation," Rouse wrote, "but what is the use, you like every one else use common sense in such cases regardless of what the New Testament 'recommends' except the point in question!"[34]

After acknowledging "jest" in Rouse's argument, Bowser insisted that God gave specific commandments but allowed Christians the freedom of devising the method by which to execute them. "The order is to 'sing' and this embraces pitch, time, harmony, words, song books, etc., but never an organ or piano." Bowser continued, "Instrumental music is adding to God's expressed plan of making music in the worship."[35]

In the sixth exchange, Rouse suggested that members of Churches of Christ opposed instrumental music in worship for sociological reasons. "Objection to instrumental music in the worship originated back in 'horse and buggy days' when ignorance was the rule and intelligence the exception, and was destined to die when these conditions are reversed."[36] Bowser, in contrast, argued that moral corruption and disrespect for divine authority influenced people to resort to using musical instruments in worship. "The introduction of instrumental music was made as the rule and respect for God's order was the exception, and is destined to die when and where people love the Lord." Bowser concluded that using instrumental music in God's service simply mirrored the violation of Nadab and Abihu whom God destroyed for incorporating "strange fire" (Lev. 10:1–2), and "it proves one is miserably disrespectful."[37]

In the concluding dialogue, Rouse accused members of Churches of Christ of deceiving people by placing baptism and musical instruments in worship on the same spiritual plane. "If I believed in such rot," Rouse wrote, "I would explain the Great Commission thus, 'Go ye into all the world and preach the gospel to every creature, he that believeth in Christ (but not in instrumental music) shall be saved.' I would preach it at the first and not wait to 'hoodwink them into it later.' Deception is fraud!"[38] Bowser held that the Great Commission must be accepted "as it is written." He added, "I challenge T. K. to point to one that has been 'hoodwinked' into the church of Christ under the impression that instrumental music in the worship was right. He worshipped as a member of the church of Christ for years and cannot point to one that used the instrument. He has heard me from his boyhood and knows that I fought it, so he practiced deception by impressing us that he was against it."[39]

In 1941 Rouse and Bowser briefly renewed their debate. Rouse wrote that he was sending Bowser a year's subscription to the *Christian Standard*, an influential periodical among the Disciples of Christ established by Isaac Errett in 1866 in Cincinnati, Ohio. "It is now 75 years old and without doubt," Rouse noted, "the very best paper in the brotherhood. Notice how much 'broader' or 'liberal' it is now, yet solid as a granite stone. Read it carefully; let it digest well."[40] Rouse described the *Christian Standard* as "broader" and "liberal" to criticize Bowser's paper, the *Christian Echo*, insinuating that the latter was narrow and legalistic because of its firm stance against instrumental music in worship and missionary societies.

Rouse further contrasted the prosperous Jarvis Christian College in Hawkins, Texas, with Bowser's struggling school, the Bowser Christian Institute in Fort Smith, Arkansas. "Jarvis Christian College has an oil well now and is expecting more soon," Rouse wrote. "It is succeeding fine. Remember Jarvis is about the same age of Silver Point, or do you still remember it?" After poking fun at Bowser's defunct Silver Point Christian Institute, A. M. Burton's Southern Practical Institute, and Peter Lowery's Nashville Labor and Manual University—all of which fizzled out in Middle Tennessee—Rouse then explained the cause of their failure. "We all know the answer, no organization behind them, just scattered aids here and there, acting independently; without system, no one willing to let the other have the leadership and such like. Will the present attempt suffer a like fate?" With these statements Rouse underscored his staunch support of missionary societies and other organizations that pooled their resources and structured their entities to uphold and sustain preachers and schools. "Organization," maintained Rouse, "is the life source of any movement."[41]

Bowser thanked Rouse for sending the *Christian Standard*, and he read it "with appreciation." He then argued that schools operated by members of Churches of Christ failed, "not for lack of organization," but "lack of support." Bowser listed Disciples of Christ schools that either failed or struggled even "with Christian church organizations." Here the *Christian Echo* editor had in mind the New Castle Bible School and the Louisville Bible School in Kentucky and the Lum Grade School in Alabama; all of these Disciple-controlled institutions collapsed because of insufficient financial support.[42]

The Bowser–Rouse exchange reveals that the divide between Churches of Christ and Disciples of Christ continued to deepen into the twentieth century, and that the doctrinal tension that disturbed white congregations was mirrored in black churches in the Stone–Campbell Movement. Further, G. P. Bowser, strongly influenced by the writings of Alexander Campbell and John W. McGarvey, appropriated the same

G. P. Bowser (1874-1950), a former Methodist preacher, converted to Churches of Christ and worked effectively as an educator, evangelist, and editor. His legacy lives on in the evangelistic work of R. N. Hogan, J. S. Winston, and especially Southwestern Christian College in Terrell, Texas.
(Photo taken from G. E. Steward's Our Pulpit*)*

argument that white leaders used to oppose instrumental music in worship—the "silence" of the New Testament. Bowser also believed that Rouse and his cohorts who worshiped with instrumental music stood in religious error, yet he refused to insist that they be re-baptized and align themselves with Churches of Christ. Despite Bowser's disagreement with Rouse, he treated him cordially and allowed him space in the *Christian Echo.* In the end, Rouse represented an unknown number of blacks in the Stone–Campbell Movement who felt uncomfortable with what they judged as the legalistic and narrow posture of the "loyals." Yet a significant number of black ministers plainly felt that Rouse and his Christian Church fellows had moved too far from their origins.

The Question of the Decade

Gradually a fuller separation came as the difference between the Churches of Christ and the Christian Churches grew more pronounced. Throughout the decade of the 1940s, G. P. Bowser fielded a constant barrage of questions from concerned readers of the *Christian Echo* who wanted to know whether people coming from the Disciples of Christ to Churches of Christ should be re-baptized. One reader asked: "I do not understand why the church of Christ takes one from the Christian Church and does not baptize him. Are people of the Christian church in Christ?" Bowser answered: "The Christian Church is part of the church of Christ who went off into unscriptural practices. They, however, teach the plan of salvation just as we do, hence baptize 'for the remission of sins.' We are trying to correct them from the error of their way [James 5:19]."[43]

The next year Sarah J. Acox asked: "Is the Christian Church and the church of Christ the same?" and Bowser replied: "There was a time when the terms 'Christian Church' and 'church of Christ' referred to the same people. Mechanical instruments were brought into the worship at Midway, Ky. in 1859; in St. Louis shortly afterwards this faction split the church. They are now registered in Washington as two separate bodies: The Christian Church (Disciples of Christ) and the 'Church of Christ.' The Christian Church has departed so far from the truth that they are rank sects, digressive brethren. We cannot claim fellowship with them."[44] Bowser indirectly refers to L. L. Pinkerton, the leader in Kentucky, who introduced an instrument—a melodeon—into the worship, igniting a storm of controversy among Stone–Campbell Churches. The St. Louis comment probably indicates the 1869 decision in the congregation during which seventy-eight members voted for the musical instrument in worship, while ten cast ballots against it. The larger group initially agreed to keep instruments out for the sake of peace. Within a two-year period, however, proponents of musical instruments in worship gained control and forced the "loyals" out.[45] Bowser tended to view this date—1869—as a turning point in the relationship between the Churches of Christ and the Disciples of Christ.

In the fall of 1942, O. Z. Mitchell inquired of Bowser, "If a member of the Christian Church comes to the church of Christ should they [*sic*] be baptized again?" Bowser answered, "If baptized into the Christian Church, it is scriptural as they are a part of the church of Christ—our digressive brethren." When George Garrett, another reader of the *Christian Echo*, posed the same question, Bowser reiterated that "If they have been baptized under the Christian Church teaching it is not necessary as the Christian Church is a digressive faction of the church of Christ, hence our brethren. They teach faith (Heb. 11:6); repentance (Acts 17:30); confession (Matt. 10:32); baptism for remission of sins (Acts 2:38) just as we do."[46]

In 1944 a writer to the *Christian Echo* reported a good meeting in Leesburg, Texas. "This meeting was held in the Christian Church. We were able by the help of God to get them to see how unloyal they were to Christ as Lord. Seeing their mistake the whole church repented of their error, confessed their fault. Now we are happy to say that they are our faithful brethren. We got the building, elders and all."[47] The black editor later commented, "The Christian Church is part of the Church of Christ who went off in 1869 after instrumental music, societies and other worldly innovations. They however teach the first principal [*sic*], and baptism as in Acts 2:38. Those baptized under Christian Church teaching are scripturally baptized."[48]

In 1947, after Abraham Davis raised the same question in the *Echo* and received the same answer, Bowser re-emphasized that since members of the Christian Church had been immersed for the remission of sins they did not need "to be baptized again."[49] Two years later "W. J. H." asked, "If one has been Scripturally taught, and Scripturally baptized, will he be a member of the Christian Church or Church of Christ?" Bowser retorted: "The term Christian Church is not in the Bible, it would not however be wrong to use the term Christian Church, which means a church made up of Christians. For years, the Church of Christ, and Christian Church were identical. Finally, some of the members pulled off after mechanical instruments of music, society organizations and other innovations. They however held to the doctrine that made Christians. They are now beginning to compromise with the sects, and can hardly be recognized as part of the Body or Church of Christ. The plan of salvation as taught by them will make Christians. To be consistent and safe, one should quit the so-called Christian Church."[50]

Throughout the 1940s the questions to Bowser and his answers remained the same. The *Christian Echo*'s editor consistently argued that African Americans in Churches of Christ and in the Disciples of Christ shared the same spiritual heritage as descendants of Barton W. Stone and Alexander Campbell. Therefore, he never required that those moving from the "digressives" to the "loyals" be re-baptized. His ministerial colleagues, Marshall Keeble, Luke Miller, R. N. Hogan, among many others, also held this position.

Additionally, several lesser-known black preachers in the Stone–Campbell Movement worked and worshiped among the Disciples of Christ before aligning themselves with the Churches of Christ. One of these, James M. Butler, a native of Stillwater, Oklahoma, grew up in Wichita,

Kansas, where he received his education as he and his family attended the Christian Church. Young James sang in the congregation's choir as a teenager, and one day during practice Butler recalled, "two very meek men walked in and sat down on the front seats. Before dismissing they were asked to have something to say." The two men, Marshall Keeble and Luke Miller, invited members of the black Christian Church to their meeting. During the Keeble–Miller campaign, Bulter and his close friend, Russell H. Moore, "walked down the aisle together and identified ourselves with the church of Christ."[51]

Alonzo Rose, born in 1916 in Valdosta, Georgia, had to leave high school because of his father's death and the resulting harsh economic conditions. At age twenty he met and married a Christian girl who influenced him to be "religiously inclined." Rose soon became a member of the Disciples of Christ and congregants urged him into the preaching ministry. After delivering five sermons in various Christian Churches, Rose, convicted by his wife and his own conscience, "submitted to the doctrine of Christ and was baptized into the Church of Christ by D. M. English in 1940."[52] Alonzo Rose went on to have a distinguished ministerial career in Churches of Christ across the country. He and his wife produced several gifted children. Rose's sons, Floyd, Jimmy, Marshall, and Richard, became renowned preachers and similarly stamped indelible marks on the history of black Churches of Christ. Sylvia Rose, Alonzo's daughter, became the most prolific songwriter in the history of black Churches of Christ.[53] Along with Butler and Rose, other black preachers such as F. F. Carson and E. W. Anderson attended Jarvis Christian College, a Disciples of Christ school in Hawkins, Texas. These latter two, among many others, benefited from academic training in a "digressive" school, yet they committed themselves to building up African American Churches of Christ.

The lives of Butler, Rose, Carson, and Anderson open windows into the formative years of black Churches of Christ in Texas and elsewhere when many black leaders in Churches of Christ had early connections with their "digressive" brethren before aligning themselves with the "loyals." Others who shared this experience included S. W. Womack, Alexander Campbell, Samuel Robert Cassius, and G. P. Bowser; all of these men transitioned from the Disciples of Christ into the Churches of Christ. Thus, the history of black Churches of Christ cannot be fully encompassed without exploring the development of black Disciples of Christ, since the two groups were in many ways inseparable in the late nineteenth and early twentieth centuries.

The well-trained and well-educated G. P. Bowser understood this history intimately and refused to re-immerse those who transitioned from the Christian Church to the Churches of Christ. Perhaps Bowser never re-baptized his black "digressive" brethren because he himself was never re-immersed when he withdrew from the Christian Church and entered the ranks of Churches of Christ. Through the pages of the *Christian Echo* Bowser solidified his position as the theological paladin in African American Churches of Christ. And before he died in 1950 he bequeathed his militant mindset to his spiritual progeny, especially J. S. Winston and R. N. Hogan, who profoundly impacted the course of African American Churches of Christ in the Lone Star State and beyond.

Chapter 8

"A Fighter from the Heart"

J. S. Winston and the Quest for Leadership in African American Churches of Christ in Texas

Fight the good fight of faith, lay hold on eternal life, to which you were also called and have confessed the good confession in the presence of many witnesses.

—1 Timothy 6:12

John Steve Winston invaluably contributed to the growth and stabilization of African American Churches of Christ in Texas. This chapter reveals him as more than a passionate and committed church planter; he also championed church leadership and black education. In his push for the establishment of the Southern Bible Institute in Fort Worth, which evolved into Southwestern Christian College in Terrell, Winston manifested his deep desire to equip and prepare young black men for leadership roles in Churches of Christ. Indeed, the presence of Southwestern Christian College is, in many ways, a testament to Winston's passion for and preoccupation with church leadership. This institution, established in 1949 with white and black collaboration, still continues its substantial contribution to the numerical strength and stability of black Churches of Christ in Texas. Finally, Winston also became the first bona fide historian for African American Churches of Christ.

Details of Winston's early life remain obscure. Born in Conway County, Arkansas, Winston lost his father at age three. Four years later, Winston's mother, Julia, relocated with her son to Muskogee, Oklahoma. In 1917 John returned to Arkansas where he attended school and where he was baptized by Steve Mitchell in the Church of Christ. Two years later, John returned to Muskogee and aligned himself with the Disciples of Christ since the town lacked a Church of Christ.[1] In the first quarter of the twentieth century, African Americans in both the Disciples of Christ and the Churches of Christ, even though viewing each other as "estranged brethren,"[2] often mingled and interacted with each other.

J. S. Winston, however, grew dissatisfied with the practices of the Christian Church and left that fellowship. In 1931 white members of the Spaulding Boulevard Church of Christ in Muskogee organized a gospel campaign with Marshall Keeble, designed to reach African Americans in that community. Keeble's meeting engendered a remarkable 204 baptisms and inspired young Winston to return to the Churches of Christ; T. W. Brents, Muskogee's white preacher, encouraged him "to prepare for the ministry." Three years later Winston met and married Mizetta Bridges, a native of Muskogee and convert of Keeble. Mrs. Winston faithfully and diligently labored alongside her husband. When J. S. ministered in Guthrie, Oklahoma, he recalled that his wife "with the sisters hauled the stones from the river bed" to erect a church building there. The marriage lasted for fifty-two years; Mizetta died in 1986.[3]

Evangelist and Church Builder

Winston had in G. P. Bowser and R. N. Hogan his most influential mentors. Bowser, founding editor of the *Christian Echo* and a determined educator, taught Winston the art of preaching by taking him on evangelistic excursions. Winston gained further knowledge and experience from working with R. N. Hogan, a native of Arkansas and a rising ministerial star in African American Churches of Christ. In 1934 Winston, an apt song leader, and Hogan, a dynamic preacher, collaborated in Okmulgee, Oklahoma, baptizing 189 people and leaving behind a new congregation.[4] Winston then assumed oversight of this new flock as well as congregations in Langston and Guthrie before relocating to Texas.

In the spring of 1930, a bloodthirsty mob in Sherman, Texas, stormed the county courthouse, burned the building, and "roasted alive" George Hughes, a black man accused of raping a white woman. After the fact, Gov. Dan Moody called out the Texas National Guard to quell the lingering violence. Eight years later, R. N. Hogan arrived in this hotbed of racism, preaching and teaching for eighteen days. Hogan's powerful sermons stirred forty-seven conversions, and after the successful campaign white Christians agreed to furnish Winston support to help stabilize the congregation. Winston wrote, "At the close of this meeting the white brethren formulated plans whereby I could be supported in carrying on the work established by Bro. Hogan." Winston's own arduous efforts then "added twenty-three other people to the church which brings our membership up to seventy." He kept the seventy-member congregation busy, "conducting several classes during the week." On Thursday and Friday Winston instructed the men of the church, while on Saturday Verda Holton, a white member of the Walnut Street Church of Christ in Sherman, instructed the women. Winston remarked that Sister Holton "is to be highly commended for the fine work which she is doing."[5]

Six influential leaders in African American Churches of Christ. Seated on the front row: T. H. Busby (ca. 1879-1970), G. E. Steward (1906-1979), and J. S. Winston (1906-2002). Standing: Levi Kennedy (1899-1970), R. N. Hogan (1902-1997), and Marshall Keeble (1878-1968). This photo was probably taken at Southwestern Christian College in Terrell, Texas, in the early 1950s.

(Photo taken from G. E. Steward's Our Pulpit*)*

Winston stressed the importance of developing church leaders. As with Booker T. Washington, who believed that bodily cleanliness reflected "self-respect" and "virtue," Winston emphasized the importance of black church leaders exhibiting pride and personal hygiene. "Training in church leadership is being done and it is sincerely hoped that we can succeed in developing some good material for this responsibility in the church. Also training in civic pride and hygiene is being taught. It is highly important that those who lead in church affairs should be clean in person and also their homes should reflect their characters in that they are kept clean and in good repair."[6] Winston's sentiments mirror Booker T. Washington's. "I sometimes feel that almost the most valuable lesson I got at the Hampton Institute was in the use and value of the bath," Washington wrote. "I learned for the first time some of its value, not only in keeping the body healthy, but in inspiring self-respect and promoting virtue. . . . I have also tried to teach my people that some provision for bathing should be part of every house."[7]

Winston reached beyond the city of Sherman, making monthly visits to Denison, Greenville, Bonham, and Savoy, Texas. "We are encouraging the work at these places," reported Winston, "and it is our wish that we can in the near future have some capable young men who will be able to take charge of some of these places and carry on the work." The visionary Winston viewed northeast Texas as "a great field which needs development." He explained that "there are a number of good towns within a radius of fifty miles of Sherman and if concentrated effort is made here and let the work spread to the other places we will witness great things for the cause of Christ in the next year or two."[8]

In the 1940s, Winston, still ministering in Sherman, found time to reach out to neighboring communities. In the fall of 1941, he preached three weeks in Van Alstyne, eliciting sixty-six responses, fifteen baptisms and fifty-one additions from the local Christian Church. Ruby Mae Potts, a member of the Sherman congregation, reported that the "Christian church and property were donated to the church of Christ, so we now have a nice building there."[9] L. M. Wright, reflecting on Winston's success in Van Alstyne, reported less sensitively: "Brother Winston tore up the Christian church and baptized several from the sectarian churches. There was no church of Christ in this town until Brother Winston held this meeting."[10] Like mentors Bowser and Hogan, Winston refused to re-baptize persons who came from the Christian Church since he viewed them as merely erring brethren.

Owing to Winston's leadership skills and preaching prowess, other congregations sought his services on a fulltime basis. Annette Cash expressed relief when the Third Ward Church of Christ in Houston agreed to allow Winston "to stay with us." Cash explained, "The completion of our building depends upon Brother Winston, since he planned it and also did most of the work. He has outlined a program to complete the building, which has resulted in the finishing of the rest rooms, baptistery and all of the plumbing."[11] Cash's comments portray Winston as a practical man who possessed more than biblical knowledge alone; he had keen carpentry skills along with good preaching ability. Furthermore, he could lead and organize church members, guiding and inspiring them. Through Winston's tireless labor, the church completed a rock building and dedicated it on Music Street in Sherman in the fall of 1942.[12]

The following year, Winston relocated to Fort Worth and assumed the oversight of the New York Church of Christ.[13] He had conducted a successful meeting there in the fall of 1942, which yielded twenty-six responses, twenty-four baptisms and two restorations.[14] Just as he did in small-town Sherman, Winston worked effectively in the city. Earthy Miller reported: "Bro. Winston is wonderful. I have lived here for thirty-five years, I have never seen as bright a prospect for the expansion of the Lord's kingdom in Ft. Worth."[15] Winston himself announced that the congregation on New York Street in Fort Worth had increased in attendance as he baptized two or three people every Sunday, and the church's contribution increased from $14 to $52 each week. While Winston labored primarily to advance the "pure gospel" in Texas, he also sought to help sustain G. P. Bowser's fledgling school in Fort Smith, Arkansas, the Bowser Christian Institute.[16]

Just as he had done while preaching in Sherman, Winston continued traveling to areas beyond Fort Worth to preach the Word. In the summer of 1943, he held a tent meeting in Sweeny, Texas, baptized ten women, and established a congregation there. Ezekiel Z. Webster assumed spiritual oversight of this new flock upon Winston's departure.[17]

Winston also found time to minister to various congregations in Fort Worth. In Fort Worth's Lake Como community, Winston's preaching yielded fourteen responses—six baptisms, five restorations, and three membership transfers. Visitors from the all-black Stop Six Church of Christ and the support from white Christians contributed to Winston's meeting in Lake Como. "Brother Winston did not fail to preach the gospel of Christ," reported Ardelia Griffin. "With the help of God and Brother

Winston we are going to do more in the future for the cause of Christ."[18] Winston also lent his services to the Stop Six congregation in Fort Worth by teaching Bible classes there on Wednesday and Friday nights.[19]

Two years after Winston had relocated to Fort Worth, several members stood in awe of his success as a church builder. Ardelia Griffin continued praising her new minister, noting, "Attendance, offering and all services are better than we have ever known."[20] Annette Cash, a Bible class teacher at Winston's former congregation in Sherman, glowingly reported of her congregation there, yet she reflected, "We will always love and remember Brother Winston for what he is, and what he has done for us."[21]

During 1944, black preachers who traveled through Texas often made reference to J. S. Winston and his evangelistic activity. H. H. Gray, a black minister in Dallas and an editor of the *Christian Counselor*, briefly stopped in Fort Worth where Winston preached. Gray, after calling him "that great worker, dreamer and builder," remarked, "That church is really doing things." He also observed that Winston's congregation had "an unusually splendid group of Sisters there, including Sister Erthly [*sic*] Miller, who is truly a mother in Israel."[22] Marshall Keeble, when en route to Carlsbad, New Mexico, from Nashville, Tennessee, also stopped in Fort Worth. Keeble praised Winston as "the hardest worker that we have," and noted that his congregation was "preparing to build a real nice meeting house." Winston and his flock, added Keeble, gave "a fine offering" to the Nashville Christian Institute, a K–12 school for black students in Tennessee.[23]

Winston continued to live up to his reputation as a tireless church builder and a hard worker in the summer of 1944 when he and Paul Settles, a preacher and song leader from Houston, collaborated to plant a small congregation in Marlin, Texas. For a two-year period, Winston and his congregation in Fort Worth guided the fledgling flock in Marlin by helping them secure a preacher and by assisting them in erecting a new church building.[24] In 1945, as G. P. Bowser's health declined, several of his protégés worked to keep his periodical, the *Christian Echo*, in circulation. Levi Kennedy, T. H. Busby, and E. W. Anderson edited the journal, and H. H. Gray served as news editor, while J. S. Winston, from his ministerial post in Fort Worth, worked as managing editor. G. E. Steward lauded Winston as "that tireless worker and prince among men."[25]

Two months later Russell H. Moore, a black preacher in Dallas, similarly praised Winston for doing a work that "can not be excelled in the brotherhood." Moore reported that Winston led the church in erecting a church parsonage "second to none" and a church building that will be "one of the finest buildings in the brotherhood." Moore also commended Winston's singing ability. "Brother Winston is leading the song services fine each night for the meeting now in progress and doing a mighty fine job of singing." Astonished by Winston's indefatigable zeal, Moore added: "He is a go-getter from his heart. He never seems to tire in the work of the Lord. Sometimes I believe he will drop in his tracks working with both hands and mind. J. S. Winston is a fighter from his heart, and God has many places for men of his ability." To sum up his feelings for Winston, Moore honored him in verse.

> Work on, J. S. Winston,
> Be faithful to your employ
> At last the God of Heaven
> Invites you to great Joy.
> Amidst strife and complaint
> Not shirking any task
> A crown of life to those who won't faint,
> God gives to those who ask.
> So when your work is done, my boy
> And time has all passed by
> For you my prayer will always be
> Sweet mansions in the sky.[26]

A Passion for Christian Education and Trained Leaders

Winston, more than an arduous evangelist and a gifted song leader, was also a determined educator. Even though Winston himself possessed no impressive academic credentials, he devoted his life to ensuring that African American youth had the opportunity to receive a Christian education. He understood that white racism barred black students from white Christian colleges and universities in the South, so he poured time and effort into building a school to educate African Americans in the liberal arts and in the Bible.[27]

With the closure of the Bowser Christian Institute and Orphan Home in Fort Smith, Arkansas, in 1946, black leaders in Churches of Christ decided that the state of Texas offered "more advantages for school work." After carrying their "cause to the white brethren of Texas," African American leaders formed a Board of Trustees consisting of thirty-two whites and thirteen blacks and founded the Southern Bible Institute in

Fort Worth, Texas.[28] No complete roster of the board members survives, but certainly black leaders understood that the success of their evangelistic and educational endeavors hinged upon monetary support from white Christians. The board chose Fort Worth as the site for the Southern Bible Institute largely because of the person and work of J. S. Winston.

The forty-five members of the Board of Trustees appointed Winston as president of the Southern Bible Institute. They selected Grover C. Washington, a gifted preacher and well-educated teacher with degrees from Samuel Huston College in Austin and Bishop College in Marshall, Texas, as academic dean. Imogene McIntyre, a graduate of Langston University, served as registrar. G. P. Bowser, suffering fragile and ailing health, was appointed Bible teacher while LaBerta D. Phillips, Mabel M. Smith, and Hattie Lavera Sansom Iverson—all college graduates, public school teachers, and devout members of Winston's New York and Leuda congregation—completed the instructional staff. President Winston explained that the school, housed in the Lake Como Church of Christ building in Fort Worth, would "meet the great need of the Negro brotherhood of the Churches of Christ for trained leadership, thus a course of study that will aid preachers and prospective preachers to become effective workers for the Lord."[29]

The Southern Bible Institute opened Monday night on October 11, 1948, with thirty-seven students. The students, divided into elementary and advanced classes, studied English, Bible, Church History, Arithmetic, and Public Speaking. Winston proudly announced, "For the first time in history there began in Texas a program of Christian education for Negro people sponsored by the members of the Church of Christ. This project is an indication of the faith with which we look to the future of the Lord's work."[30]

To help sustain the new school, Winston arranged an annual lectureship and meeting. On November 22–25, 1948, approximately 1,500 people from six different states attended the lectureship. On the opening day of the meeting, Winston incorporated a "timely innovation": Preachers in attendance "donned overalls and with hammer and nails went whole heartedly to work helping to complete the buildings. Sessions were begun according to schedule Tuesday night and the remainder of the meeting was as usual, lively and educational." With this enthusiastic launch, Winston reported a few months later that $11,095.87 was spent to support the faculty, publications, classroom and dormitory construction, and incidentals pertaining to operation of the school. "We are thankful to God that we can say that we are completely free of indebtedness, and with your aid, we have been able to meet our monthly obligations."[31]

Winston attributed much of the success to white leaders in Churches of Christ, singling out Dr. John G. Young, an elder of the Sears and Summit Street Church of Christ and "prominent physician" who chaired the Board of Directors. J. H. Richards, a "highly esteemed" elder of the Polytechnic Church of Christ in Fort Worth, oversaw the local committee, while W. C. Lippord, secretary and treasurer for the Polytechnic congregation, served in those same capacities for the Southern Bible Institute. Foy Lee Kirkpatrick, a graduate of Abilene Christian College, worked as business manager for the new school and served as "public relations man among the white people."[32] Winston also commended the efforts of G. E. Steward, R. N. Hogan, H. H. Gray, Levi Kennedy, and Grover C. Washington, black leaders who sat on the Board of Directors. The president then reminded his supporters that the driving force behind his work at the Southern Bible Institute was "prepared leadership!"[33]

Even though Winston traveled extensively and worked diligently to raise support for the Southern Bible Institute, he somehow found time to fulfill other responsibilities. In the winter of 1949, he took his ailing mentor, G. P. Bowser, to "one of the best white doctors in Fort Worth." A thorough examination showed that "Yellow Jaundice had set in." The physician recommended that Bowser's needed surgery be postponed until he could regain his strength. When Bowser pondered how to raise funds for the procedure, Winston replied, "Do not worry about expenses, he would raise it." After Bowser received a $200 check for his medical expenses, he said, "my heart leaped with joy at the liberal response, which has gone far beyond our expectation. I feel so uplifted, and have not words with which to express my gratitude to the churches and Christians who are aiding me."[34] In addition to caring for his beloved teacher and mentor, Winston continued to fill preaching appointments. In the summer of 1949, Winston closed a "fine meeting" in Edna, Texas. Lelia Brigham reported that Winston "brought unity in the church which was very much needed. He shall long be remembered by this congregation for the fine Christlike Spirit he manifested."[35]

Despite Winston's best efforts to develop the Southern Bible Institute, the young school eventually closed in Fort Worth and relocated to Terrell, Texas, becoming Southwestern Christian College in 1949. The following year G. P. Bowser died, but not before his dream of educating African American youth had become a reality. Bowser dreamed the dream, but his protégés, R. N. Hogan, Levi Kennedy, and J. S. Winston, executed his dream.

In 1952 Winston and his family relocated to Cleveland, Ohio, to work with a small congregation of thirty-seven members. It remains unclear as to why Winston abruptly left the educational enterprise in Texas. Perhaps when the college relocated to Terrell, he felt confident that the school was finally in a secure place and under the oversight of more competent leaders. Notwithstanding the lack of information, Winston carried his effective preaching and skillful leadership to the Buckeye State where the church membership increased to 227, and in 1966 the flourishing flock built a $362,000 edifice and became known as the University Church of Christ.

While ministering in the Midwest, Winston continued to stress the significance of church leadership through the columns of the *Christian Echo*; in 1954 he explained that most church conflicts stem from incompetent leaders. "Wherever the church suffers from hinderances [*sic*], there are causes, and hinderances cannot be eliminated without first locating and remedying the causes. As this is true with the physical body, so it is with the spiritual body." Winston maintained that "one unqualified preacher can do more harm to the church and the brotherhood at large, than two or three elders of the local congregation; for his influence and work are national," wrote Winston. "Paul was a well-educated man and very religious, but, when the Lord selected him to be an apostle unto the Gentiles and to bear his name before kings and governors, he did not permit him to start preaching immediately after his conversion, but brought him into Arabia and by revelation taught and trained him for his work. (Gal. 1:11)."[36] From Winston's viewpoint, a well-trained minister was essential to a flourishing congregation.

Winston's article on church leadership struck a chord in African American Churches of Christ, as several leaders and members thanked him for his discourse on the important subject. The following spring, Winston elaborated: "Leadership is requisite to the maintenance and development of the church and its work." In other words, a strong leadership was indispensable for a strong membership. "We must emphasize the need of leadership in the church. Much has been done to inspire men to become preachers, and this is good, but we must do more to inspire men to become elders, deacons and teachers, for when a church has a qualified group of elders, to teach and lead it, the evangelist is then able to give more time to preaching the gospel and helping needed congregations.... I maintain that a church is not fully developed nor can it maintain the program of working that it should until it has qualified men for deacons and elders." He concluded, "Strong leadership will result in a stronger church."[37] A couple of months later Winston reiterated this theme: "Where the church has no elders and deacons, its progress is greatly hindered."[38]

Winston, practicing what he preached, poured his heart and soul into the lives of many young men. One of Winston's signal accomplishments in Cleveland might have been the conversion of Tony E. Roach. Taught and trained at the University Church of Christ, Roach married Candyce Winston, J. S. Winston's daughter. In the late 1970s, the young couple moved to Abilene, Texas, gathered a few members, and established the T & P Lane Church of Christ (now the Minda Street Church of Christ). Like his spiritual father, Roach proved himself an effective church leader and church builder, developing one of the most racially diverse congregations in Texas. Willie Tucker, a powerful black preacher from Dallas, visited the Minda Street congregation and praised its "Rainbow Membership." Tucker observed: "A typical gathering is composed of Blacks, Whites, Mexicans, Asians, Africans, Haitians, and perhaps, others I could not identify. I am not speaking of token representation, but a genuine fellowship of multi-races who have been drawn together in Christ. People who genuinely love one another, trust one another, accept one another, and who work together to build up the body of Christ."[3] Roach also became the first African American to earn a Doctor of Ministry degree from Abilene Christian University and developed "God's Love Book" ministry, a program aimed at building "'New Self-Love' in people of all ethnic, social, and economic backgrounds," and used by congregations across the country.[39]

In the late 1970s, Winston relocated from Cleveland to Dallas, and from there he traversed the country, conducting leadership workshops, preaching in gospel meetings, and uniting feuding congregations. The subject of church leadership remained close to his heart, and in 1973 Winston contributed several articles addressing the topic in the *Christian Echo*. For those who asked why black congregations had so few elders, Winston explained that while whites' ready access to Christian education had enabled them to create a renewable body of trained leaders, blacks enjoyed no such system. The Stone–Campbell Movement produced such schools as Alexander Campbell's Bethany College (founded in 1840), David Lipscomb's Nashville Bible School (in 1891), and Abilene Christian College (1906)—all rejected blacks until the 1960s. Exclusion from such Christian training, Winston contended, thwarted the development of black leadership in Churches of Christ. White Christians "have had educational high schools, colleges, lectureships, orphan homes, etc., for years, while at

J. S. Winston (1906-2002) was one of the most influential preachers in the history of African American Churches of Christ in Texas and beyond, serving as an evangelist, educator, and historian. His abiding passion was to train and develop leadership for black congregations.

the same time the brethren of black congregations, because of the practice of Racism have been deprived of all these advantages. It was not until the establishment of Southwestern Christian College, 23 years ago, that the black members had any established Christian education program."[40]

J. S. Winston understood that the future of black Churches of Christ depended largely on the preacher's ability to teach and train faithful leaders. "The minister may be doing a marvelous job of preaching the gospel, and increasing the membership, keeping peace, building adequate church buildings, and inspiring the congregation in mission work," Winston wrote, "even so, that congregation cannot reach its full potentials in the Lord's work without the organization of Elders and Deacons to serve it."[41] From Winston's perspective a well-equipped and biblical leadership was indispensable to church growth.

The Historian

In addition to his evangelism and educational efforts, Winston was the first noteworthy historian of black Churches of Christ. In 1947 Winston wrote a historical sketch of African American Churches of Christ. In this article, Winston, after highlighting the pioneering work of black preachers such as S. W. Womack, Alexander Campbell, T. H. York, T. H. Merchant, T. H. Busby, and D. J. Bynum, singled out G. P. Bowser and Marshall Keeble as "the leading evangelists" who "suffered very much in their efforts to preach the gospel to their people." Winston then highlighted white benefactors such as A. M. Burton who took "great interest in the gospel being preached to the colored people." Winston's piece also provided chronological and statistical information, finding 35,000 black congregants in 250 congregations served by 175 ministers in 1947. It further pointed out that the Churches of Christ were "strongest" in Texas, Tennessee, Florida, California, Michigan, Alabama, and Illinois.[42]

Despite the work of a number of courageous black preachers, Winston commented that many African American congregations were "not very strong. Some of them have quit meeting." Winston attributed the dissolving of some churches to the "lack of capable leadership." Because of this lingering problem, he tirelessly pushed for the establishment of a Christian college for blacks in Churches of Christ. He recalled, "In February, 1945, Brother G. E. Steward and I carried our plea to Brother R. L. Watson of Austin and D. B. Rambo of Huntsville, Texas, for the need of Christian Education for the colored people. These Christian men were greatly stirred by our plea and immediately went to work to create an interest in our plea."[43] The response of white leaders led to the formation of the Southern Bible Institute in Fort Worth.

Pursuing his interest in the subject of history and encouraged by Alex Haley's landmark book, *Roots*, Winston appealed to readers of the *Christian Echo* to send him material about their congregations so that he could compose a history of African American Churches of Christ. He received historical information from several ministers and members of Churches of Christ, dating back to the "Restoration Period." His wife's heart attack, however, prevented him from completing the project, which he tentatively called, "A History of Black Members of the Church of Christ: 'Tracing Our Roots from the Restoration Movement.'"[44] Annie C. Tuggle's 1945 compilation, *Our Ministers and Our Songleaders*, likely the first attempt at a history of African American Churches of Christ, contains significant biographical and historical information. But Winston's 1947 article represents an academic treatment of the history of African American Churches of Christ, and sets the author apart as the first and most knowledgeable historian of his chosen fellowship. His 1985 article on the history of choral groups in black Churches of Christ emerged from his broad historical knowledge. He dated the first black chorus in Churches of Christ to 1938 when R. N. Hogan organized a group of singers from his Los Angeles congregation for his radio program in Southern California. Four years later Hogan put together a chorus from the Fifth Ward Church of Christ in Houston, Texas, and in 1943 Winston himself directed a radio choir at the congregation he served in Fort Worth.[45]

Winston, indeed a "fighter from the heart," planted, built, and led congregations, pouring his blood, sweat, and tears into African American Churches of Christ. As an evangelist, he fought those whom he deemed to be in religious error, even transforming some instrumental Christian Churches into a cappella Churches of Christ in Texas. As an educator he labored to establish and develop church leadership through the short-lived Southern Bible Institute in Fort Worth, but his legacy lives on through the "J. S. Winston Sound Doctrine Foundation" at Southwestern Christian College. His desire to train qualified church leaders consumed his life and fired his passion for Christian education. Winston not only mounted the podium to advocate church leadership, but he also used his pen in the pages of the *Christian Echo* to accentuate the necessity of well-trained preachers, elders, and deacons for African American Churches of Christ in Texas and the wider world.

Chapter 9

"Just Want to Be the White Man's Brother"

R. N. Hogan and the Race Problem in Churches of Christ

No doubt you have heard Keeble, Miller, Bowser and others as well as Hogan. I have heard several of them but Hogan is the boy who can do the job.

—James L. Lovell to Mr. J. A. Jones, 1937

In 1944 G. P. Bowser composed a celebratory poem in honor of one of his most effective protégés, R. N. Hogan. The poem read, in part:

Little Emma soon became a woman,
Joined hand with Willie Hogan;
To this union three were born,
Of which R. N. was the slogan.

Nathan Cathey took charge of him,
'Till G. P. Bowser came along;
Nathan and Francis soon decided
To let him join the Bowser throng . . .

He began preaching about fourteen,
Then only in knee pants;
He was not ashamed of the gospel of Christ,
And folks did fairly prance.

He left our home when near eighteen,
He said to see his mother;

But met a girl named Maggie Bullock,
AND AT ONCE MADE HER HIS LOVER.

They lost no time in getting married,
Maggie is a true wife;
For when six years Nath went astray,
She helped him back to life.

They moved to Chicago, Illinois,
And started life anew;
We do not hesitate in saying,
His equals are but few.

Much credit is due one, Jimmie Lovell,
A white brother from the coast;
He picked up Hogan as his son,
And never stops to boast,

Richard N. Hogan is too useful,
To ever let him down;
Near two thousand through him obeyed,
And some will wear the crown.[1]

This eulogistic poem provides an instructive outline of Richard Nathaniel Hogan's life.

The Making of a Church Planter

Born in 1902 to Willie and Emma Hogan in Monroe County, Arkansas, Richard grew up under the guardianship of his grandparents, Nathan and Frances Cathey, after his father's early death. When Richard turned fourteen, the Catheys gave him over to G. P. Bowser who enrolled him in the Silver Point Institute in Tennessee for training as a preacher. Under Bowser's careful grooming, R. N. Hogan's skillful preaching soon led to the baptism of over seventy people, and he earned a reputation as "the boy evangelist."[2]

At age eighteen Hogan married Maggie Bullock of Maury County, Tennessee. The young couple moved about from Tennessee to Arkansas to Kentucky and to Michigan, as he filled a variety of pulpits. In Detroit, Hogan, discouraged by the untimely death of his infant daughter, abandoned the preaching ministry and quit the church for some while until his wife encouraged him to return to God. Hogan later recalled: "I worked in the automobile factories for six years during which time I allowed Satan to discourage me but my wife remained faithful, which finally awakened my soul and brought me to repentance."[3]

Recommitting his life to God, Hogan relocated from Detroit to Chicago, where he helped establish "a good congregation with eighty-five members." He then founded several churches in Arkansas, Oklahoma, and Texas in the 1930s. By 1937 R. N. Hogan had become a household name after white journalist Jimmy L. Lovell began publishing *Hogan's Helper*, a newsletter designed to raise support for the black evangelist's travels.[4] Lovell judged Hogan as indisputably the most able preacher in Churches of Christ, lauding him as "the greatest preacher—white or black—I have ever heard."[5] Secure with such endorsements, Hogan settled in for a lengthy tenure as minister of the Figueroa Street Church of Christ in Los Angeles in the late 1930s.

While some researchers have chronicled Hogan's remarkable work in California and other far west states,[6] many have forgotten his impressive legacy in Texas. Hogan left a twofold legacy among African American Churches of Christ in Texas. First, he planted several black congregations in Texas, most of which thrive into the twenty-first century. Armed with a fiery and militant mindset inherited from both white leaders and his black spiritual father, G. P. Bowser, Hogan disturbed and disrupted a black Christian Church in Longview. His presence was "objected to by a few of the Christian church members, but we succeeded in getting in there." Three powerful sermons by Hogan persuaded seventy black members to walk out and take "a stand with the loyal body of Christ." The departure of these parishioners, Hogan reported, "caused things to get pretty hot around there and quite a lot of threats were made. They ordered us not to come back, but about 500 stood up for me to return, and we were back the next night." A fourth sermon swayed twenty-five more to "stand with the church of Christ. Then they put the law on us, putting us out of their building by securing an injunction. We kindly walked out and took with us ninety-five of their members including two preachers."[7]

Hogan's encounter with black congregants of the Christian Church in East Texas demonstrates the commitment of the black evangelist to key Church of Christ distinctions: worshiping without instruments of music and opposition to missionary societies, which he considered fundamental violations of God's will. Yet even though he viewed members of the Disciples of Christ as brethren in doctrinal error, he refused to require that they be rebaptized. Hogan maintained this position throughout his early evangelistic career. In all-black Langston, Oklahoma, he planted a church with forty-one conversions—"forty by baptism and one from the Christian Church."[8] In nearby Guthrie, Hogan's passionate preaching engendered "eighty additions—seventy-five baptisms and five from the Christian Church."[9]

In 1936 a Hogan meeting in Gladewater, Texas, left behind a congregation of twenty-six members.[10] Two years later Hogan spent several days in Sherman, engendering forty-seven baptisms and establishing the present-day Grand Avenue Church of Christ.[11] From 1941 to 1943 the Figueroa Church of Christ in Los Angeles gave Hogan a two-year leave of absence to work with the Fifth Ward Church of Christ in Houston. Before he left Southern California, the members there surprised Hogan and his family with a going-away party. "[They] gave us a pleasant surprise gathering at my home in Los Angeles just before we left there for Houston, Texas," Hogan wrote. "As we were sitting in conversation with two or three friends, our front door immediately opened and the members started marching in singing the song, 'I'll be Happy with You up There.' They kept pouring in until seventy-five or a hundred had marched in. They brought us plenty to eat and we sang, prayed and enjoyed the very best of Christian fellowship. We haven't altogether given up the work in Los Angeles; no sir, our work continues there. I have agreed to return to them in the near future."[12] Encouraged by this emotional and spiritual support from black Christians in California, Hogan held a brief but successful tenure in Houston. Believing that African Americans should control their own resources and their own congregations, he helped the Fifth Ward congregation attain economic independence from the all-white Heights Church of Christ.[13]

While ministering in Houston, Hogan found time to evangelize nearby areas in south Texas. After preaching in Edinburgh in 1941, he described his success there in militant terminology.

> We invaded the devil's territory in Edinburgh, Texas from February 9th through February 27th in the way of a gospel meeting sponsored by the church of Christ (white) of that city.
>
> We bombed several of the enemies' bases (erroneous teachings) and several explosions (sect's complainings) were heard.
>
> One lady exploded about our loud speaker, to not only the chief of police but to the mayor also. They were very nice to us.
>
> One of the enemies' bombers (a Baptist preacher) attacked us the last night of the meeting. . . .[14]

GOSPEL MEETING

The Church of Christ

PRESENTS

R. N. HOGAN

of

Muskogee, Okla.

OUTSTANDING EVANGELIST

Services Each Night During the Week at 7:30 - Except Saturday

BEGINNING

Feb. 27 - 2:30 P. M.

Look for the Big Tent Located at:

11 + California St

YOU HAVE NEVER HEARD A MAN PREACH LIKE HOGAN BEFORE. HIS SLOGAN IS "THE BIBLE ONLY MAKES CHRISTIANS ONLY."

THIS SPECIAL INVITATION IS EXTENDED

— TO YOU —

R. N. Hogan (1902-1997), a protégé of G. P. Bowser, indelibly marked African American Churches of Christ in Texas and beyond. As a fierce debater and editor, Hogan opposed both religious error and racial injustice.

(Photo courtesy of the Center for Restoration Studies, Abilene Christian University, Abilene, Texas)

Hogan deemed his evangelistic work in Edinburgh "a victory," producing six baptisms and three restorations. Clearly his preaching in the Rio Grande Valley aroused the ire of members of various denominations. Hogan's rhetoric reflected the "fighting-style" mentality which then pervaded Churches of Christ. He added that "the morale of our soldiers in Edinburgh is high and they are well prepared for the fight. They are real fighters and are at all time pleased with the orders of our captain (Christ Jesus, Heb. 2:10), and are doing their best to carry them out. . . . Therefore, the fight is on. The orders to fight came from headquarters. 1 Tim. 6:12, 1 Cor. 9:26."[15] From Hogan's perspective, God sanctioned the fighting style.

R. N. Hogan's Fight against Racism in Churches of Christ

In addition to his fiery and energetic evangelistic preaching in Texas, Hogan used the columns of the *Christian Echo* to contest the racism of whites in Texas and other states in the South. He fought to help open the doors of Christian colleges that had traditionally excluded black students. No other black preacher in Churches of Christ was more vocal on the race issue in the United States during the Civil Rights era than R. N. Hogan. Carroll Pitts, an African American preacher in Churches of Christ, commented in 1969 that "During the years between 1954 and the 1960s the voice of R. N. Hogan, editor of the *Christian Echo*, and other black writers were raised against segregation in Christian colleges and in congregations."[16]

In 1955 Hogan and Marion V. Holt proudly announced that Southwestern Christian College in Texas had graduated twenty young black preachers to fill empty pulpits in Churches of Christ. Of the twenty ministers mentioned in the laudatory article, six of them served congregations in Texas. Andrew Hairston preached in Waco; Winter I. Johnson ministered in Wichita Falls; Bonnie Matthews assumed oversight of the Eastside congregation in Corsicana; Woodie Morrison worked with a church in Knox City; Joe C. Simon served in Ennis; and Woodrow Wilson led a flock in El Paso. Other alumni included Alvertice Bowdre who preached in Ada, Oklahoma; Cloys Cecil in Terre Haute, Indiana, A. C. Christman in Seattle, Washington; Issac Dedrick in Baton Rouge, Louisiana; Arthur Fulson in Benton, Arkansas; Archester Houston in Green Pastures, Oklahoma; Marion Holt in Los Angeles, California; John Jackson in New Orleans, Louisiana; T. H. Johnson in Wichita, Kansas;

Warrick Jones in Savannah, Georgia; Lewis Montgomery in Natchez, Mississippi; James Tinsley in Holdenville, Oklahoma; Isaac Webb in Morrilton, Arkansas; and Roosevelt Wells in Okmulgee, Oklahoma.[17] The reports of Hogan and Holt underscore Southwestern Christian College's profound impact on the growth and development of African American Churches of Christ. Many young men, after receiving academic and biblical training at the all-black college, went on to lead distinguished ministerial careers as they enlarged and stabilized congregations established by their mentors.

Even though the newly formed school graduated many talented students, no other Church of Christ-related school, with the exception of Pepperdine College in California, accepted African Americans for more advanced degrees before 1961. Like many of their white contemporaries in the South, most white leaders in Churches of Christ imbibed a neurotic fear that the admission of African American men into their schools would lead inexorably to sexual mixing. This phobia gripped the mind of the white South. Theodore G. Bilbo, a rabid racist, rigid segregationist, and twice governor of Mississippi, spoke for many southerners when he asserted: "the real and true white man is willing to accept the Negro as his brother in Christ. However, he does not prefer to take him on as a son-in-law in his family. . . ."[18] Margaret Halsey, a white counselor on a U.S. Army base, called bi-racial sex "the white American's Achilles heel." She insisted that "What the white people are afraid of is not that the Negro men will propose to the white girls, *but that the white girls will say yes.*"[19]

When the U.S. Supreme Court declared segregation unconstitutional in *Brown v. Board of Education*, its decision aroused a deeply felt "sex fear" through the South. One scholar has pointed out that before the desegregation ruling, white and black southerners listened to the same radio stations, danced to the same music, read the same magazines, and perhaps drifted toward racial harmony, but the *Brown* case shattered all hopes for racial peace as white segregationists felt white supremacy threatened. "The real fear was the white female staying out of reach of the Negro man."[20]

White defenses quickly arose in a variety of guises. The *Brown* decision inspired the emergence of the White Citizens' Council in Indianola, Mississippi. Founded in 1954 by Robert Patterson, a graduate of Mississippi State University, the white supremacist organization sought to oppose and subvert the desegregation ruling. The following year the White Citizens' Council came to Kilgore, Texas, and virtually put the

National Association for the Advancement of Colored People out of business.[21] The *Brown* verdict similarly troubled religious groups, including Churches of Christ, now confronted with the "flushed question of intermarriage."[22] Resistance often reverted to its traditionally violent stance as well. Emmett Till, an African American teenager from Chicago, was brutally murdered in the Mississippi Delta for allegedly "whistling" at a white woman, and he became "the sacrificial lamb of the civil rights movement" in the summer of 1955.[23] African American preachers in Churches of Christ, who traversed the South and beyond, were keenly aware of the social taboo of a black man interacting with a white woman, but very few contested such racist assumptions.

White Texans in Tarrant County revealed their deeply rooted anti-black sentiment and opposition to mixing with African Americans in 1956. That year white residents in Mansfield, a small Fort Worth suburb, used mob rule and threatened racial violence to prevent a court desegregation order. Declaring that African Americans possessed "repulsive skin" and that they were intellectually inferior, whites in Mansfield displayed effigies and signs warning black students not to enroll at Mansfield High School. An inflammatory sign on one effigy admonished: "this negro tried to go to a white school" and "wouldn't this be a horrible way to die." Such dangling effigies and incendiary signs—flaunted by white citizens, supported by Texas Gov. Allan Shivers, and ignored by Pres. Dwight D. Eisenhower—helped forestall desegregation in Mansfield for eight years.[24] The Mansfield episode offers a telling example of how many white Texans viewed their black neighbors, illustrating that many Anglos in the Lone Star State were still willing to resort to racial violence to maintain white supremacy as a way of life.

Unlike Marshall Keeble and other prominent black preachers in Churches of Christ who remained virtually silent on the race problem in the United States, R. N. Hogan worked consistently to disrupt the racial status quo in Church of Christ schools. Hogan constantly critiqued and criticized white church leaders and white school administrators who excluded black students from the so-called "Christian" colleges and universities. Three encounters, among others, significantly shaped Hogan's racial perspectives. First, he developed deep aversion for white racism from his mentor, G. P. Bowser. In 1920, when white superintendent C. E. W. Dorris of the all-black Southern Practical Institute in Nashville required black pupils to enter the building through the back door, Bowser opposed the practice, then "packed up and went home." The newly established school closed abruptly.[25] Hogan never forgot the firm stand his spiritual mentor took against white racism.

Second, while residing in Nashville, Hogan stayed temporarily with wealthy entrepreneur, A. M. Burton. When reflecting on his living arrangements with Burton, Hogan called him "prejudiced" because he had Hogan live in his basement; here Hogan echoed the sentiment of other black preachers who resented staying in the basement of white hosts. G. P. Holt, G. P. Bowser's grandson and Hogan's co-laborer, complained that "We as Negroes have in the past laughed when we were not tickled, scratched when we were not itching, making the white man think that what he was doing and saying was right and that we liked it. But brethren, we were lying to you,—and may God forgive us. We made you think that putting us in your basement or attic was all right with us, even though we knew what James taught. Brethren, we lied to you."[26] Both Hogan and Holt understood that even though whites in Churches of Christ could be kind and generous, some of them yet espoused white supremacist views.

Third, in 1941 Foy E. Wallace Jr., a white preacher from the South, excoriated Ira Y. Rice, the white editor of the *Christian Soldier*, for staying in the same house and sleeping in the same bed with R. N. Hogan. Wallace accused Rice and Hogan of advocating "social equality." Hogan denied the accusation and pointed out that Wallace was actually jealous that more white believers attended Hogan's meetings than his own.[27] Rice later explained that he and Hogan were "caught in a freak South Texas blizzard one night—and had to stay at the same house." Rice also called his dispute with Wallace "the most gruesome knock-down-drag-out editorial battle this brotherhood has gone through in the 20th century—and it has seen some dillies!"[28]

The Hogan–Rice relationship illustrates the rigidity and complexity of race relations in Churches of Christ. On the one hand, white preachers such as Rice vehemently opposed segregation, yet the very assault on racial discrimination in white churches and schools attests to how entrenched racism was among Churches of Christ. Rice explained that Hogan often arrived at his preaching engagements in Texas "completely exhausted" because, when driving from Los Angeles to Texas, the black evangelist "had to keep right on going, day and night, without stopping but for gas and oil, all the way through." Rice railed that this happened in supposedly "'Christian' America! Christian my eye! He would have received more 'Christian' treatment than that among the pagan barbarians of Asia

In the 1950s, Jack Evans (standing right) conducted a meeting at the Figueroa Church of Christ in Los Angeles for his close friend and mentor, R. N. Hogan (1902-1997). Through such encounters, Hogan exerted profound influence on young Evans.

(Photo courtesy of Jack Evans, Sr.)

who had never even *heard* of Jesus Christ!" Rice then recalled accompanying black preachers, Hogan, J. S. Winston, and J. M. Butler, from Weslaco, Texas, to Reynosa, Mexico, to treat them to a "game-dinner." The owner, however, refused to serve them in the dining room because if "'regulars' from the Texas side" came in and saw blacks eating there "it would 'ruin our business.'" After the owner agreed to serve them "*behind* the out-house," Rice lamented, "Oh, I really got 'indoctrinated' as to what our colored brethren were having to put up with, not only as their normal course of life, but often as not from their own white brethren in the Lord."[29]

Shortly after the *Brown* decision mandated the desegregation of public schools, Hogan understood both the repercussions and the opportunities the verdict presaged for African Americans in Churches of Christ seeking to improve their lives. Thus Hogan began attacking the racism and segregation that gripped white colleges controlled by Churches of Christ. Taking his instruction and inspiration from James 2:9, Hogan argued that race hatred was sinful and that it carried eternal consequences. "It is my personal observation," averred Hogan, "that most of our Brethren who are in high places in the church of our Lord, are going to lose their souls because they are respecters of persons."[30]

Whites in Churches of Christ, declared Hogan, allowed cultural and traditional racial practices to color their view and treatment of African Americans. "Because of tradition and racial prejudice Negroes are not wanted and not allowed to worship with some white congregations. If they go, they are directed to the basement, balcony or a dressing room, or if given a seat in the main auditorium, there is usually enough room around him to lie down on the Pew and stretch out his full length. Thus making it very embarrassing and uncomfortable. These congregations are suppose [*sic*] to be ruled by scriptural Elders." Here Hogan's testimony is strikingly similar to Carl Spain's indictment of white Christians in the South who wanted "no niggers in the house of God."[31]

The anti-black sentiment espoused by many white church leaders spilled over into their schools. Hogan lamented that "A fine young gospel Minister, as clean as christians [*sic*] come, well qualified, has just received a letter from one of the biggest so-called christian schools in the Brotherhood turning him down, rejecting his application to enter a christian (?) school to be taught the word of God only because he is a Negro, only because of the color of his skin. They use [*sic*] to hide behind the law, but our government has informed the entire country that the practice of segregation because of race or color is unconstitutional." Knowing that Christian schools were no longer able to maintain legally segregated institutions, Hogan indicted white leaders in Church of Christ colleges for admitting all other ethnic groups except African Americans. "Philippinos [*sic*], Koreans, Mexicans, and every nationality but the Negro are welcome to these schools, and they call them christian schools." Hogan also argued that the exclusion of African Americans from white "christian" schools was "proof that God is not there; for where God is, no man is barred because of the color of his skin."[32]

For Hogan, the "most embarrassing" fact was that colleges connected to members of the Christian Church or Disciples of Christ and others controlled by secular state governments welcomed African Americans, but Church of Christ schools rejected them. "One of our Ministers graduated at T. C. U. (Texas Christian University) a Christian Church school, but he couldn't go to Abilene Christian College. However, Bro. Figueroa of Mexico graduated there. Negroes are admitted to the State school in Fayetteville, Ark., but they cannot enter Harding College, a christian (?) school. They are admitted in State supported schools in Tennessee, but they cannot attend David Lipscomb College in Nashville, Tenn., nor Freed–Hardeman College in Henderson, Tenn. If these schools will disassociate the name christian from them, their practice would not reflect so badly on the Cause of Christ."[33] At the end of his biting article, Hogan, on the one hand, thanked white Christians for supporting Southwestern Christian College. "Some of our white brethren are supporting S.W.C.C. because they know that the Negro needs Bible training and due to the practice of our so-called Christian schools they cannot get it otherwise. These men have the right spirit. They are doing what they can to help." On the other hand, Hogan charged some white believers with supporting the all-black school for the wrong reason. That is, they gave money to Southwestern Christian College to keep African Americans out of their own schools. "Others are doing it to keep the Negro out of their so-called Christian (?) schools and knowing that they are doing wrong in the sight of God, they support S.W.C.C. to sooth a guilty conscience."[34] Segregationists willingly gave money to black causes—educational or religious—as long as their white children did not attend school with black children.

Hogan's co-worker, Ira Y. Rice Jr., similarly noted that the racist practices of white Christians in Texas were responsible for Southwestern Christian College's existence. Rice argued that Jesus Christ himself would not have been welcomed in some Church of Christ schools because of "the color of his skin." He then referenced Timothy's mixed racial heritage and asked if "such a *half-breed* would get in Nashville or Henderson or Montgomery or Searcy or even-now-to-some-extent Abilene?" Rice further inquired: "Oh, but, I'm told, things are so much better in Abilene! Think so? If they really are, then why does *Southwestern Christian College still exist* at Terrell? There never *would* have been a segregated college for Afro-Americans at Terrell, if ACC had been truly *Christian*. To talk about colleges being 'Christian' when *Christians* in fellowship still can not gain admission to the lower levels because of *race* or *color*—Well, how hypocritical can you get?"[35]

That segregationists found a home in Churches of Christ can be seen in the testimony of Leon C. Burns, minister of the West Seventh Street Church of Christ in Columbia, Tennessee, who vociferously denounced the *Brown* verdict. Burns argued from the pulpit that the case marked a negative shift in race relations in the South, turning white southerners against African Americans. "The Negro has truly become an outcast race," preached Burns. "He is no longer trusted as a race, by his White friends and neighbors. Prior to 1954 the South was deeply conscious of the Negro's sad economic and social plight, and was doing everything possible to improve these conditions, but now the South is totally indifferent in attitude to him." Like many in the white South, Burns interpreted the *Brown* verdict as an endorsement of bi-racial sex between black men and white women. "These are simply means to an end, and the end is free and unrestrained intermarriage between Negroes and Whites, and they will not be satisfied until they get it. Unless you believe in intermarriage between Negroes and Whites, and hence the creation of a mongrel race in America, you cannot possibly believe in integration in our schools." Burns added in his 1957 sermon that "In a survey made among several thousand Negroes a few years ago, it was found that the secret desire of almost every Negro man questioned was to be able to sleep with a White woman."[36]

C. A. Cannon, a white believer in Saratoga, Arkansas, took exception to Hogan's editorials on race, accusing the black evangelist of being a sorcerer and a pretender. Cannon claimed that "White people built many of the very best schools for the Negro. But, no good Negro wants to force himself on the White race, nor want the White man mixed with his race domestically or publicly." Hogan conversely charged Cannon with pretending. "Mr. Cannon, you are wrong about Bro. Hogan wanting to be associated with people who pretend to be Christians. May God keep me from pretenders. However, I maintain that my rightful place is with all true children of God regardless of race or color of their skin." Hogan maintained that Cannon expressed the visceral issue for most whites in Churches of Christ, that is, the fear of racial and sexual mixing of black men with white women. "The trouble with Mr. Cannon and many like him, they think that the Negro just want [sic] to mix with the White race. This is not so."[37]

Even though Hogan detested the inhumane racial views of some whites in Churches of Christ, he clearly understood that some white leaders denounced racism and discrimination before their members. In 1960 Hogan praised David Lipscomb, longtime editor of the *Gospel Advocate*, for rebuking white Christians in McKinney, Texas, who in 1878 barred a black man who desired membership in their congregation. Hogan expressed gratitude for "this pioneer gospel Minister who had the intestinal fortitude and the love of God so inbedded [*sic*] in his heart that he spoke out in no uncertain terms in exposing the soul damning sin of racial prejudice and segregation in the Lord's church." Hogan also commended white ministers in Churches of Christ, especially Carl Spain, M. T. Tune, and James Willeford, for their fierce opposition to racial discrimination. "These men are men of integrity who are not afraid to speak up for the truth that is in Christ Jesus our Lord. Bro. Spain did it at Abilene; Bro. Tune did it through his paper and Bro. Willeford did it over the Herald of Truth program when he presented the sermon on 'Call No Man Common.' I predict that Abilene college will be the first to stop the ungodly practice of segregation and admit Negroes in their school where they can be prepared to help in leading the millions of the dark races to Christ."[38]

Hogan correctly predicted that Abilene Christian College would indeed be among the first Church of Christ schools to admit black students after Carl Spain's 1960 blistering speech at the school. Aware that some Methodist and Baptist schools welcomed African Americans, Spain indicted his colleagues at Abilene Christian College. "We fear the mythical character named Jim Crow," Spain asserted, "more than we reverence Jesus Christ."[39] Roosevelt Sams, an African American preacher and educator in Churches of Christ, recalled that "After he [Spain] gave his lecture on racial segregation it seemed as if a ton of dynamite had exploded. His lecture was the 'talk' during the remainder of the lectureship." Ira Rice, after reading what Spain had said, "shouted."[40]

In 1963 Hogan continued to express his displeasure with whites in Churches of Christ who discriminated against African Americans. "I'll be

Jimmy Lovell (1896-1984), a genuine friend and passionate supporter of African American preachers in Churches of Christ, used his papers, *Hogan's Helper* and the *West Coast Christian*, to garner monetary support for R. N. Hogan and other black preachers.

glad to meet any preacher in public debate on this racial issue. However, I am not expecting anyone to accept the challenge, for they know that God Almighty condemns the prejudicial and hateful segregation that is existing in the so-called Churches of Christ and so-called Christian schools today." Hogan was also distraught with white Christians who remained silent about the bombings and murders of African Americans in the Deep South. "Where are the Churches of Christ in Birmingham, Ala., Jackson, Miss. and other places during all of those disgraceful racial struggles in these places?"[41] Like many white Christians across the South in the civil rights era, most Anglos in Churches of Christ felt no moral obligation to get publicly involved in purely social matters. "What good will it do a man," one writer declared, "to have equal rights if he loses his soul in hell after getting it, because some foolish 'gospel' preacher was more interested in his physical welfare than his spiritual."[42]

Hogan understood that for many whites in Churches of Christ their opposition to integration derived from their fear of racial and sexual mixing of black and white Christians. Frequently asked, Do you think that Negroes and whites should marry? Hogan consistently replied that it was a matter of preference. "I believe that I would marry one of my own race; not because of prejudice nor because I think it is wrong, but only because I prefer my own race." He then put his finger on the heart of the race problem in Churches of Christ: "The fact of the matter is, that about all Negro men in the Church of Christ, just want to be the white man's brother and *not* his brother-in-law."[43] Hogan understood that for most white southerners, including those in Churches of Christ, the issue of racial and sexual mixing lay at the heart of the United State's race problem. Jack Evans, an admirer of Hogan and a renowned preacher in black Churches of Christ, voiced a similar observation when he debated a white Baptist minister, Vernon L. Barr. Continuing Hogan's fight against racism in America, Evans declared in 1976 that "The very heart of the racial problem in America, whether we admit it or not, is intermarriage."[44]

Certainly R. N. Hogan's aggressive stance on the issue of race set him apart from the giant among black preachers, Marshall Keeble. In Texas both men founded numerous congregations and both left indelible marks on the history of African American Churches of Christ. Hogan's most avid and diligent white supporter, Jimmy L. Lovell, repeatedly called the black evangelist "the greatest preacher—white or black—I have ever heard."[45] Hogan was probably not a "better" preacher than Keeble; but the former was certainly a different preacher than the latter. While Keeble remained virtually mute on the explosive issue of racial discrimination and school segregation in U.S. society, Hogan unabashedly and consistently refused to keep silent. Of course Keeble preached mostly in the rigidly segregated South while Hogan labored largely in the more egalitarian culture of Los Angeles, California. Whatever his comparative talents, Hogan felt deep concern about rescuing both the souls of white folk from the sin of racism as well as the minds of black folk from the sin of spiritual ignorance. And Texans, black and white, could not mistake how he felt on both of these matters as R. N. Hogan marched in the vanguard of "the hard-fighting soldiers."

PART IV

The Education of Black Disciples of Christ and Black Churches of Christ in Texas

Chapter 10

THE BOOKER T. WASHINGTON OF TEXAS

J. N. Ervin and the Jarvis Christian Institute Experience

Booker [T.] Washington could not have accomplished his great work but for the financial assistance of the whites, and [J. N.] Ervin is our Texas Booker [T.] Washington.

—Christian Courier, 1920

Any study of the history of African American Churches of Christ in Texas would be incomplete without an examination of the historically black Jarvis Christian Institute in Hawkins.[1] Long before members of Churches of Christ founded Southwestern Christian College in Terrell in 1949, black ministers and members in Churches of Christ received a cordial welcome at the Jarvis Christian Institute. Since racial discrimination barred them from white schools, and Churches of Christ had not yet founded educational institutions for blacks, Jarvis seemed a reasonable choice. The establishment of this East Texas school also reveals much concerning the racial thought of white Disciples of Christ, its principal benefactors. The institution drew its name from Maj. J. J. Jarvis and his wife Ida Van Zandt Jarvis, both of whom felt a strong sense of moral obligation to African Americans. Indeed, Mrs. Jarvis and other supportive white Disciples especially delighted in the school's first president, J. N. Ervin, because he exhibited a non-threatening racial mien and, more importantly, because his demeanor reminded them of Booker

T. Washington, the most influential black American in the Progressive era, whom whites in the Stone–Campbell Movement esteemed highly.[2]

The Philanthropy of J. J. and Ida Van Zandt Jarvis

White Disciples of Christ in Texas awoke to the intellectual and spiritual plight of African Americans under the prompting of W. M. Williams, editor of the *Christian Courier* from 1917 to 1931. In 1920 he indicted white Disciples in Dallas who "have too long neglected the Negro." Quoting Dr. John G. Slayter, a leader of the East Dallas Christian Church, who rebuked saints in Texas for showing more interest in "the Africans away down on the equator" than in "the vast Negro population right here at our doors," Williams concluded that "The only hope for the solution of the Negro problem lies in the Christian religion, and the Disciples of Christ with their zeal for evangelism must not overlook their great opportunity to carry Christ to this people and to educate the race along the line of Christian civilization."[3]

The following month Williams again reminded white Disciples in Texas of their "debt" to both Hispanic and African Americans. After encouraging his readership to reach out to the Mexican, he then lamented: "But what depresses me is the fact that Texas Disciples are making no worthy effort to do mission work among Texas negroes; and not only so, but they are not interested in such missions, and not personally concerned as to whether or not the negro gets New Testament Christianity or goes to hell without it." Williams cited E. T. McFarland, secretary of the Dallas Missionary Fund, who reported many Disciples eagerly supported foreign missions but felt no obligation to engage in domestic outreach. Editor Williams then confessed that "I fear that is the attitude of most of our people in other places; for I think Dallas brethren are not very different from others."[4] He then warned that "God will curse every people who disregard his will; and Texas Disciples can not afford to neglect their duty and opportunity in connection with the Mexican and negro."[5]

Apart from Williams, other Disciple principals recognized that white Disciples owed a debt to African Americans. John B. Lehman, head of the Southern Christian Institute in Edwards, Mississippi, and general superintendent of the Negro work of the Christian Woman's Board of Missions, pled with Disciple ministers to condemn publicly the practice of lynching, urging preachers to affirm the Fatherhood of God and the brotherhood of man, to pray, and to preach on the wicked practice. The administrator in Mississippi concluded that "It is high time for Christianity's place at the bat, and if we fail God will call off the game by a social upheaval which will make our hair rise on end."[6]

Three years later Lehman praised Jarvis Christian Institute as a "moral and spiritual asset." He explained: "Texas has a vast Negro population. If this is neglected and it reverts to the vices of its barbarian ancestors it can easily pull down the entire white population down to its level. In fact it has already done that in some sections. There is no hope for the higher development of the white race except as it lifts up these people."[7] An obvious proponent of Social Darwinianism, which advocated the retrograding of former slaves who were no longer under white supervision,[8] Lehman insisted that the elevation of white Americans went hand-in-hand with that of black Americans. He consequently encouraged white Disciples to support the fledgling college in Hawkins. "Jarvis Christian Institute is already the pride of Texas and we are sure that all they need is to know their duty and they will aid."[9]

Ida Van Zandt Jarvis drove the emergence of the Jarvis Christian Institute. Born in Washington, D.C., in 1844, Ida grew up in Texas where she met and married Maj. J. J. Jarvis, a committed member of the Christian

Ida Van Zandt Jarvis and her husband, J. J. Jarvis, were the impetus behind the emergence of what is now Jarvis Christian College. Both were life-long champions of black education.

(Courtesy of Disciples of Christ Historical Society, Nashville, Tennessee)

Church. Mr. Jarvis, a native of North Carolina and a former Confederate officer, became an influential lawyer and a successful recruiter for the Texas and Pacific Railroad to Fort Worth. The substantial contributions by the Jarvises helped establish and stabilize Add–Ran College, a growing Disciples college and forerunner of Texas Christian University in Fort Worth, serving whites only in the race-ridden society of the time.[10] But Jarvis Christian Institute was essentially the brainchild of Mrs. Jarvis. Feeling a certain sense of obligation to her former slaves, she dreamed of establishing a school for black people in East Texas. Mrs. Jarvis testified in 1922: "It goes without saying, that I have always felt we owed a debt to the loyal and warmhearted negroes of the old South, and my husband, Major J. J. Jarvis, and I felt glad that in a small way we could pay that debt by the gift of the land on which Jarvis Christian Institute is built. It was the best investment either of us ever made."[11] For Jarvis, the creation of a school for African Americans in East Texas afforded her an opportunity to "take up the White Man's Burden,"[12] or in this case, the white woman's burden.

A sense of moral obligation prodded Major Jarvis as well. "About 1905 my husband, J. J. Jarvis, decided that he could put a certain tract of land in East Texas to no better use than to help the people of 'Aunt Milly,' his old Black Mammy, and the Negro playmates of his childhood." Mr. Jarvis then advised C. C. Smith, Corresponding Secretary of the Negro Board of Education and Evangelization, to inspect the land to see if it was "suitable for the school." Mrs. Jarvis recalled fondly the imagined racial harmony that existed between whites and blacks in the Old South. "Well do I remember the comradeship existing between the white people and their slaves before and during the war. All were members of one common family, and each in a measure dependent on the other. These 'hewers of wood and drawers of water' with loving hearts and willing hands, carried out the plans of the white women who had the management of the affairs at home."[13] Like many white southerners, Mrs. Jarvis imbibed the "lost cause" mythology which caused them to yearn for the antebellum life replete with faithful and obedient slaves, a facetious and self-serving construct unshared by the victims of the malevolent system.[14]

Mrs. Jarvis perhaps acquired her compassion for African Americans during her personal encounters with slaves, likely inheriting her sense of duty from her mother. "The first missionary work I ever did was reading the Bible to the Negroes in their cabins on Sundays evenings," she wrote. "The first educational work I ever did was teaching the dining room boy and the five little house girls their letters by the light of blazing pine knots—my head and the little black ones bending together over the same page. My mother encouraged me in this, for she felt that her responsibility for the souls of her Negroes could only be shifted to them by teaching them to read the Bible." Mrs. Jarvis, likely insulated, as were many aristocratic white women, from slavery's more odious aspects, never forgot these experiences with her black servants. "There is a tender memory in my heart of these good old days, but the crying need is help for the young Negroes of today, the children and grandchildren of those old playmates of my childhood."[15]

Factors other than sentiment lay behind the establishment of Jarvis Christian Institute. The presence of such Texas black schools as Wiley College, Bishop College (both in Marshall), and Texas State College in Tyler also stirred the interest of the Disciples. The Negro Woman's Society of the Disciples generated interest and appealed to the Disciples' National Board of the Missionary Society. The latter group proposed to donate $10,000 if the black organization could raise $1,000, and in 1910 the pledge was met. Mr. Jarvis, after some prodding by his wife, agreed to give 418 acres of land in Hawkins to start a school. When Jarvis consented to donate the land, his wife laughed, cried, embraced him, and said, "You are the greatest man in the world."[16]

J. N. Ervin: The Booker T. Washington of Texas

Two years later J. B. Lehman sent Thomas B. Frost, an alumnus of the Southern Christian Institute, his wife, and four children to Hawkins to launch construction of the campus. They brought with them chickens, turkeys, household goods, and farming utensils in a private car. C. A. Berry, another graduate of the Southern Christian Institute, helped the Frosts clear the land, erect a cabin and schoolhouse, and open the school with thirteen students in 1913.[17] The following year Mrs. Jarvis, attending a Disciples conference in Toronto, Canada, met J. N. Ervin. One writer noted: "So much impressed with Ervin was Mrs. Jarvis that she sought and obtained a conference with him. She thought she observed in him the combination of Booker T. Washington, whom she had met, and Addison Clark of Add–Ran, and who, in the opinion of her and her husband, was the greatest educator the Southwest had thus far produced."[18]

Ervin, born into slavery in 1844 in Tennessee, belonged to a renowned political family, the Taylors. Bob Taylor, an ex-governor of Tennessee, assumed responsibility for young Ervin's elementary education. His mother inspired him to pursue education beyond elementary

J. N. Ervin (1844-1938), a former slave from Tennessee, went on to earn degrees from Columbia University in New York before becoming the first president of the Jarvis Christian Institute in 1914.

(Courtesy of Disciples of Christ Historical Society, Nashville, Tennessee)

and high school, and Ervin earned a bachelor's and a master's degree from Columbia University in New York. In 1914 Ervin left a lucrative administrative post in Johnson City, Tennessee, to become the first president of the Jarvis Christian Institute. An eloquent and erudite black leader, Ervin visited and preached in churches across Texas, and after one passionate and articulate sermon, a white listener commented, "I declare, no nigger's got a right to be that smart."[19]

Ervin won widespread support from white Disciples, certainly because of his impressive academic credential, but also because he exhibited the white-comforting qualities of an "old Negro." Unlike the assertive and abrasive new Negro, the old Negro was faithful and obedient[20]; in 1921 J. L. Clark, a white Disciple and faculty member at Sam Houston State University, divided black men into two categories: "One is radical; the other is conservative and safe."[21] In the minds of white Disciples, J. N. Ervin clearly fell in the latter group. Mrs. W. W. Phares, wife of a reputable editor of the *Christian Courier*, described Ervin as "meek and humble" as a child.[22] Ervin's "meek and humble" bearing reminded white Disciples of the old-time Negro of the slavery era, allowing them in turn to assume a complacently paternalistic attitude among themselves. Just as importantly, Ervin reminded white Christians in Texas of the famed educator, Booker T. Washington. Ervin never revealed his own perspective on such matters, but he well understood the narrow latitude of any black educator in a South shadowed by "Judge Lynch."

In 1922 Henry Dorsey, a Dallas business owner and member of the Christian Church, lavished praise on Ervin. "The school and the brotherhood are most fortunate in having President Ervin at the head of this institution," Dorsey wrote, "for he enjoys the confidence and esteem not only of the colored people, but of the whites also, because of his sterling Christian manhood, his genuine consecration to the upbuilding of his race, and his devotion to the cause of New Testament Christianity. He is not only an educator along industrial and intellectual lines, but he has a fine appreciation of racial relations and knows the importance of the moral training for the children of his people. He is our Booker [T.] Washington."[23] Like many other white southerners in the early twentieth century, Disciples sought to educate African Americans to remain in subservient roles, preferably in the manner exemplified in educators with a "fine appreciation of racial relations" such as J. N. Ervin.[24]

In the spring of 1922 George Washington Carver, distinguished agricultural scientist, visited the Jarvis Christian Institute for one week, and while there displayed and explained "his innumerable products from the peanut and the sweet potato." The *Christian Courier* praised him, explaining, "He stands in a class by himself. He is also a naturalist, horticulturist and landscape gardener. With his wonderful personality and with faultless English he held his audience spell bound, while he unfolded the glory and beauty of nature and his marvelous discoveries. Farmers and visitors thronged to hear this wonderful man."[25] The editor of the *Christian Courier*, W. M. Williams, also included a picture of Carver. The following month a subscriber of the paper lambasted Williams for inserting the picture of "a nigger in its columns." The correspondent asserted that "I was born and reared in Texas and have always treated a negro fair and square as long as he stayed in a negro's place. But when such favors are shown in a publication which is interested strictly for the white race, it seems that you are in favor of social equality, and will only serve to cause more hatred towards the black race."[26]

Williams in turn defended his right to include a picture of George Washington Carver since presidents Woodrow Wilson and Warren G. Harding had invited the black agriculturalist to give them advice about farming innovations. Williams praised the Jarvis Christian Institute for inviting Carver "to assist this negro school in lifting the young of this child-minded race out of ignorance and into a life of Christian service." The editor took the opportunity to commend J. N. Ervin for his opposition to "social equality," concluding: "The Courier knows that social equality, as between whites and blacks, is unthinkable, and the leading negroes of the country are of the same position and are so teaching their people; as for example, President J. N. Ervin, of Jarvis Christian Institute, who impresses upon them that they must keep their place and improve their minds and morals and render unselfish service to mankind by being industrious, honest and efficient in whatever lines their talents lead them."[27] In advising African Americans to stay in a place of subordination, Ervin secured encomiums from white Disciples.

The subscriber's criticism of Carver's picture so disturbed Ida V. Jarvis that she got up from six weeks of bed confinement, shook off her "acute sciatic neuritis," and rose to the defense of the black race. Mrs. Jarvis confessed that "I could write enough on this subject to fill a whole number of the Courier, but I just want to tell two stories of Aunt Adaline, an old-time cook of ours, who had come from Tennessee."[28] Mrs. Jarvis then related stories common among white southerners who longed for an imagined antebellum era of contented slaves and kindly masters.[29] Aunt

Adaline's faith, fidelity, and courage left an indelible imprint on the mind of Mrs. Jarvis, stirring her to rise to the defense of George Washington Carver and other African Americans. The *Christian Courier* announced Carver's plans to visit in 1923, but this time the paper included no picture of the black horticulturalist.[30]

Mrs. Jarvis especially admired J. N. Ervin. With Booker T. Washington, Ervin argued that the South presented African Americans the best opportunities for progress, that the "Southern Anglo-Saxon" understood the black man better than anyone else, and that most intelligent blacks opposed racial—certainly sexual—mixing. Ervin asserted: "White and black must live here side by side in the South. Their destinies are linked together. All right thinking negroes are as much opposed to amalgamation of the races as are the whites."[31] Ervin's rhetoric, mirroring the racial thought of Booker T. Washington, endeared the Jarvis Christian Institute president to white Disciples.

Visitors to the Jarvis Christian Institute regularly praised Ervin's educational work. Three women from Forney, Texas, after spending two days at the East Texas campus, commended Ervin as "a strong and capable man, doing his work in a remarkable way." The competence of the teachers, the cleanliness of the school's ten-building campus, the work ethic of its 150 students, and the prospect of a new hospital further impressed the women. The Forney trio "met several men living in the vicinity of the school who spoke in the highest terms of President Ervin and his work. They especially complimented the students on their conduct in the town and community."[32]

When W. W. Phares visited the Hawkins campus the following year, he remarked that the school's plentiful livestock and sawmill provided food for the students, and furnished them "material for building and the means of instructing the youth in useful vocations." In a sewing room, instructors taught girls how to make clothes and household linen. Such instruction, Phares insisted, could only "add to their usefulness." He then lauded Ervin as "a most capable, polished, Christian gentleman."[33] White southerners did not mind educating black southerners as long as they gained knowledge in manual and agricultural skills. William H. Baldwin Jr., a railroad entrepreneur, reported in the *Raleigh Morning Post* that "the Negro should be taught to work, to work at the trades and in the fields, and a common school education along with their work is not only unharmful but a great benefit to them [and] to their employers." White Disciples in Texas similarly delighted in the curriculum at the Jarvis Christian Institute because it trained both the minds and hands of black youth. In 1928 the Disciples happily reported that "There is a growing interest among the southern people in the education of the Negro. They appreciate the fact that the educated Negro is a more valuable asset to any community than the uneducated one, especially if his education is of an industrial character." In this regard, the Jarvis Christian Institute imitated the curricula of both the Hampton Institute and the Tuskegee Institute.[34]

For Jarvis Christian Institute, however, the Bible stood at the core of the curriculum. Phares explained that "every student, in public assembly, has a portion of the Scripture expounded to him every day; a two-year course in Bible study in classes is provided and the students spend practically all of the Lord's day in worship, Bible study, Y.M.C.A., Y.W.C.A. and Y.P.C.E. activities. At the tap of a bell at 8 a.m. every voice is hushed, every hand is stopped and every head is bowed in silent prayer." Biblical instruction went hand-in-hand with practical training. "The courses offered are the Bible, literature and music, besides the industrial course, which includes everything from 'slopping' a pig and milking a cow to making a dress and building a house."[35]

In the fall of 1922, J. B. Holmes gave a similar report. As with Phares, Holmes appreciated the balance of academic with practical training, and that the students learned "neatness along with usefulness. They not only get the knowledge from books, but are given practical experience in farming, stockraising, dairying, handling of poultry, sewing, cooking, housekeeping, music and a little of the fine arts." The deportment of Ervin's students so impressed Holmes that he believed that white youth "could learn much in courtesy, decorum, and devotion from the Jarvis Christian Institute at Hawkins."[36] The next year students at the East Texas school sent W. M. Williams farm products including peppers, onions, and tomatoes. The *Christian Courier* editor thanked Ervin and his school for "producing gardens, farms and orchards [which] have been made to take the place of jungles by these aggressive Christian educators and workers."[37]

In 1924 Leon Williams visited the Jarvis Christian Institute and heaped more praise on Ervin. "He is intensely interested in this school and the development of the Negro race. He is keenly desirous to remove from his race all traces of racial prejudices and hatred, and his whole being throbs for the greatest longing of his soul—the education of the Negro, softened by religious influences." Williams particularly commended Ervin for his desire for racial harmony. "Prof. Ervin is not only president, but he is also a preacher of the gospel. His influence on the surrounding Negro

Disciples of Christ standing in front of the first building at the Jarvis Christian Institute in Hawkins, Texas. Founded in 1913, the Jarvis Christian Institute welcomed and trained black preachers from Churches of Christ before the opening of Southwestern Christian College in Terrell in 1950.

(Courtesy of Disciples of Christ Historical Society, Nashville, Tennessee)

An early chapel service at Jarvis Christian College. The date of the photo is unknown.

(Courtesy of Disciples of Christ Historical Society, Nashville, Tennessee)

community has been marvelous. He told me recently of a woman who, through ignorance, was saturated with racial hatred. He said that he finally was instrumental in removing the scales from her eyes and at the prayer meeting service she never fails to say, 'God bless the white man.'"[38]

Three years later, W. M. Williams attended the State Fair in Dallas. He was thrilled to see black people giving whites "the right-of-way on a day that seemed to mean so much to them." Williams was particularly thrilled to see African Americans who "could be together, in holiday spirit, among white people, many of them having to get food and drink from places kept by whites, and yet none of them should do anything that reflected upon his race." Williams attributed the cordial behavior of blacks at the fair partly to the leadership of Ervin. "I am boasting about facts and not philosophizing about the causes, but I must express hope that this excellent behavior of a multitude of Negroes was inspired in part by the improved attitude of the white people toward their colored neighbors. The teaching and example of men like J. N. Ervin must be looked to for further explanation."[39]

In addition to Ervin's non-threatening demeanor, the melodious voices of the Jarvis Jubilee Singers delighted white Disciples in Texas as well. Building on the long and rich legacy of the Fisk Jubilee Singers who began fundraising tours in the 1870s, the chorus from East Texas similarly traveled across the Lone Star State to raise funds for their school. In the summer of 1923, the Jarvis Jubilee Singers sang "negro folk lore songs" at the Texas Christian Missionary Convention in Fort Worth. The *Christian Courier* reported that "These singers were repeatedly and enthusiastically called back to the platform in Fort Worth, in spite of the fact that the program was crowded and time therefore limited."[40]

Enthralled over their excellent performances, white Disciples in Texas invited the black choir to community after community. Their stirring songs, according to the *Christian Courier*, appealed to white listeners even in areas where racial tension was stifling.

> In spite of the fact that this is the heated period of the year, and many of the leaders in the church life are away on vacation, crowds even beyond expectation have greeted them wherever they have appeared. This has been quite noticeable even in places where there has been strong race feeling, in one of which a thousand people turned out for the concert, packing the church house, and filling the spaces around the building, and automobiles drawn up within ear shot. Encore after encore

> has been given with enthusiastic hands, and the program has repeatedly run a half hour beyond the period assigned because the audiences would not let them go.[41]

The Jubilee Singers showcased their talents across Texas, giving "members of the Christian church an opportunity to see first hand what the money expended at Jarvis Christian Institute is accomplishing and to acquaint the church with opportunities to thus assist the Negro race."[42] On occasion, the Jubilee Singers toured cities beyond Texas; in the fall of 1925 they performed the Negro spiritual, "Swing Low, Sweet Chariot," in Oklahoma City. The *Christian Courier* commented that "Music conveys a subtle meaning which is too ethereal for words. Nothing finer, nothing more beautiful, nothing more soul-inspiring was ever heard at our National Conventions than the exquisite rendition of 'Swing Low, Sweet Chariot' during the Wednesday session."[43]

After performing in Mineola, Texas, the chorus received a check from the Ku Klux Klan. The terrorist group attached a note reading: "In order to show the appreciation the better element of the white population has for those of your race who are striving to make it a better people and to cultivate the right ideals and bring about a better understanding of your race and their White neighbors, we make this small donation for your encouragement."[44] The Mineola Klan, likely consisting in part of local Disciples, supported African Americans who did not challenge the racial status quo, which kept blacks in a subservient role.

Certainly some members of the Disciples of Christ in Texas aligned with the Ku Klux Klan. In 1921 the *Christian Courier* cast its full support behind the Texas Klan, claiming it protected girls and women, opposed sexual relations between blacks and whites, and maintained law and order. The editor of the *Christian Courier* expressed the view of many white Texas Disciples, shared by many in other churches, when he asserted that "the Courier trusts the Ku Klux Klan of 1921 is of that high order as those following immediately after the Civil War over which General Bedford Forrest ruled. And there is evidence that only the best men of the community are solicited or invited to become Ku Klux." W. M. Williams, blithely linking religion and thuggery, concluded that the *Christian Courier* "is for the Ku Klux or any other organization that stands for true Americanism, high moral ideals, and clean government—for the enforcement of the law."[45]

In 1924 W. M. Williams visited the Jarvis Christian Institute and lauded the efforts of J. N. Ervin. The editor of the *Christian Courier* added that the East Texas Ku Klux Klan has "notified the Jarvis school authorities that they are their friends and ready to assist them in any way possible." Williams remarked on the peaceful and harmonizing race relations among whites and blacks in Hawkins, owed, he claimed, to their refusal to practice "racial amalgamation." Instead "they are coming to mutually understand each other on a friendly and neighborly basis and to work together for the common good of the country and the salvation of all. And no man among the Negroes is better fitted for leadership along these lines than President Ervin, who so fully enjoys the confidence of both white and black."[46] The racial harmony between the Jarvis Christian Institute and the Ku Klux Klan in East Texas again suggests that some in the white supremacy group held membership in the Disciples of Christ as well.

Other Disciple ministers and their co-religionists in other denominations supported the Klan. J. W. Underwood, preacher for the Magnolia Avenue Christian Church in Fort Worth, approved of the Klan's supposed mission "to get certain low-down skunks which can't be gotten in any other way."[47] In San Marcos the Klan interrupted a service and handed a note to D. A. Leak, a white preacher for the Disciples of Christ, who had addressed the topic, "The Greatest Menace to Christianity." The letter thanked Leak for his "kindly attitude toward the Klan." Leak then applauded the Klan "for one hundred per cent Americanism, the American educational system of public free schools, the separation of church and state, freedom of speech and the press, the sanctity of the home, religious liberty, the fatherhood of God, the brotherhood of man, the Fiery Cross—everything that goes into the highest ideals of citizenship and Christianity." Leak then concluded, "No man . . . can be a good Klansman without fully subscribing to the tenets of the Christian religion."[48] For Leak, the practices of the Ku Klux Klan complimented the teachings of Christianity.

Editor W. M. Williams attended a worship service at the Rosemont Christian Church in Dallas where Alexander Campbell Parker served as preacher. Williams praised Parker for his "virile, practical, scriptural" sermon. Parker, added the editor, "has no patience with a 'sissy' brand of Christianity, and he fights the great battles of life with the faith and courage of a crusader, and does not allow the making and losing of a million dollars to break his morale. Here's to Alexander Campbell Parker—a winner!" Lodge No. 66 of the Invisible Empire of the Ku Klux Klan had chosen Williams' "winner" as its "Cyclops." Across much of the nation,

J. N. Ervin (front row, center) sits with members of the Jarvis Christian College faculty. The photo date is 1933.

(Courtesy of Disciples of Christ Historical Society, Nashville, Tennessee)

whites had deftly enfolded religion and malign racism, glossing over lynch-law fury with a patina of "the fatherhood of God and the brotherhood of man."[49]

While the Jarvis Christian Institute found few to challenge its passive stance on the racism of the time, some did express unhappiness with the school's educational philosophy. Some black Disciples such as Vance Smith, a graduate of the Southern Christian Institute, Butler University, and the University of Chicago, maintained that Disciple schools placed too much emphasis on manual training. Smith asserted: "Not that I mean to decry all industrial training, far from it, but I do believe a man can be a good, moral, intelligent citizen and Christian, yea, even a leader, without knowing how to pick cotton or hoe corn, and a woman may be as true a wife, as loving a mother and as perfect a neighbor, without the knowledge of canning wild plums or washing dirty overalls. But, so far, each and everyone of our schools has a farm attached, with sometimes a saw mill, planning mill, power house, blacksmith shop, laundry, cannery, garden, et cetera, ad infinitum." Smith further lamented that when colleges divert their resources between the "mental development" and "manual training" of young people, they produced "half-baked artisans and retarded scholars. It is splendid for all people, white and black, to have industrial training, but it is costly when it is bought at the expense of all else." Smith concluded that "the Negro of today is the progressive Negro." Therefore, the goal of schools like the Jarvis Christian Institute should be to provide an "advanced, adequate and serviceable training to carry on the work of Christ in positions of leadership and intelligent laymanship. That these essentials are lacking now in our brotherhood is apparent and the Negro is willing to support any plan that assures his more adequate training along academic lines."[50]

The Jarvis Christian Institute, however, kept to its bi-educational path, and J. N. Ervin's ability to navigate the treacherous racial waters of the Lone Star State endeared him to white Disciples, who in turn gave their full support to his school. More than a skillful peacemaker, Ervin also worked adroitly as an administrator. In 1931, when a fire destroyed a boys dormitory and killed a student, Disciples of Christ across Texas "rallied to the aid of Pres. J. N. Ervin and the school."[51] Ervin confessed that he had often received compliments about his administrative work at the Jarvis Christian Institute, but he sometimes wondered if the remarks were sincere. After the fiery tragedy he saw firsthand "the genuineness of our friends." Ervin testified that "Less than 12 hours later one automobile of clothing for relief was brought to us from Longview. Close behind this delivery 3 other carloads came from other points, including McKinney and Greenville. Several days later a truck full of clothing was sent from the churches of Dallas."[52] That so many Disciples gave monetarily and materially to help rebuild the boys dormitory and to alleviate grief testifies to their unfeigned concern for J. N. Ervin and his work at the Jarvis Christian Institute.

Ervin remained at the school's helm until March 2, 1938, when he suffered a paralyzing stroke, and five months later he died in his son's home in Los Angeles.[54] Through Ervin's tireless efforts, the Jarvis Christian Institute grew numerically and financially. The enrollment increased, buildings multiplied, and the acreage grew. If Ervin had displayed the traits of the "new" Negro, he would not have enjoyed the twenty-four year tenure he had in Hawkins, Texas. His meek, non-threatening, and

Booker T. Washington-like persona won the trust and respect of white Disciples in Texas. And this support, coupled with Ervin's zeal and determination, transformed the Jarvis Christian Institute into a viable, prosperous, and reputable college to train African American youth from Texas and beyond.

More significantly, Ervin cordially welcomed black ministers and members in Churches of Christ to a Disciples school when they lacked their own colleges. Some of these preachers included E. W. Anderson, who ministered to congregations in Texas and Oklahoma; F. F. Carson, who sprang from the "mother church" of black Churches of Christ in Texas and preached across the state before taking up residence in California and then doing missionary work in Nigeria; and Woodrow A. Wilson, who worked effectively with congregations in El Paso, Texas, and Detroit, Michigan.[55] These men, among others, received knowledge and training from a black Disciples of Christ institution, but they led distinguished ministerial careers among black Churches of Christ in Texas and beyond.

Chapter 11

"A Young Moses Arose"

Jack Evans and the Legacy of Southwestern Christian College

Then Moses stretched out his hand over the sea, and all that night the Lord drove the sea back with a strong east wind and turned it into dry land. The waters were divided.

—Exodus 14:21

During his four-decade presidential tenure, Jack Evans transformed Southwestern Christian College (SWCC) in Terrell, Texas, from a fledgling, unaccredited institution to a fully accredited liberal arts college with a four-year Bible degree program. In the process, Evans became perhaps the most influential figure in black Churches of Christ in Texas and even beyond. Eugene Lawton, SWCC's academic dean from 1969 to 1971 and a renowned black preacher, captured the essence of Evans's significance: "Frustration, agony and uncertainty characterized a struggling college that seemed to be headed for nowhereville. It was during these critical days of Southwestern that a young Moses arose to lead the college from the valley of despair to the mountaintop of success."[1] After highlighting Evans's skills in increasing SWCC's student enrollment and expanding the school's physical plants, Lawton again compared Evans's labor to the biblical prophet: "For his administrative expertise and electrifying charisma, we salute Dr. Jack 'liberating Moses' Evans."[2]

A native of Houston, Evans became a member of Churches of Christ under the preaching of Paul Settles and at age sixteen began preaching himself. After attending Houston's public schools, he enrolled in high school at the Nashville Christian Institute in Tennessee, under the tutelage of the renowned Marshall Keeble. Evans imbibed there the exclusivistic theological posture of Keeble and the racial combativeness of G. P. Bowser. From the Nashville Christian Institute, Evans moved to SWCC, graduating from the two-year program in 1959. Because no white Church of Christ colleges apart from Pepperdine University admitted black students, Evans sought academic advancement outside his religious fellowship, earning his BA degree in History and Religion at Eastern New Mexico University in Portales, New Mexico. In 1963 he received his MA degree in History and English from Texas Western College (now the University of Texas at El Paso), writing his thesis on "The History of Southwestern Christian College of Terrell, Texas."[3] The same year, Evans returned to SWCC and assumed the deanship of his alma mater. He succeeded Roosevelt Sams whose eight-year tenure reached across the fledgling years of SWCC and a time of evolving race relations in Churches of Christ and the broader U.S. society.

The Deanship of Roosevelt Sams

Native to Dime Box, Texas, Roosevelt Sams graduated from his local high school at the age of twenty. After serving in World War II and receiving four medals, he converted to Churches of Christ in Waco, Texas, in 1949. In the same year, he completed a BS degree in education at Waco's Paul Quinn College, and four years later he received a Masters of Education in Administration from Texas Southern University in Houston.[4]

Sams became the third academic dean at SWCC in 1955, succeeding Vanderbilt Lewis who held that post from 1950 to 1951 and Grover C. Washington, dean from 1952 to 1955. Sams and his wife Izetta relocated to Terrell at a time when racial strife engulfed the United States. *Brown v. Board of Education*, which struck down segregation in public schools in 1954, coupled with the brutal murder of Emmett Till in Mississippi and the racially charged Montgomery Bus Boycott in Alabama, illustrate the racial clashes that destabilized the South in the 1950s.[5] In this intensely charged milieu, Sams sat in SWCC's dean's chair for eight years.

More than an academic dean at the struggling school, Sams worked as coach, dean of men, and instructor, as well as treasurer of the Living Endowment Association. His 1989 memoir, *My Experience Relevant to My Work at Southwestern Christian College, Terrell, Texas,* briefly recounts his experiences at SWCC. It attests to the multiple roles he held during SWCC's infant years while revealing the financial struggles and racial challenges the young college faced. According to Sams, SWCC's financial status in the mid-1950s was "very bad with meager support," requiring faculty members to take extra jobs since their pay trickled in sporadically. Sams acknowledged that SWCC's subsistence depended largely on white Christians, and this prompted such comments as: "To support Southwestern Christian is to support segregation," or "The Caucasian gave support to keep the blacks out of the White colleges." Such allegations—true or false—discouraged many supporters from giving to the black college.[6]

Like many other college campuses in the mid-twentieth century, SWCC had its share of racial difficulties. During an annual lectureship gathering in Terrell, Columbus Grimsley, a black preacher from Florida, took his text from Acts 10 and denounced racial bigotry. A. V. Isbell, white president of the all-black college, responded in a "belligerent way," and "his message disturbed the audience tremendously." Details of Grimsley's sermon and Isbell's response remain nebulous, but Sams noted, "racial tension was rather inflammable everywhere during that time."[7]

On another occasion, as President Isbell made what many interpreted as racially insensitive remarks during a chapel assembly, Arthur L. Smith, a student from Valdosta, Georgia, "yelled" at him. Smith's irate outburst "was extremely obnoxious to the president." Isbell called both Smith and Sams into his office and demanded that the latter expel the student "from school before the student body." Sams refused, stating that Smith "was wrong for interrupting you without your calling his name, and you were wrong for saying such things as an administrator of this school." Unfortunately, Sams never divulged Isbell's remarks, but they were obviously racial slurs in Sams's view. Notwithstanding Sams's omission of details, he noted that the president threatened to fire him if he refused to "dismiss that student from school." After meeting once more with Isbell and Smith, Sams convinced them to reconcile their differences "on the basis of Christian principles."[8] In addition to his administrative work, Sams also functioned as a racial reconciler.

Arthur L. Smith later graduated from SWCC with an AA degree. He then graduated from Oklahoma Christian College with a BA, Pepperdine University with a masters degree, and the University of California, Los Angeles with a doctorate in communications. In the process he evolved into a racial radical. He moved into the Black Power Movement in the 1960s, changed his name to Molefi Kete Asante, and helped establish the first doctoral program in the field of African and African American studies at Temple University in Philadelphia. More significantly, Asante created a new field of study, "Afro-centricity," which places Africa and the African experience at the center of the intellectual world.[9] Asante's negative experiences with Isbell at SWCC perhaps started him down a path to racial hostility.

Racial animosities frequently surfaced at black colleges in the volatile era, reflecting the anti-black sentiment across the South. One morning at SWCC when Sams's wife approached campus she saw a "big doll hanging in the entrance of the gate with one side of it's [*sic*] face painted black and the other side white and lips painted red with KKK in big black letters." Izetta immediately alerted her husband who then informed the president. Isbell ordered the dean to "Get it down before the students see it." Sams objected: "No, we did not put that thing there," but Isbell quickly disposed of the doll before students discovered it.[10] The virulent racism, which plagued the nation, forced leaders in black institutions to cope, not only with sudden eruptions, but also with the more ordinary vagaries of segregated life. Even hotels in Terrell, Texas, as in other southern communities, created obstacles, welcoming only white visitors, forcing black visitors to SWCC to stay in the homes of black hosts.[11]

Sams sometimes dealt with racial troubles away from his college campus. When Ansen A. Essien, a SWCC student from Africa, traveled by bus to fulfill a preaching engagement in Houston, he was arrested in Henderson for sitting near the front. As Essien reached into his pocket to show his passport, a police officer struck him on the head. Learning of Essien's situation, Sams dashed to Henderson to pay the student's bail, only to discover that Essien had paid his own fine and caught another bus to Houston.[12] Sams genuinely cared for and loved his students, and upon their completing classes at SWCC, he followed their careers. Noting that senior colleges only conditionally accepted transfer students from SWCC before granting them credit for their previous academic work, Sams worked diligently to improve SWCC. He later proudly announced that "Graduates of Sw.C.C., who enrolled in the senior colleges, did so well in their studies until the senior colleges began accepting the credits from Sw.C.C."[13] Sams understood that SWCC's future advancement depended largely on the achievements of its alumni.

The deanship of Roosevelt Sams portrays in microcosm the race problem in the larger U.S. context. As African Americans endeavored to prepare themselves for better lives, they often had to overcome the formidable obstacles of a violent and implacable racism. Some white believers, Isbell among them, willingly worked with blacks in a Christian and academic context, but often disdained the very people with whom they interacted. Working through this distressing paradox, Sams served as academic dean until 1963 in an eventful eight-year tenure. He left with SWCC still amid economic difficulties and racial conflict, replaced by a new academic dean, Jack Evans, who served in that capacity for four years before ascending to the presidency. Evans then launched his alma mater on a trajectory of unprecedented success even as he exercised extraordinary influence on black Churches of Christ in Texas and the wider world beyond.

Jack Evans as Educator

In 1967 Evans became the fourth president of Terrell's SWCC, succeeding E. W. McMillan, H. L. Barber, and A. V. Isbell. Within seven years, Evans led the school to full accreditation as a two-year junior college,[14] then in 1982 the college began offering a four-year Bible program to train preachers. Its board of trustees called this achievement "a tremendous stride in strengthening the college, the church and the world," and Evans viewed the four-year Bible program as an opportunity to produce more qualified Gospel preachers. "Thus the program," he explained, "is designed to prepare young men to preach the *Bible as the Word of God*, and to apply its principles to the many problems confronting the world and the church today."[15]

While Evans deserves much of the credit for SWCC's impressive accomplishments, he did not achieve them alone. James O. Maxwell, Evans's diligent assistant for almost forty years, worked faithfully to advance the cause of SWCC among African American Churches of Christ. A native of Tulsa, Oklahoma, Maxwell earned an AA degree from SWCC in 1959 and a BA degree from Pepperdine University in 1961. Nine years later, he received the Masters of Religious Education from Central Theological Seminary in Kansas City, Kansas. In 1979 Maxwell earned his doctoral degree from Southern Methodist University in Dallas, Texas, with his dissertation entitled, "The Communication Aspects of Preaching, Worship and Ministry in the Black Church."[16]

While advancing his academic training, Maxwell effectively served congregations across the country. From 1962 to 1964 he worked with a Church of Christ in North Gulfport, Mississippi; for the next four years he ministered to the Cleveland Avenue Church of Christ in Columbus,

Jack Evans, a native of Houston, came under the influence of Marshall Keeble (1878-1968) and R. N. Hogan (1902-1997). Upon becoming president of Southwestern Christian College in Terrell, Texas, in 1967, Evans has wielded considerable influence on African American Churches of Christ in Texas and beyond.

(Photo courtesy of Jack Evans, Sr.)

Ohio; in 1968 Maxwell preached for and built up the Roswell Church of Christ in Kansas City, Kansas. Three years later he returned to his alma mater in Texas as academic dean, moving in 1978 to the vice presidency, ably seconding Evans for three decades while simultaneously preaching for congregations in Texas and nearby states.[17]

Evans's wife, Patricia, has also helped train young men and women for Christian service. After graduating from SWCC, Bishop College, and East Texas State University (with an MA in English and French), Mrs.

Evans returned to her alma mater in 1965. As an astute English teacher and an accomplished vocal soloist, she has touched the lives of many black youths affiliated with Churches of Christ.[18]

Evans as Evangelist

Since entering the preaching ministry as a teenager, Jack Evans has endeavored "to live the life and preach the Word." Developing his skills as a gifted and powerful preacher, Evans gained experience as a local minister by serving congregations in West Texas while pursuing his BA and MA degrees. And like his own mentors, Paul Settles, Marshall Keeble, and R. N. Hogan, Evans understood that morally upright preachers were prerequisites for building effective and vibrant congregations. Likewise, he has urged his young protégés at SWCC in this direction. Evans's solid character, booming voice, sharp eloquence, fiery passion, and apt humor have endeared him to black and white listeners across the country and throughout the world.[19]

Since 1981 President Evans has been the featured speaker at the biannual Crusade for Christ across the United States. This biennial campaign held in major cities for one week helped establish Evans as a national evangelist and one of the premier preachers in black Churches of Christ. As the keynote speaker for the nationally televised event, Evans has led countless numbers of people into the fold of Churches of Christ. And while serving as president of SWCC, Evans continues to preach in gospel meetings and to mediate in church disputes across the county. His son Jack Evans Jr., a SWCC administrator and the preaching minister for the Lake Como Church of Christ, perpetuates the preaching legacy in the Evans family.

Evans as Debater

In addition to juggling responsibilities as a gospel preacher and college administrator, Evans solidified himself as a fierce debater for Churches of Christ. Exhibiting a combative style in his sermons, writings, and debates, he has debated white Baptists, black Muslims, and even some of his own fellow white and black preachers in Churches of Christ. In 1974 Evans clashed with Vernon L. Barr, pastor of the Missionary Baptist Church in Dallas, over theological and racial issues.[20] Three years later, the SWCC president disputed with Iman Wallace D. Muhammad, a spiritual leader of black Muslims in North America.[21]

In 1984 and 1985 SWCC's president debated Floyd Rose, his classmate at both the Nashville Christian Institute and SWCC, and a noted black preacher in Churches of Christ. Their disagreement carried over into print when Rose, in his book *Beyond the Thicket*, explained why he left Churches of Christ and sought "unity in diversity" with believers in Christ beyond his own religious fellowship. In responding to the account recorded in *Before the Thicket*, Evans argued that Rose's withdrawal from Churches of Christ was "heretical" and "dangerous" and denounced Rose's theological view that Christians may be found in other churches as "totally false."[22]

The Evans-Barr Debate

Among all Evans's debates, the one with Vernon L. Barr best furnishes insights into the racism that lingered among many white evangelical churches in the South even after the Civil Rights era. At the same time, it reveals how white ministers misappropriated Scripture to construct racist theologies. More importantly, Evans represents well both the Bowser legacy of racial militancy and the Keeble legacy of theological exclusivity.

The debate's key proposition was whether it was "God's will for members of the black race and members of the white race to intermarry." Barr began his first speech by referring to Jesus' prayer in John 17. Jesus, insisted Barr, "prayed for oneness for His children, His church, in love, in doctrine; but never did He pray for oneness of union in marriage of the white and black races."[23]

Barr then delineated ten reasons why he vigorously opposed racial integration between whites and blacks and why he believed God rejected bi-racial marriage. Based on his assessment of Genesis 6:1–7, Barr argued that immorality ran rampant on earth "by habitation of two different races, the Cainites and the Sethites."[24] The Lord, he maintained, separated three primary races onto three different continents: Ham in Africa, Shem in Asia, and Japeth in Europe.[25] Barr then interpreted Genesis 9:24–27 and Jeremiah 13:23 to mean that God forbade the changing of his laws "advocating the intermarriage of the two races."[26] Referring to Genesis 12 and 25, Barr argued that racial and sexual mixing produced "emotional compatibility" and led to "multiplied troubles,"[27] noting that Abraham specifically instructed his house servant not to select for his son a wife of the Canaanites.[28]

Barr, after commenting that God "made the beast of the earth after his kind" in Genesis 1:25, concluded that bi-racial marriages violated "God's law of like producing like."[29] Citing Deuteronomy 7:1–3, Barr stressed that "Intermarriage of black and white persons is forbidden, punished, and prevented by racial segregation and intimate social relationships."[30] Barr then linked the intermarrying of African Americans and Anglo Americans with the work of Communists, referencing Booker T. Washington and George W. Carver as black leaders who openly denounced "mixed marriages between the two races."[31] Barr pointed out that since it was contrary to God's natural law for birds and beasts "to mix," it was equally dishonorable for blacks and whites to amalgamate.[32] Barr put forward Acts 17:28 to show that God taught against "the fusion of the black and white races," observing further that both white Baptists and whites in Churches of Christ, with whom Evans identified, believed that it was "wrong for blacks and whites to intermarry."[33] Barr concluded his first speech by lamenting the past mistreatment of black people during slavery and segregation, by arguing for the equality of all people, and by rejecting the corollary of black inferiority and white superiority.[34]

In his initial retort, Evans explained he wanted to debate the white Baptist minister to show "that we still have some around, such as Mr. Barr, who are responsible for the mess that this world is in."[35] He then compared Barr to Rip Van Winkle who slept through the American Revolution without knowing that events had raised another "George" to command, and like Rip Van Winkle, Barr did not know that racist ideologies were "on their way out." Evans even thanked other Baptists from Oklahoma City for attending the debate in East Texas, pointing out that "Mr. Barr and his bunch do not represent all Baptists."[36]

Seeking to show the fallacy of Barr's use of Scripture, Evans cited Numbers 12 to show that God did not oppose intermarriages. "I remember that Aaron and Miriam criticized Moses for marrying this Ethiopian woman; and Miriam, as a results [*sic*] of here criticizing Moses, you remember, God turned her white. (Amens and laughter) And I mean really white! I want you to deal with that, Mr. Barr."[37]

In a comedic yet combative demeanor, Evans argued that Barr misinterpreted Acts 17:26, insisting that "God here in this Bible dealt with nations, not races." Evans added: "So if, according to Mr. Barr's position, it is a matter of God's forbidding marriages between members of certain nations, then that simply means that Americans can't marry Germans, for example."[38] After his opponent quipped, "this is supposed to be a college president," Evans explained: "I am not debating you as a 'college president,' I am debating you as a gospel preacher. (Amens) If you want the 'President' in me, you get your President of your Baptist Institute, and I'll take him, too. I'll take on the whole bunch of you Missionary Baptists."[39]

Evans urged young Baptist preachers in the audience to "study your Bibles, and I'll guarantee you that you will come out of that false church, teaching such a racist doctrine."[40] As far as Evans was concerned, Barr not only espoused erroneous racial views, but he also preached in a "false church." Furthermore, because Martin Luther King Jr. held membership in the Baptist Church, Evans argued that the Civil Rights leader, while having done commendable social work, was a false teacher. "Don't you think that I am afraid to say it, Mr. Barr. Dr. Martin Luther King, Jr., was not a gospel preacher! (Amens and Amens)."[41] Evans, with Marshall Keeble and G. P. Bowser, contended that only members of Churches of Christ were true Christians, making him a "radical exclusivist."[42] While Evans denounced King as a false teacher, illustrating his adherence to both the Bowser and Keeble legacy, he declared that the racism of preachers like Barr created the venomous anti-black environment in which King was slain, demonstrating his embrace of the Bowser and Hogan legacy of racial militancy.[43]

Throughout the debate Evans demonstrated the tenacious fighting style so characteristic of twentieth-century Churches of Christ. Astonished that Evans did not conduct his "part of the debate in an orderly way," Barr said: "When you take all of the bombast, hollering, the coming over to the table and seeking to josh the moderator, find out what's left in the refutation of the proposition."[44] Evans's combativeness and contentiousness in his debate with Barr shows clearly.[45]

> Now if some of you, even members of the church, don't like the way I'm talking, that's too bad. Somebody will say, 'Well, brother Evans, if I were you, I wouldn't say that.' Well, you are not me; and you are not saying it. (Laughter) Mr. Barr is a false prophet! And those who represent what he represents are false prophets, false teachers, who are teaching people those things that are erroneous. And they are on their way to hell. (Amens) John said, 'Beloved, believe not every spirit, but try the spirits, whether they be of God; for many false prophets are gone out into the world,' 1 John 4:1. If you want to see one of these false prophets, there he is (pointing to Mr. Barr). There he is![46]

After giving Barr what he called a verbal and scriptural "whipping," Evans then offered to debate leaders of Bob Jones University in either Greenville, South Carolina, or Terrell, Texas, "for the benefit of your and my inquiring students and constituents."[47] After Evans wrote to officials of Bob Jones University to challenge their racial theories, Henry Ward, executive assistant of the South Carolina college, replied, calling Evans's missive a "silly letter" from a "Campbellite." Ward concluded: "It is too bad that you folks are not more interested in reaching people for Christ than you are in having debates."[48] Ward's observation tellingly indicts Jack Evans and the legacy of SWCC. Heirs of the debating tradition established by Alexander Campbell in the nineteenth century,[49] many white and black members of Churches of Christ have been more preoccupied in winning verbal skirmishes than they were in winning lost souls to Jesus. But Evans and many other black preachers in Churches of Christ considered verbal disputation one of the most effective ways of leading the lost to Christ.

Sons and Daughters of Southwestern Christian College

Myriads of spiritual children went out from the corridors of SWCC and have made important contributions to black Churches of Christ in Texas and the world. For example, Ralph H. Draper, a 1979 graduate of SWCC, has served bi-vocationally as an educator and preacher for Churches of Christ in Missouri, Tennessee, Maryland, and Texas. Having completed his doctorate in education from Stephen F. Austin University, Draper serves as superintendent for one of the largest and fastest growing school districts in Texas. Jamal K. Hamilton, a noteworthy and studious preacher, ministers effectively to the Mountain View Church of Christ in Dallas. A native of St. Louis, Missouri, Lovell Hayes attended both Nashville Christian Institute and SWCC before filling pulpits for congregations in California, Illinois, and Tennessee. A well-trained minister with a masters degree from the University of Illinois at Springfield and a doctorate in ministry from Southern Christian University (now Regions University), Hayes serves as pulpit minister for the thriving East Jackson Church of Christ in Jackson, Tennessee. Jefferson R. Caruthers Jr., a former Californian and SWCC alumnus, preaches for one of the largest black Churches of Christ in North Carolina.

Rick Hunter, a former SWCC student and administrator, earned a Doctor of Ministry degree from United Theological Seminary in Dayton, Ohio. A passionate and skilled organizer, Hunter has built up churches in Texas, Michigan, Ohio, Indiana, and California. A longtime SWCC administrator, Gerald Lee now leads a thriving congregation in Houston, the South Union Church of Christ. Lawrence Murray, a native of California and former SWCC student, earned a Ph.D. from the California School of Professional Psychology. Murray now preaches in Oklahoma and teaches at Oklahoma Christian University. SWCC has trained other Californians as preachers, including Fate Haygood and Anthony Stokes, among others.

A native of New York, Frederick Aquino, after converting to Churches of Christ, enrolled at SWCC in the mid-1980s and earned an AA degree in Bible. A passionate preacher, teacher, and Greek student, Aquino advanced his education at Abilene Christian University by earning bachelor and masters degrees in biblical studies before receiving his Ph.D. in systematic theology from Southern Methodist University; he presently serves as a professor of theology at Abilene Christian.[50]

Darryl Bowdre descends from a family of talented preachers, with his grandfather and father respected ministers in black Churches of Christ. An alumnus of SWCC, Bowdre served congregations in Cleveland and Youngstown, Ohio, before relocating to East Texas in 1982. A gifted communicator, song leader, and administrator, Bowdre has done his most impressive work as an evangelist and community leader in Tyler, Texas. After serving for seventeen years as the preaching minister for the North Tenneha Church of Christ, he now serves the South Central Church of Christ in the same community. In addition to his ministerial work, Bowdre publishes a weekly black newspaper, *Ebony News Journal*.[51]

Billy Curl attended SWCC after finishing high school in Nachodoches, Texas. Upon completing his AA degree from SWCC, Curl was among the first black students and graduates of Abilene Christian University. He and his wife then served as missionaries to Ethiopia for six years. The recipient of honorary doctoral degrees from both Abilene Christian University and SWCC, Curl remains heavily involved in Christian education, serving as a board member at both of his alma maters. Perhaps more importantly, Curl has ministered effectively to the Crenshaw Church of Christ in Los Angeles, California, for thirty-two years.[52]

A son and grandson of preachers, Shelton Gibbs III graduated from SWCC and Abilene Christian University before ministering to congregations in Illinois and Texas. Gibbs currently preaches for the Greenville Avenue Church of Christ in Richardson, Texas, the largest black Church of Christ in the Lone Star State. While effectively edifying its own members, this congregation has assisted domestic ministries and foreign missions. Domestically, it contributes to SWCC, World Bible School in Dallas, a television program in East Dallas, Worldwide Spanish Literature Ministry in Wichita Falls, Sunset International Bible Institute in Lubbock, and congregational ministries in High Point, North Carolina, and Clarksville, Tennessee. Internationally, the Greenville congregation supports missionary efforts in Rio de Janeiro, Brazil, Freeport, Bahamas, Crusade Mission in Kingston, Jamaica, and NCI Medical Ministries in Nigeria, Haiti, the West Indies, Transkie, Kwa Zulu Natal, and Liberia.[53]

A native of Winston Salem, North Carolina, Ken Greene enrolled at SWCC in the late 1970s. Upon graduation he studied at Abilene Christian University where he earned both Bachelor of Science and Master of Divinity degrees. In 1983 Greene joined the Texas Army National Guard's chaplaincy program and retired as a Colonel after twenty-three years of distinguished service. In 1991 Greene earned a Doctor of Ministry from Fuller Theological Seminary in Pasadena, California. Around the same time he used his practical experience and academic training to launch STAAF (Strengthening the African American Family). Disturbed by the alarmingly large black prison population, the disproportionate number of black homes led by women, and the exorbitant unemployment rates of blacks, Greene designed his annual conferences "to liberate African-American families as well as equip them for service, encouragement, and a call for evangelizing other hurting African-American families." Greene secured renowned preachers in Churches of Christ to address these complex issues, and invited marriage and family therapists and other professionals to participate.[54] For almost twenty years Greene has ministered to the Metro Church of Christ in Cedar Hill, Texas.

Ervin Seamster, an outstanding athlete from Shreveport, Louisiana, enrolled at SWCC where he converted to Churches of Christ. After completing the four-year Bible program with distinction, he matriculated at Southern Methodist University in Dallas where he earned a Master of Divinity degree. He then enrolled in United Theological Seminary in Dayton, Ohio. A gifted leader, an adroit administrator, and a powerful pastor–teacher, Seamster has broken from the conventional practices of African American Churches of Christ. The Light of the World Church has made a strong commitment to addressing the socio-economic needs of African Americans in the Dallas–Fort Worth Metroplex and beyond. The Light of the World Praise Team leads a celebratory and enthusiastic worship experience. Seamster, through electrifying preaching and illuminating teaching, then seeks to stir the congregation to higher levels of spiritual ecstasy.[55]

The ministries of Ken Greene and Ervin Seamster exhibit striking parallels. Both men have appropriate advanced degrees: Greene, a Doctor of Ministry from Fuller Theological Seminary; Seamster, a Doctor of Ministry from United Theological Seminary. Both preachers are young, dynamic, energetic, and creative, and both birthed congregations out of the Marsalis Avenue Church of Christ in Dallas. The two ministers have shifted away from the traditional worship services of black Churches of Christ, and have assumed a more open and embracing posture toward the Christian Church and other Christian groups. Greene spoke in the summer of 2007 at the North American Christian Convention of the Christian Church, while Seamster employed as a consultant a black woman, Evelyn Parker, an Associate Professor of Christian Education at Perkins School of Theology and a Lay Leader for Carter Temple Christian, Methodist Episcopal Church, to design the educational ministry at the Light of the World Church of Christ. More significantly, Greene and Seamster reflect the evolving character of African American Churches of Christ in Texas.

One of the most talented black preachers in Churches of Christ is Jerry Taylor. A Tennessean, Taylor enrolled at SWCC in the early 1980s and was among the first graduates of the SWCC's newly instituted four-year Bible program. Taylor went on to earn a Master of Divinity degree and a Doctor of Ministry degree from Southern Methodist University. While preaching for congregations in Sulphur Springs and Port Arthur, Texas, and Greensboro, North Carolina, Taylor regularly received invitations from churches across the country to preach and stir up their members.

More than a powerful preacher and a melodious songster in Churches of Christ, Taylor in 2000 found the time and temerity to launch the New Wineskins Retreat "to create a safe and welcoming place where ministers and church leaders can come without hidden agendas and find encouragement, spiritual nurture and fellowship." Black ministers in Churches of Christ who openly challenged the traditional views and practices of their chosen fellowship often found themselves ostracized and condemned. For this reason, Taylor and a group of other young ministers felt the need to establish a "City of Refuge for the persecuted who speak prophetically about the legalistic dogmatism that runs rampantly throughout the national body." Taylor considered it a "haven of hope for those who feel the only option they have is to totally disconnect from churches of Christ."[56]

In the 1980s and 1990s George Pendergrass (left) and Wayburn Dean, both graduates of Southwestern Christian College, became world-renowned singers with the pioneering vocal group Acappella.

(Photo courtesy of George Pendergrass)

Sylvia Rose, a native of Georgia and a member of a distinguished preaching family, worked as chorus director at Southwestern Christian College for several years and left a lasting mark on African American Churches of Christ as a songwriter. Rose's melodious and meaningful compositions are sung each Sunday by black members of Churches of Christ.

(Photo courtesy of Sylvia Rose)

Since 2003 Taylor has been Assistant Professor of Bible at Abilene Christian University. In addition to his teaching responsibilities, Taylor serves as Associate Preaching Minister for the Highland Church of Christ in Abilene, while traveling and preaching nationally and globally. In 2006 Taylor delivered the keynote address at the North American Christian Convention in Louisville, Kentucky, an annual conference of the Christian Church.

While focusing on training such preachers as these, SWCC has prepared a plethora of competent young singers. Wayburn Dean and George Pendergrass became world-renowned singers in the vocal group Acappella. Dean, a native of Hobbs, New Mexico, and Pendergrass, a native New Yorker, sang in SWCC's choir before graduating from the college in 1980. Both men afterward connected with the recently formed group Acappella. After working with Acappella for several years, Dean continues to showcase his dynamic voice as a Christian solo artist, incorporating both vocal and instrumental arrangements. Pendergrass, who went on to earn a bachelors degree in Bible and education from Lubbock Christian University in Lubbock, Texas, and a masters in community leadership from Duquesne University in Pittsburgh, Pennsylvania, left Acappella in 1995. Known for his ability to excite crowds of worshippers with his melodious tenor voice, Pendergrass presently serves as director of multicultural enrichment at Abilene Christian University.

The most influential hymnist in black Churches of Christ has been Sylvia Rose. Certainly one of SWCC's greatest gifts to the fellowship of African American Churches of Christ, this daughter of a family of preachers distinguished herself as an outstanding musician and hymn writer.[57] After graduating from SWCC, Rose became the school chorus director. In that capacity the Georgia native trained and developed young voices, but she also composed more than two hundred songs that are widely sung by black Churches of Christ. Additionally, Rose has emerged as an evangelist outside the fellowship of Churches of Christ and has established herself as an effective and cogent writer. In her 2004 book, *Rise Up: A Call to Leadership for African American Women*, Rose challenges black women to arise and assume leadership roles in homes and churches left vacant by men.[58]

The Legacy of Southwestern Christian College

SWCC has bequeathed an extraordinary legacy to black Churches of Christ in Texas and beyond. Born in a climate of racial hostility, SWCC emerged in East Texas because African Americans affiliated with Churches of Christ seeking a college education had no place else to go. At SWCC young black high school graduates found a warm welcome. The emergence of Jack Evans as president of the college in 1967 signaled a turning point in race relations in Churches of Christ as its black members were determined to move in a more independent direction. At the same time the legacies of Marshall Keeble and G. P. Bowser remained conspicuous at SWCC as its leaders have maintained a position of theological exclusivity toward other denominations as well as a stance of racial militancy when confronted by white racism within and outside of the religious world.

The Keeble–Bowser legacy, however, has been challenged by a growing number of young ministers who have acquired advanced degrees and training beyond the corridors of SWCC. The emergence of Ervin Seamster's Light of the World Church of Christ, Ken Greene's STAAF ministry, Jerry Taylor's New Wineskins Retreat, Wayburn Dean's incorporation of instrumental music, and Sylvia Rose's writing and preaching beyond the fellowship of Churches of Christ—all attest that the Keeble–Bowser legacy as manifested in the theological and racial postures of its current leadership has been contested. Instead of fighting, debating, and berating other religious groups, many former students of SWCC have chosen to fight for stronger black homes, safer black neighborhoods, racial and social justice, as well as gender equality. In brief, the legacy of the hallowed SWCC remains both distinguished and divided.

Epilogue

"HARD-FIGHTING SOLDIERS"

African American Churches of Christ in Texas in the Twenty-First Century

From their emergence in 1865 when a former slave owner and former slaves in Madison County, Texas, birthed the first black Church of Christ in the Lone Star State, African Americans affiliated with the Stone–Campbell Movement have sought to serve God diligently, according to the Scriptures. The early black seed planters from 1900 to 1930, although now virtually forgotten, worked among members of denominations as well as the unchurched, seeking to draw converts into the fold of Churches of Christ. But it was not until Marshall Keeble, the premier black evangelist from Middle Tennessee, appeared in Texas that African American Churches of Christ experienced a marked advance. Keeble's legacy lives on in the presence of the Hood Street Church of Christ in Waco, the North Tenneha Church of Christ in Tyler, the Tudor Street Church of Christ in Paris, the Thomas Boulevard Church of Christ in Port Arthur, and many other congregations in the state. Keeble's spiritual sons such as Luke Miller, L. H. Alexander, and F. A. Livingston also lastingly imprinted black Churches of Christ in such towns as Jacksonville, Lufkin, Temple, Midland, and Odessa.

Even though Keeble remains the most widely revered black preacher in Churches of Christ, in some ways G. P. Bowser's legacy may be more abiding and more influential. Bowser's potent heritage not only survives in the congregation he planted in Marshall, but it also shapes the numerous churches his protégés, R. N. Hogan and J. S. Winston, left behind in locales such as Longview, Gladewater, Sherman, Fort Worth, and Houston. More significantly, Terrell's Southwestern Christian College stands as Bowser's greatest enduring legacy. The East Texas college, the only accredited school under the auspices of African Americans in Churches of Christ, has produced a large and growing number of church leaders and song directors who daily touch the lives of people worldwide. Perhaps most importantly, the Keeble and Bowser legacies in Texas intersect in that the former funneled many of his graduates from the Nashville Christian Institute in Tennessee to the latter's college in Texas. Many NCI and SWCC graduates ingested both Keeble's theological exclusivity and Bowser's racial frankness, and they vigorously fought what they perceived as aberrant religious practices and anti-black sentiment in Churches of Christ and in the broader American culture. SWCC graduates have perpetuated this joint legacy into the early twenty-first century.

The year 2000, however, reflected a shift in the combative styles of African American Churches of Christ. In that year Jerry Taylor, one of SWCC's most skilled graduates, launched the New Wineskins Retreat for young ministers who had been "marginalized by the power structure of African American churches of Christ because of views they had publicly espoused or because of questions they had raised in honest evaluation and critique of Churches of Christ."[1] Taylor and other former SWCC students, rather than censuring and castigating black Baptists, Methodists, and others who have surrendered their lives to Jesus apart from the Churches of Christ, have focused their energies on addressing issues that have devastated black families and communities.

In 2005 the North Richland Hills Church of Christ invited New Wineskins participants to convene in their Fort Worth church building. The conference theme was "Undoing Racism in Churches of Christ and Beyond." SWCC's president, Jack Evans, true to his combative tradition, castigated the group, derisively referring to the New Wineskins gathering as the "'new coonskins,' both white and black." Evans branded the conference a "socio-religious retreat from truth," and charged African American participants with being ensnared in a "doctrinal change movement unaware of the real purpose."[2] Evans's indictment tellingly testifies that the fighting tradition lives on in black Churches of Christ. For Evans, doctrinal and theological issues such as the impossibility of there being true Christians beyond the fellowship of Churches of Christ bear greater importance than racial and social concerns; but for increasing numbers of former SWCC students and those whom they lead, racism, poverty, black-on-black crime, and unstable black families have emerged as more visceral issues than combating believers in Jesus outside the circle of Churches of Christ.

In 2003 Kenneth Greene, a SWCC alumnus, preacher in Dallas, and founder of Strengthening the African American Family (STAAF) conference, contributed four chapters to a book, *Unfinished Reconciliation:*

Justice, Racism, and Churches of Christ. He indicted African Americans who abandoned God and the church for hedonism and materialism. "Like a weary antelope plodding through a sun-parched wilderness and suddenly coming upon a body of water," Greene wrote, "African-Americans came out of slavery and happened upon the Lake of Materialism, knelt down, and lapped its addictive liquid until their minds became numbed in drunkenness and their eyes blinded to the road that lay before them. Materialism quickly became the end sought by African-Americans, rather than the freedom found in Jesus Christ." Greene cited perturbing statistics concerning high school dropout rates and suicide rates among African Americans and attributed the demoralization of black families to the lack of loving parents. "Neither racism nor the lack of money plays the biggest role in the dysfunctional development of African-American children. Caring, loving parents remain the greatest factor in creating a self-reliant, upwardly mobile, confident child."[3]

Greene acknowledged that while blacks must continue to confront white racism, African Americans must assume personal accountability and moral responsibility. He challenged African American churches to deal with the economic problems decimating black families. "Economic genocide cripples the African-American male's ego; his self-esteem is lost," Greene explained, "he cannot compete with the welfare laws, and he is unable to be the provider, protector, producer, and nurturer of his home. Thus, a growing number of men turn their backs on their wives and children." Unlike many older black preachers of the Keeble–Bowser background who have appropriated the Book of Acts to accentuate baptism for the remission of sins, church government, and the plan of salvation, Greene challenged readers to revisit the benevolent work of the first Christians. "The early church was not only sharing their God, but they were also sharing their goods." He insisted, "The African-American church has to address this economic genocide. African-American men need money, job opportunities, business resources, and relevant skill training. The African-American church collects money, but it does little to create opportunities through which it can make money."[4]

In his chapter, "What White Churches and Institutions Need to Hear," Greene uncompromisingly assaulted the white power structure of American religion and society, contending that attitudinal and institutional racism, from the slavery era to the present, has victimized African Americans. "Does *White Racism* mean that every White person is racist? Yes, every White person is part of the problem, but not necessarily with personal racist intent. We are assuming that most White Americans do not want to be racist, even though every White person participates in and benefits from the system of racism, even if it is against their will." Greene then offered a solution. "The answer is in the hands of White-Americans. The solution cannot come from African-Americans. Expecting an answer from them is like expecting the lion to look at the lamb and say, 'What is the answer to your fear and frustration, little lamb?' We know what the problem is; it has been well outlined statistically and historically. The problem is White Racism."[5] For Greene, the fight continues—but a fight very different from that of his predecessor. He endeavors to lift up and build up struggling African American families from the social and economic disaster that is their lot, while simultaneously stamping out the debilitating effects of white racism. While the men featured in this book fought their own era's battles, Greene embarked on a different campaign, plotted an alternative strategy.

The bold work of Taylor, Greene, and others attests that the fighting spirit of the men whose foundational work this book describes has indeed endured but has radically changed. They shifted away from their predecessors' focus on proper forms of worship and evangelism to focus their ministry instead on applying Jesus' teachings to modern-day circumstances—the economic paralysis, black-on-black crime, the AIDS crisis, the exorbitant number of single family homes, and the white racism that continue to plague black homes and lives. The "fighting style" of earlier Texas preachers, though certainly successful in preceding times, is giving way to different techniques and practices appropriate to a twenty-first-century American culture.

One of the most popular songs in African American Churches of Christ remains "Hard-Fighting Soldier."

> I'm a hard-fighting soldier on the battlefield.
> And I'm bringing souls to Jesus by the service that I give.

Yet in the twenty-first century, while African American Churches of Christ in Texas have brought forward their fathers' "hard-fighting" spirit, these modern soldiers, finding new battlefields and new foes, have pressed the attack with their forebears' implacable determination and undaunted courage.

APPENDIX I

Church Planter	Date	Place	Congregation
Hugh P. Hayes	1865	Midway	Antioch COC
Marshall Keeble	1932	Lubbock	20th & Birch COC
Marshall Keeble	1937	Greenville	Eastside COC
Marshall Keeble	1936	Wichita Falls	Welch Street COC
Marshall Keeble	1933	Bonham	Katy Blvd. COC
Marshall Keeble	1935	Port Arthur	Thomas Blvd. COC
Marshall Keeble	1941	Wellington	?
Marshall Keeble	1932	Paris	Tudor Street COC
Marshall Keeble	1929	Houston	Fifth Ward COC
Marshall Keeble	1935	Tyler	North Tenneha COC
Marshall Keeble	1935	Waco	Hood Street COC
Marshall Keeble	1935	Abilene	North 10th & Treadaway COC
R. N. Hogan	1935 (?)	Longview	East Cotton COC
R. N. Hogan	1936	Gladewater	South Main & West Sinclair COC
R. N. Hogan	1936	Corinth	?
R. N. Hogan	1937	Gilmer	?
R. N. Hogan	1937	Easton	?
R. N. Hogan	1938	Sherman	Grand Avenue COC
R. N. Hogan	1940	San Antonio	Laurel Street COC
R. N. Hogan	1941	Welasco	?
R. N. Hogan	1943	Huntsville	Northside COC
R. N. Hogan	1938	Houston	Third Ward COC
J. S. Winston	1941	Van Alstyne	Eastside COC
J. S. Winston	1943	Sweeny	Third Street COC
J. S. Winston	1944	Marlin	Bernard Street COC
G. P. Bowser	1928	Marshall	Westside COC
S. T. W. Gibbs I	1939	Center	Greer Street COC
S. T. W. Gibbs I	1937 (?)	Ennis	Eastside COC
Luke Miller	1943	Beaumont	Eleventh Street COC

Luke Miller	1933	Corsicana	Eastside COC
Luke Miller	1940	Jacksonville	Seminary Heights COC
Luke Miller	1940	Midland	Lee Street COC
Luke Miller	1935	Palestine	Sterne Avenue COC
Luke Miller	1942	Sulphur	COC on Martin Luther Springs
Luke Miller	1930s (?)	Bryan	COC
Luke Miller	1940	Temple	South Tenth COC
Paul D. English	1939	Neches	School Road COC
Paul D. English	1940	Troup	Sinclair COC
Paul D. English	1939	Kilgore	?
Paul D. English	1939	Mineral Wells	Sixth Avenue COC
H. C. Tyner	1940	Big Spring	Highway 80 COC
A. L. Cassius	1940 (?)	Pampa	Southside COC
George Robin	1950	Cisco	?
L. H. Alexander	1950	Colorado City	Dallas & College Street COC
L. H. Alexander	1954	Monahans	?
L. H. Alexander	1956	Synder	?
L. H. Alexander	1939	Spur	?
L. H. Alexander	1942	Odessa	Highland & Bunche COC
L. H. Alexander	1939	Kermit	Westside COC
L. H. Alexander	?	Sweetwater	?
L. H. Alexander	1944	Midland	Lee Street COC
E. W. Anderson	1940	Giddings	?
Walter Weathers	1949	Conroe	Eastside COC
Eugene Derrick	1942 (?)	Willis Point	?
P. E. Walker	1941	Greggton	?
R. B. Thurmond	1938	Hallsville	Sweet Home COC
R. B. Thurmond	1938	Marshall	Sweet Home COC
Levi Kennedy	1943	Henderson	South Hill COC
F. F. Carson	?	Rankin	?
F. A. Livingston	1936	Vernon	?
K. C. Thomas	1924	Dallas	Cedar Crest COC
K. C. Thomas	1928	Dallas	Lawrence & Marder COC
T. H. Merchant	1923	Fort Worth	Eastland COC
A. A. Thomas	1951	Dickens	?
A. A. Thomas	1951	Croton	?

APPENDIX II

An incomplete list of former students who were trained to be ministers at Southwestern Christian College in Terrell, Texas:

Harold Alexander
Frederick D. Aquino
Molefi Kete Asante
(Arthur Lee Smith)
Johnny Barton
David Benford
Robert Birt
Joseph Bouye
Alvertice Bowdre
Darryl Bowdre
Ryan Bowman
Lewis Brabham
Wesley Brown
James Carter
Courtney Caruthers
Jefferson R. Caruthers, II
Luis Casiano
Billy Cason
Cloys Cecil
Alex Chambers
A. C. Christman
Creig Christman
Ronnie Cook
Norvie Cottingham, Sr.
Norvie Cottingham, Jr.
Allen D. Cross
Billy Curl
Timothy Daniels
Willie Davis
I. W. C. Dedrick
Mack Dillingham
Eric Doss
Ralph Draper
Harvey Drummer
Reginald Dulin
Rodney Dulin
John Edmerson
Jack Evans, Jr.
Jack Evans, Sr.
Jacque Evans
Michael Evans
Fred Every
Michael J. Feimster
Cedric Finley
Lester David Fisher
Thomas Fitzgerald
Ben Foster
Arthur Fulson
Carl E. Gaines
Barry Gainey
Dennis Gamble
Kenneth Garnier
Jerome Garrison
Bernard B. Gaston
Joe Gibbs
Shelton Gibbs III
Shelton Gibbs IV
Ken. W. Gilmore
Willie R. Gray
Charles Greene
Kenneth Greene
Jamal Hamilton
John Hamilton
Eddie Harper
Robert Harper
Andrew Hariston
Ivan Harris
James D. Harris
Lovell Hayes
Fate Haygood
Cecil B. Herndon
Willie Ray Hill
Marion Holt
Archester Houston
Douglass Howie
Rick Hunter
John E. Jackson
Ivory James, Jr.
George Johnson
Thomas H. Johnson
Winter I. Johnson

Grady T. Jones
Warrick Jones
James Jones, Jr.
Dennis King
Willie Kreigler
David Lane
Lewis Lanham
James Lauderdale
Eugene Lawton
Christopher Lee
Gerald Lee
Horace E. Lee, Sr.
Ernest Lemon
Gary Lodge
Jerry Macon
Charles Martin
Peter Martin, Jr.
Bonnie Matthews
Apollos Maxwell
James Maxwell
Noah McArthur
Zachary McChristian
Michael McClendon
Alvin McCoy
Douglass McDuffey
John Michael
Mark Miles
Matthew Miles
Luke Miles
Christopher Mitchell
Lewis Montgomery
Woodie Morrison
Lawrence Murray
Stephen W. Nixon
Waydell Nixon
George Pendergrass
Russell Pointer, Sr.
Harold Rawlinson
Edward J. Robinson
Nokomis Rogers
Floyd Rose
Jimmy Rose
Richard Rose
Thomas Sampson
James Scates
Ervin D. Seamster
Timothy Sells
Joe C. Simon
Charles Smith
Daniel Smith
Herman Smith
James Stewart
Anthony Stokes
Ryan Stuckey
Reginald Tarpley
Gerald Taylor
Jerry Taylor
John Taylor
Matthew Terry
J. C. Thomas
Martin Thomas
Orlander Thomas
Mark Thompson
Philip Thompson
Stephen Thompson
James Tinsley
John Tillman
Willie Tucker
Sonny Turner
Benny Walls
Isaac Webb
Varner Webb
Marcus Welch
R. C. Wells
Darryl Wesley
Herman Wesley
Gary White
George White
John C. Whitley
David Wilson
Woodrow Wilson
Dwayne Winnrow
Ron Wright
Narleski Wyrick
Jonathan Young
Paul Young, Jr.

ENDNOTES

Prologue

[1]John T. Ramsey, "Among the Colored People," *Gospel Advocate* 58 (January 6, 1916): 21.

[2]The term "loyals" refers to the Churches of Christ, who opposed instrumental music in worship and evangelizing through missionary societies, while the labels "digressives" or "progressives" denote the Disciples of Christ, who supported instrumental music in worship and evangelism through missionary societies. Furthermore, the term "pure gospel" denotes those who worshiped without using instrumental music and evangelized without the help of missionary societies.

The Stone–Campbell Movement or Restoration Movement traces its origins to the early nineteenth century and to four principal leaders: Barton W. Stone (1772–1844), Thomas Campbell (1763–1854), Alexander Campbell (1788–1866), and Walter Scott (1796–1861). These men essentially championed the unity of all Christians based on the Bible alone. Their battle cry was: "Where the Bible speaks, we speak; where the Bible is silent, we are silent." The best reference work on this movement is Douglas A. Foster, Paul M. Blowers, Anthony L. Dunnavant, and D. Newell Williams, eds., *The Encyclopedia of the Stone–Campbell Movement* (Grand Rapids: Eerdmans, 2004).

[3]Richard T. Hughes, *Reviving the Ancient Faith: The Story of Churches of Christ in America* (Abilene, Tex.: Abilene Christian University Press, 2008 [1996]), 176. See also John L. Robinson, *David Lipscomb: Journalist in Texas, 1872* (Wichita Falls, Tex.: Nortex Offset Publications, 1973), 1.

[4]Chalmers McPherson, *Disciples of Christ in Texas: A Partial History of Disciples of Christ in Texas during the Past Forty-One Years, Together with Personal Remembrances of Both the Living and the Dead, Addresses, Forms, Etc.* (Cincinnati: Standard Publishing, 1920); Colby D. Hall, *Texas Disciples: A Story of the Rise and Progress of That Protestant Movement Known as Disciples of Christ or Christian Churches, As It Developed in Texas; Including, through the Nineteenth Century Decades, A Story of the Kindred Movement, the "Churches of Christ"* (Fort Worth: Texas Christian University Press, 1953); and Stephen D. Eckstein Jr., *History of the Churches of Christ in Texas, 1824–1950* (Fort Worth: Star Bible Publications, 1992 [1963]).

[5]Vesta Rea Melton, "The Outlook," *Christian Echo* 45 (November 5, 1949): 8.

[6]Kyle Haselden, *The Racial Problem in Christian Perspective* (New York: Harper & Row, 1959), 29. For the McKinney, Texas, episode, see David Lipscomb, "Race Prejudice," *Gospel Advocate* 20 (1878): 120-121.

[7]When David Lipscomb (1831–1917) toured Texas in 1884, he marveled over the number of Tennesseans who had taken up residence in the state. "It is strange how many Tennesseans are there. For some years after the formation of its government, nine tenths of the members of its congresses and legislatures were Tennessean born, as were several of its Presidents, Governors and Congressmen. We have concluded that Tennessee has been the prolific spawning ground for the South and Southwest." Lipscomb, "A Trip to Texas," *Gospel Advocate* 27 (January 24, 1885): 50.

[8]C. Leonard Allen and Richard T. Hughes, *Discovering Our Roots: The Ancestry of Churches of Christ* (Abilene, Tex.: Abilene Christian University Press, 1988). This insightful book argues that most whites in Churches of Christ have virtually ignored, and some have blatantly denied, their indebtedness to Barton W. Stone, Alexander Campbell, and other Christian groups who espoused restorationist views. This argument applies to African American Churches of Christ as well.

[9]Cokie Roberts, *Founding Mothers: The Women Who Raised Our Nation* (New York: Harper-Collins, 2004), 61. Abigail Adams made this statement to her husband, future president of the United States, John Adams, in 1776 when he was a delegate to the Continental Congress.

Chapter 1

[1]"The Oldest Continual Black Church of Christ in Texas," *Madison County Patriot* (February 20, 1991): 5. The writer is keenly aware that there were actually two black congregations that originated during the Reconstruction era. The Antioch Church of Christ in Midway, Texas, was established in 1865; the Southside Church of Christ in the same city was established in 1879. This book, however, focuses on the former congregation and its descendants.

[2]Among the best current studies of the Stone–Campbell Movement are David Edwin Harrell Jr., *Quest for a Christian America: The Disciples of Christ and American Society to 1866* (Tuscaloosa: University of Alabama Press, 2003 [1966]); David Edwin Harrell Jr., *The Social Sources of Division in the Disciples of Christ, 1865–1900* (Tuscaloosa: University of Alabama Press, 2003 [1973]); Richard T. Hughes, *Reviving the Ancient Faith: The Story of Churches of Christ in America* (Abilene, Tex.: Abilene Christian University Press, 2008 [1996]); and Douglas A. Foster, Paul M. Blowers, Anthony L. Dunnavant, and D. Newell Williams, eds., *The Encyclopedia of the Stone–Campbell Movement* (Grand Rapids: Eerdmans, 2004).

[3]African American preachers in Churches of Christ often used the terminology, "pure gospel," denoting their opposition to using musical instruments in worship and their aversion to evangelizing through missionary societies. Like

their white compatriots, blacks in Churches of Christ believed that such "innovations" violated New Testament teachings. See Edward J. Robinson, "'The Two Old Heroes': Samuel W. Womack, Alexander Campbell, and the Origins of Black Churches of Christ in the United States," *Discipliana* 65 (Spring 2005): 3-20; and Edward J. Robinson, *To Save My Race from Abuse: The Life of Samuel Robert Cassius* (Tuscaloosa: University of Alabama Press, 2007).

[4]*U. S. Census, Leon County, Texas* (September 5, 1850).

[5]*Slave Inhabitants in Leon Division in the County of Leon, Texas* (1850).

[6]*Slave Inhabitants in Leon Division in the County of Leon, Texas* (1860).

[7]*U. S. Federal Census: Free Inhabitants* (Madison County, 1880).

[8]*A History of Madison County, Texas* (Madisonville, Tex.: Madison County Historical Commission, 1984), 265; Langston James Goree V, ed., *The Thomas Jewett Goree Letters: The Civil War Correspondence* (Bryan, Tex.: Family History Foundation, 1981), 1:269; Mary Nolley Jackson, "As I Remember the Early Days in Madison County," *Madisonville Meteor* (June 1954).

[9]Randolph B. Campbell, *An Empire for Slavery: The Peculiar Institution in Texas, 1821–1865* (Baton Rouge: Louisiana State University Press, 1989); Barry A. Crouch, *The Freedmen's Bureau and Black Texas* (Austin: University of Texas Press, 1992); Alwyn Barr, *Black Texans: A History of African Americans in Texas, 1528–1995* (Norman: University of Oklahoma Press, 1995 [1973]); Quintard Taylor, *In Search of the Racial Frontier: African Americans in the American West, 1528–1990* (New York: W. W. Norton, 1998); and Carl H. Moneyhon, *Texas after the Civil War: The Struggle of Reconstruction* (College Station: Texas A&M University Press, 2004).

[10]George P. Rawick, ed., *The American Slave: A Composite Autobiography* (Westport, Conn.: Greenwood Press, 1979), 9:413.

[11]Ibid., 9:3441, 3443, 3446.

[12]F. F. Carson, "Meet Our Ministers," *Christian Echo* 35 (August 20, 1940): 2.

[13]Elisha Bailey and Mack C. Bailey, "Mack Allen Bailey," in *A History of Madison County, Texas* (Madisonville, Tex.: Madison County Historical Commission, 1984), 1:127; Wiley A. Johnson, "History of the Antioch and Midway Church of Christ, Midway, Texas" (Wiley Johnson, 1959), 4, 7.

[14]Johnson, "History of the Antioch and Midway Church of Christ," 5.

[15]Declara Nixon Bailey, *From Whence We Came: The History of the Antioch Church of Christ, Midway, Texas* (MTR & Company, 1992), 12.

[16]F. F. Carson, "Meet Our Ministers," *Christian Echo* 35 (August 20, 1940): 2. Carson preached his first sermon in 1938 at the Thomas Avenue (now the Lawrence and Marder) Church of Christ. See E. E. Starks, "The Outlook," *Christian Echo* 38 (November 5, 1943): 7.

[17]"Richmond, California Dedicates New Edifice," *Christian Echo* 59 (July 1964): 4. In 1965, Carson and his Richmond flock were lauded as "the first Negro church to send a white person to a foreign field as a Missionary." See F. F. Carson, "The People Had a Mind to Work," *Christian Echo* 61 (February 1966): 5.

[18]Claudia Washington, "Women at Work," *Christian Echo* 83 (February 1986): 6.

[19]J. S. Winston, "A Tribute to Francis F. Carson," *Christian Echo* 84 (October 1987): 3.

[20]Bailey, *From Whence We Came*, 17; Johnson, "History of the Antioch and Midway Church of Christ," 10-12.

[21]R. N. Hogan, "Southside Church of Christ Shining in Los Angeles," *Christian Echo* 83 (June 1985): 1, 4; Carl C. Baccus, *I Can Tell the World about This* (Los Angeles: Baccus Publications, 1982), 3-4; and Calvin H. Bowers, *Realizing the California Dream: The Story of the Black Churches of Christ in Los Angeles* (n.p., 2001), 124-127.

[22]Johnson, "History of the Antioch and Midway Church of Christ," 15; *First Annual Texas State Lectureship Booklet, 1976* (n.p., n.d.), 9.

[23]Wiley W. Johnson, a former member of the Antioch Church of Christ, listed several other noteworthy preachers who originated from the congregation in Midway, Texas. Those preachers included W. A. Adams, Allen Bailey, Oscar Bailey, J. M. Johnson, Wesley Johnson, Wiley Johnson, David Johnson, Benjamin F. Johnson, Jessie Lee, Robert Lee, Horace Lee, W. A. McGilbra, Karie Manning, Maceal Nixon, Cornell Nixon, George Nealy, O. D. Nealy, Otis Thompson, Lacy Lee Washington, and Jimmy Lacy Washington. See Johnson, "History of the Antioch and Midway Church of Christ," 27.

[24]Bailey, *From Whence We Came*, 2.

[25] Stephen D. Eckstein Jr., *History of the Churches of Christ in Texas, 1824–1950* (Fort Worth: Star Bible Publications, 1992 [1963]), 225. For an excellent discussion on the topic of "baptism for the remission of sins" and its controversy in the Stone–Campbell Movement, see David W. Fletcher, ed., *Baptism and the Remission of Sins: An Historical Perspective* (Joplin, Mo.: College Press, 1992 [1990]).

Chapter 2

[1]Garna L. Christian, *Black Soldiers in Jim Crow Texas, 1899–1917* (College Station: Texas A&M University Press, 1995), xiv.

[2]Ibid., 69-91.

[3]Ibid.

[4]Patricia Bernstein, *The First Waco Horror: The Lynching of Jesse Washington and the Rise of the NAACP* (College Station: Texas A&M University Press, 2005), 58-59, 111.

[5]Robert V. Haynes, *A Night of Violence: The Houston Riot of 1917* (Baton Rouge: Louisiana State University Press, 1976), 16, 23, 29.

[6]Norman D. Brown, *Hood, Bonnet, and Little Brown Jug: Texas Politics, 1921–1928* (College Station: Texas A&M University Press, 1984), 49, 57.

[7]Ibid., 362-363. For the discussion of black Texans being "outsiders," see Alwyn Barr, *Black Texans: A History of African Americans in Texas, 1528–1995* (Norman: University of Oklahoma Press, 1995 [1973]), 112-172.

[8]Marshall Keeble, "From the Wide Harvest Field," *Firm Foundation* 51 (June 19, 1934): 6.

[9]John Thomas Ramsey, "The Work in Dallas, Texas," *Gospel Advocate* 57 (January 28, 1915): 89.

[10]Ibid.

[11]John Thomas Ramsey, "Among the Colored People," *Gospel Advocate* 58 (January 6, 1916): 21.

[12]Ibid.

[13]John Thomas Ramsey, "Among the Colored People," *Gospel Advocate* 59 (May 10, 1917): 471.

[14]John Thomas Ramsey, "Among the Colored Folks," *Gospel Advocate* 59 (December 6, 1917): 1199.

[15]Ibid.

[16]John Thomas Ramsey, "Appreciation," *Gospel Advocate* 60 (January 10, 1918): 47. David Lipscomb died in 1917. Stephen D. Eckstein Jr., *History of the Churches of Christ in Texas, 1824–1950* (Fort Worth: Star Bible Publications, 1992 [1963]), 268.

[17]John Thomas Ramsey, "Among the Colored Folks," *Gospel Advocate* 60 (March 7, 1918): 237.

[18]John A. Howland, "Among the Colored Folks," *Gospel Advocate* 61 (October 9, 1919): 997.

[19]John Thomas Ramsey, "Among the Colored Folks," *Gospel Advocate* 62 (April 1, 1920): 332. Ramsey does not provide the specific location of the Mitchell Chapel Church of Christ, even though it was probably in close proximity to Beaumont, Texas.

[20]John Thomas Ramsey, "Among the Colored Folks," *Gospel Advocate* 62 (May 27, 1920): 532.

[21]For an overview of Cassius's eventful life, see Edward J. Robinson, *To Save My Race from Abuse: The Life of Samuel Robert Cassius* (Tuscaloosa: University of Alabama Press, 2007).

[22]Samuel Robert Cassius, "At Work for the Colored Folks in Texas," *Gospel Advocate* 57 (September 30, 1915): 997.

[23]Samuel Robert Cassius, "Among the Colored People," *Gospel Advocate* 57 (November 11, 1915): 1150.

[24]Samuel Robert Cassius, "The Heathen at Home," *Christian Leader* 42 (April 3, 1928): 3.

[25]Samuel Robert Cassius, "The Heathen at Home," *Christian Leader* 42 (March 20, 1928): 14.

[26]Frank L. Cox, "Negro Mission in Fort Worth, Texas," *Gospel Advocate* 66 (February 14, 1924): 165.

[27]Ibid.

[28]T. H. Merchant, "From the Brethren," *Gospel Advocate* 67 (January 15, 1925): 67.

[29]Ibid.

[30]T. H. Merchant, "From the Brethren," *Gospel Advocate* 70 (October 4, 1928): [include page number]; and *Westside Church of Christ* (Anniversary Booklet: September 23, 2001).

[31]T. H. Merchant, "News and Notes," *Gospel Advocate* 77 (May 9, 1935): 449.

[32]T. H. Merchant, "News and Notes," *Gospel Advocate* 77 (July 4, 1935): 640.

[33]T. H. Merchant, "News and Notes," *Gospel Advocate* 77 (September 26, 1935): 927.

[34]"The Outlook," *Christian Echo* 34 (August 5, 1939): 5.

[35]Willie Williams, "The Outlook," *Christian Echo* 37 (November 20, 1942): 5.

Chapter 3

[1]Samuel Robert Cassius, "A Debate," *Christian Leader* 35 (April 5, 1921): 9.

[2]Richard T. Hughes, *Reviving the Ancient Faith: The Story of Churches of Christ in America* (Abilene, Tex.: Abilene Christian University Press, 2008 [1996]), 176-185.

[3]Cassius, "Debate," 9.

[4]W. L. Oliphant, "Mitchell Street Church of Christ—Colored," *Firm Foundation* 48 (January 13, 1931): 30.

[5]Formerly the Sparks Street Church of Christ, the Mitchell Street Church of Christ became the Ninth Street Church of Christ before relocating and becoming the Cedar Crest Church of Christ in 1963.

[6]Oliphant, "Mitchell Street Church of Christ," 30.

[7]Ibid.

[8]J. S. Winston reported that he first met F. F. Carson in Dallas in 1938 when K. C. Thomas was critically ill. See Winston, "A Tribute to F. F. Carson," *Christian Echo* (October 1987): 3. A souvenir booklet, which contained the schedule for the First Annual Texas State Lectureship in 1976, indicated that K. C. Thomas passed away "some time in 1938." Thomas's wife died on February 23, 1944. See "The Outlook," *Christian Echo* 39 (March 20, 1944): 5.

[9]Sherman Jackson, "The Outlook," *Christian Echo* 34 (August 20, 1939): 4.

[10]L. M. Wright, "The Outlook," *Christian Echo* 36 (January 20, 1941): 5.

[11]Eva McIntosh, "The Outlook," *Christian Echo* 35 (July 5, 1940): 4.

[12]Wright, "The Outlook," *Christian Echo* 36 (January 20, 1941): 5.

[13]L. M. Wright, "The Outlook," *Christian Echo* 36 (July 5, 1941): 5.

[14]Russell H. Moore, "The Outlook," *Christian Echo* 37 (January 20, 1942): 7.

[15]Russell H. Moore, "The Outlook," *Christian Echo* 37 (May 5, 1942): 5.

[16]Russell H. Moore, "The Outlook," *Christian Echo* 37 (September 20, 1942): 5; and L. M. Wright, "The Outlook," *Christian Echo* 37 (October 20, 1942): 6.

[17]Russell H. Moore, "The Outlook," *Christian Echo* 38 (November 5, 1943): 6.

[18]L. M. Wright, "The Outlook," *Christian Echo* 40 (April 5, 1945): 4-5.

[19]"The Cedar Crest Church of Christ," *Christian Echo* 63 (July 1968): 9.

[20]On November 5, 1967, Locke withdrew fellowship from eighty-four delinquent members. A faithful member applauded Locke for having the courage "to break this awful Ice in the Dallas area." See L. M. Wright, "The Outlook," *Christian Echo* 63 (January 1968): 9.

[21]C. C. Locke was succeeded by Waydell Nixon from 1980 to 1992.

[22]Joe W. Pouncy, "History of the Lawrence and Marder Church of Christ" (2002): 2.

[23]Eva McIntosh, "The Outlook," *Christian Echo* 36 (April 20, 1941): 5.

[24]Eva McIntosh, "The Outlook," *Christian Echo* 37 (January 5, 1942): 4.

[25]H. H. Gray, "South Dallas, Texas Work," *Christian Echo* 37 (July 5, 1942): 4.

[26]Eva Starks, "The Outlook," *Christian Echo* 37 (November 5, 1942): 5.

[27]Eva Starks, "The Outlook," *Christian Echo* 37 (December 20, 1942): 4.

[28]Eva Starks, "The Outlook," *Christian Echo* 38 (August 5, 1943): 6.

[29]Eva Starks, "The Outlook," *Christian Echo* 38 (July 20, 1943): 5.

[30]Starks, "The Outlook," *Christian Echo* 38 (August 5, 1943): 6.

[31]Eva Starks, "The Outlook," *Christian Echo* 38 (September 20, 1943): 5.

[32]E. E. Starks, "The Outlook," *Christian Echo* 38 (November 5, 1943): 7.

[33]Mrs. K. C. Thomas, "The Outlook," *Christian Echo* 38 (November 5, 1943): 6.

[34]Eva Starks, "The Outlook," *Christian Echo* 39 (January 5, 1944): 5.

[35]Eva Starks, "The Outlook," *Christian Echo* 39 (February 5, 1944): 2.

[36]Ibid., 4.

[37]Eva Starks, "The Outlook," *Christian Echo* 40 (May 20, 1945): 5. In 1974, Grover C. Washington, an erudite evangelist and teacher, decided to relocate the Lawrence and Marder Church of Christ to Marsalis Avenue where he served as pulpit minister for several years until his retirement in 1995.

[38]*First Annual Texas State Lectureship* (Anniversary Booklet), 11; and "East Dallas Church (Negro)," *Gospel Advocate* 97 (November 17, 1955): 1040.

[39]"Hatcher Street Church (Colored)," *Gospel Advocate* 97 (November 17, 1955): 1037. In the post–World War II era, thousands of African Americans moved from rural communities and took up residence in Dallas, boosting its black population from 50,412 in 1940 to 57,825 in 1950. See Quintard Taylor, *In Search of the Racial Frontier: African Americans in the American West, 1528–1990* (New York: W. W. Norton & Company, 1998), 263. For a discussion of the post–World War II racial tension in Dallas, see Michael V. Hazel, *Dallas: A History of "Big D"* (Austin, Tex.: Texas State Historical Association, 1997), 50-51.

[40]*First Annual Texas State Lectureship*, 4.

[41]"Historical Sketch of the Greenville Avenue Church of Christ in Richardson, Texas" (in the possession of the author). Thanks to Shelton T. W. Gibbs III for sharing this information with me.

[42]Mac Lynn, *Churches of Christ in the United States: Inclusive of Her Commonwealth and Territories, 2006 Edition* (Nashville: 21st Century Christian, 2006).

Chapter 4

[1]Rayford W. Logan, *The Negro in American Life and Thought: The Nadir, 1877–1901* (New York: Dial Press, 1954).

[2]J. E. Choate, *Roll Jordan Roll: A Biography of Marshall Keeble* (Nashville: Gospel Advocate, 1974); and Edward J. Robinson, *Show Us How You Do It: Marshall Keeble and the Rise of Black Churches of Christ in the United States, 1914–1968* (Tuscaloosa: University of Alabama Press, 2008).

[3]Choate, *Roll Jordan Roll*, 21.

[4]Marshall Keeble, "Great Man Gone," *Gospel Advocate* 62 (July 29, 1920): 745. See also Edward J. Robinson, "'The Two Old Heroes': Samuel W. Womack, Alexander Campbell, and the Origins of Black Churches of Christ in the United States," *Discipliana* 65 (Spring 2005): 3-20.

[5]Choate, *Roll Jordan Roll*, 39, 41.

[6]Marshall Keeble, "From the Brethren," *Gospel Advocate* 71 (December 5, 1929): 1175. For the statistics of Houston's black population in the late 1920s and in the early 1930s, see Quintard Taylor, *In Search of the Racial Frontier: African Americans in the American West, 1528–1990* (New York: W. W. Norton, 1998), 223.

[7]Marshall Keeble, "From the Brethren," *Gospel Advocate* 72 (January 2, 1930): 20.

[8]Ibid.

[9]"Historical Sketch of the Fifth Ward Church of Christ" (n.p., n.d., in the author's possession).

[10]Marshall Keeble, "From the Brethren," *Gospel Advocate* 76 (May 17, 1934): 482.

[11]Marshall Keeble, "Keeble Closes, Chattanooga," *Gospel Advocate* 76 (May 24, 1934): 529.

[12]"Historical Sketch of the Fifth Ward Church of Christ." Despite what appeared to be an ulterior motive for erecting a church building, white members were delighted to see the black congregation grow from one to thirty-five members. Jack P. Lewis, a member of the white congregation in Huntsville, applauded Sam Cebrun Jr. for doing "splendid work" under the "sponsorship of the white congregation here. In about six months the colored membership has grown from one to thirty-five." Jack P. Lewis, "The Outlook," *Christian Echo* 39 (June 5, 1944): 5.

[13]Ibid.

[14]Ibid. The Fifth Ward Church of Christ in Houston helped establish the following congregations: Third Ward Church of Christ, Trinity Garden Church of Christ, Westside Church of Christ, Fidelity Church of Christ, Highland Church of Christ, Kashmere Gardens Church of Christ, Lafayette Church of Christ, North Houston Church of Christ, North Wayside Church of Christ, Plymouth Rock Church of Christ (Carver, Massachusetts), South Union Church of Christ, Studiowood Church of Christ, and Sugarland Church of Christ.

[15]R. L. Colley, "Keeble–Miller Meeting," *Christian Worker* 18 (November 24, 1932): 6; and Luke Miller, "Sowing and Reaping," *Gospel Advocate* 74 (December 29, 1932): 1386.

[16]Colley, "Keeble–Miller Meeting," 6; Miller, "Sowing and Reaping," 1386.

[17]Luke Miller, "From the Wide Harvest Field," *Firm Foundation* 51 (January 9, 1934): 6.

[18]Marshall Keeble, "From the Wide Harvest Field," *Firm Foundation* 54 (November 9, 1937): 6.

[19]Columbus Grimsley, "The Outlook," *Christian Echo* 40 (April 20, 1945): 5.

[20]Luella Fleeks, "The Outlook," *Christian Echo* 40 (April 20, 1945): 6.

[21]Columbus Grimsley, "The Outlook," *Christian Echo* 41 (May 5, 1946): 4.

[22]Columbus Grimsley, "Making a Change," *Christian Echo* 45 (January 20, 1948): 8.

[23]E. S. Pearson, "The Outlook," *Christian Echo* 45 (February 20, 1949): 5.

[24]Marshall Keeble, "From the Wide Harvest Field," *Firm Foundation* 52 (July 2, 1935): 6.

[25]Luke Miller, "From the Wide Harvest Field," *Firm Foundation* 53 (January 28, 1936): 6.

[26]Luke Miller, "From the Wide Harvest Field," *Firm Foundation* 54 (May 4, 1937): 6.

[27]Marshall Keeble, "From the Wide Harvest Field," *Firm Foundation* 54 (November 9, 1937): 6.

[28]Patricia Bernstein, *The First Waco Horror: The Lynching of Jesse Washington and the Rise of the NAACP* (College Station: Texas A&M University Press, 2005).

[29]Marshall Keeble, "From the Wide Harvest Field," *Firm Foundation* 52 (September 10, 1935): 6.

[30]O. L. Aker, "From the Wide Harvest Field," *Firm Foundation* 52 (September 17, 1935): 7.

[31]O. L. Aker, "From the Wide Harvest Field," *Firm Foundation* 53 (February 18, 1936): 8.

[32]Marshall Keeble, "From the Wide Harvest Field," *Firm Foundation* 52 (October 1, 1935): 6.

[33]E. W. Anderson, "From the Wide Harvest Field," *Firm Foundation* 52 (December 17, 1935): 5.

[34]E. W. Anderson, "From the Wide Harvest Field," *Firm Foundation* 53 (February 4, 1936): 6.

[35]E. W. Anderson, "From the Wide Harvest Field," *Firm Foundation* 53 (March 10, 1936): 6.

[36]Joel Thompson, "From the Wide Harvest Field," *Firm Foundation* 53 (March 17, 1936): 6.

[37]E. W. Anderson, "From the Wide Harvest Field," *Firm Foundation* 55 (November 3, 1936): 6. The black congregation in Tyler erected a small,

framed structure on North Tenneha in 1937. Constant growth continued under the leadership of Jessie Robinson, Joel Thompson, R. N. Nelson, Robert Mills, Columbus Grimsley, George Robbins, Russell H. Moore, Paul Young, Paul Hubbard, Cecil B. Herndon, Rufus Johnson, and Darryl B. Bowdre. See *A Half-Century of Praise!: A Historical Sketch of the North Tenneha Church of Christ, 1935–1985* (n.p., n.d., in the author's possession).

[38]John T. Smith, "Sowing and Reaping," *Gospel Advocate* 74 (August 18, 1932): 931.

[39]Delbert M. Gatlin, "From the Wide Harvest Field," *Firm Foundation* 52 (July 2, 1935): 6. It remains unclear whether Marshall Keeble established a black congregation in Mexia, Texas.

[40]Marshall Keeble, "With the Colored Brethren," *Gospel Advocate* 78 (June 18, 1936): 595. It is unclear whether Keeble planted a black church in Stephenville, Texas.

[41]Marshall Keeble, "From the Wide Harvest Field," *Firm Foundation* 53 (November 3, 1936): 7.

[42]F. A. Livingston, "From the Wide Harvest Field," *Firm Foundation* 54 (September 28, 1937): 7.

[43]M. C. Franklin, "With the Colored Brethren," *Gospel Advocate* 79 (June 24, 1937): 593.

[44]Marshall Keeble, "Keeble Reviews Work," *Gospel Advocate* 79 (September 9, 1937): 861.

[45]R. L. Colley, "From the Wide Harvest Field," *Firm Foundation* 54 (October 19, 1937): 7.

[46]Marshall Keeble, "Keeble Visits Churches," *Gospel Advocate* 81 (January 5, 1939): 24.

[47]Marshall Keeble, "News and Notes," *Gospel Advocate* 82 (May 28, 1940): 502.

[48]Marshall Keeble, "Keeble Held Dallas Meeting," *Gospel Advocate* 83 (January 2, 1941): 21.

[49]Marshall Keeble, "Keeble Preaches in Texas," *Gospel Advocate* 83 (July 24, 1941): 716.

[50]Marshall Keeble, "News and Notes," *Gospel Advocate* 83 (August 14, 1941): 784.

[51]Marshall Keeble, "News and Notes," *Gospel Advocate* 84 (September 17, 1942): 907.

[52]Marshall Keeble, "Among the Colored Brethren," *Gospel Advocate* 93 (July 26, 1951): 479.

[53]Marshall Keeble, "Among the Colored Brethren," *Gospel Advocate* 93 (August 16, 1951): 527.

[54]Marshall Keeble, "Among the Colored Brethren," *Gospel Advocate* 93 (October 4, 1951): 638.

[55]Marshall Keeble, "Among the Colored Brethren," *Gospel Advocate* 96 (May 6, 1954): 356-357.

Chapter 5

[1]Luke Miller, "The Negroes," *Firm Foundation* 56 (April 25, 1939): 2.

[2]G. F. Gibbs, "A Needed Work," *Gospel Advocate* 69 (June 9, 1927): 532.

[3]P. G. Millen, "The Colored Work in Florida," *Gospel Advocate* 71 (June 6, 1929): 551-552. See also Marshall Keeble, "Report of Work," *Gospel Advocate* 71 (May 9, 1929): 451-452.

[4]For an insightful discussion of the differences between the "old Negro" and the "new Negro," see Leon Litwack, *Trouble in Mind: Black Southerners in the Age of Jim Crow* (New York: Vintage Books, 1998), 184-197.

[5]P. G. Millen, "The Colored Churches in Florida," *Gospel Advocate* 72 (February 20, 1930): 191.

[6]Marshall Keeble, "From the Brethren," *Gospel Advocate* 72 (March 29, 1930): 284.

[7]Marshall Keeble, "From the Brethren," *Gospel Advocate* 72 (May 15, 1930): 473.

[8]Marshall Keeble, "Work in Florida," *Gospel Advocate* 72 (June 12, 1930): 574.

[9]Luke Miller, "Sowing and Reaping," *Gospel Advocate* 73 (January 22, 1931): 88.

[10]Marshall Keeble, "Sowing and Reaping," *Gospel Advocate* 73 (September 24, 1931): 1201.

[11]Luke Miller, "Sowing and Reaping," *Gospel Advocate* 74 (December 29, 1932): 1386. For Miller's quotation, see Luke Miller, "Sowing and Reaping," *Gospel Advocate* 75 (June 1, 1933): 524.

[12]Luke Miller, "News and Notes," *Gospel Advocate* 75 (July 6, 1933): 645.

[13]Luke Miller, *Miller's Sermons* (Austin, Tex.: Firm Foundation, 1940), 6.

[14]Marshall Keeble, "From the Wide Harvest Field," *Firm Foundation* 51 (November 20, 1934): 7. See also Marshall Keeble, "News and Notes," *Gospel Advocate* 76 (September 20, 1934): 916.

[15]Luke Miller, "News and Notes," *Gospel Advocate* 77 (August 15, 1935): 783.

[16]Luke Miller, "News and Notes," *Gospel Advocate* 79 (August 19, 1937): 787.

[17]W. G. Bass, "News and Notes," *Gospel Advocate* 79 (September 2, 1937): 834.

[18]Luke Miller, "The Negroes," *Firm Foundation* 56 (April 25, 1939): 2.

[19]Michael W. Casey, *Saddlebags, City Streets, and Cyberspace: A History of Preaching in the Churches of Christ* (Abilene, Tex.: Abilene Christian University Press, 1995), 148.

[20]Luke Miller, "News and Notes," *Gospel Advocate* 80 (June 9, 1938): 537.

[21]Luke Miller, "News and Notes," *Gospel Advocate* 80 (July 28, 1938): 704.

[22]F. B. Shepherd, "News and Notes," *Gospel Advocate* 81 (August 10, 1939): 753.

[23]F. B. Shepherd, "From the Wide Harvest Field," *Firm Foundation* 56 (September 5, 1939): 7.

[24]A. C. Payne, "A Report," *Christian Echo* 40 (April 5, 1940): 7. A historical sketch of what is now the Martin Luther King Church of Christ in Sulphur Springs, Texas, states that this congregation began in June of 1942 (in author's possession). However, the 1940 testimony of A. V. Hill in the *Christian Echo* suggests that Luke Miller started the congregation in 1938. "The Church of Christ in Sulphur Springs, Texas, brought Luke Miller to their city for two summers to preach the gospel of Christ to his people." See A. V. Hill, "The Outlook," *Christian Echo* 40 (April 5, 1940): 6.

[25]Thomas W. Wright, "The Outlook," *Christian Echo* 38 (December 5, 1943): 4; and Thomas W. Wright, "The Outlook," *Christian Echo* 39 (March 5, 1944): 5.

[26]Jack Southern, "Colored Church Started," *Gospel Advocate* 88 (August 1, 1946): 734.

[27]Luke Miller, "Among the Colored Brethren," *Gospel Advocate* 93 (January 25, 1951): 63.

[28]Luke Miller, "Among the Colored Brethren," *Gospel Advocate* 93 (May 10, 1951): 301.

[29]Louise Whitaker, "Among the Colored Brethren," *Gospel Advocate* 94 (June 5, 1952): 375.

[30]Luke Miller, "Among the Colored Brethren," *Gospel Advocate* 94 (August 28, 1952): 567.

[31]W. Ray Duncan, "Among the Colored Brethren," *Gospel Advocate* 94 (September 25, 1952): 631.

[32]Miller, "Among the Colored Brethren," *Gospel Advocate* 94 (August 28, 1952): 567; Luke Miller, "Among the Colored Brethren," *Gospel Advocate* 94 (October 24, 1952): 695; and Luke Miller, "Among the Colored Brethren," *Gospel Advocate* 100 (May 29, 1958): 351.

[33]Marshall Keeble, "Among the Colored Brethren," *Gospel Advocate* 96 (May 6, 1954): 356.

[34]W. D. Sweet, "At Rest," *Gospel Advocate* 104 (March 22, 1962): 190; and W. D. Sweet, "Luke Miller Passes," *Firm Foundation* 79 (March 27, 1962): 204.

Chapter 6

[1]*Thirty-Fifth Annual West Texas Lectureship Booklet* (n.p., n.d.), 2 [in author's possession].

[2]L. H. Alexander, "With Colored Lubbock Church," *Gospel Advocate* 78 (December 24, 1936): 1241.

[3]Cremmon Alexander, interview with the author, Saturday, June 25, 2005, Midland, Texas. Cremmon Alexander was ninety-five years old. See also L. H. Alexander, "With Colored Lubbock Church," *Gospel Advocate* 78 (December 24, 1936): 1241.

[4]Sopha Pink, "The Outlook," *Christian Echo* 37 (July 5, 1942): 4; Sopha Pink, "The Outlook," *Christian Echo* 37 (September 5, 1942): 6; and Lewis Diggs, "The Outlook," *Christian Echo* 37 (November 5, 1942): 5.

[5] *Thirty-Fifth Annual West Texas Lectureship Booklet*, 6.

[6]Rose Lee Butler, "Among the Colored Brethren," *Gospel Advocate* 94 (September 11, 1952): 598.

[7] *Thirty-Fifth Annual West Texas Lectureship Booklet*, 2.

[8]A. A. Thomas, "Among the Colored Brethren," *Gospel Advocate* 93 (April 26, 1951): 269.

[9]A. A. Thomas, "Among the Colored Brethren," *Gospel Advocate* 93 (June 21, 1951): 399. This same article shows that Thomas did evangelistic work in Lovington, New Mexico, and Brownwood, Texas.

[10]Obituary of Jefferson R. Caruthers, I [in author's possession].

[11] *Thirty-Fifth Annual West Texas Lectureship Booklet*, 2.

[12]Ibid., 6.

[13]R. L. Colley, "Starts Colored Congregation," *Gospel Advocate* 77 (May 16, 1935): 470; and R. L. Colley, "News and Notes," *Gospel Advocate* 77 (September 12, 1935): 883.

[14]Richard T. Hughes, *Reviving the Ancient Faith: The Story of Churches of Christ in America* (Abilene, Tex.: Abilene Christian University Press, 2008 [1996]), 25, 55.

[15]F. A. Livingston, "News and Notes," *Gospel Advocate* 80 (September 22, 1938): 903.

[16]Robert C. Jones, "Colored Church in New Building," *Gospel Advocate* 83 (February 6, 1941): 143.

[17]F. A. Livingston, "Among the Colored Brethren," *Gospel Advocate* 92 (December 28, 1950): 842.

[18]Carrie C. Ferrell, "Among the Colored Brethren," *Gospel Advocate* 93 (February 1, 1951): 79.

[19]F. A. Livingston, "Among the Colored Brethren," *Gospel Advocate* 93 (May 31, 1951): 349; and F. A. Livingston, "Among the Colored Brethren," *Gospel Advocate* 93 (September 20, 1951): 607.

[20]F. A. Livingston, "Among the Colored Brethren," *Gospel Advocate* 94 (June 26, 1952): 422.

[21]F. A. Livingston, "Among the Colored Brethren," *Gospel Advocate* 95 (June 4, 1953): 351. See also F. A. Livingston, "Among the Colored Brethren," *Gospel Advocate* 95 (July 23, 1953): 469; F. A. Livingston, "Among the Colored Brethren," *Gospel Advocate* 95 (August 27, 1953): 550; and F. A. Livingston, "Among the Colored Brethren," *Gospel Advocate* 95 (October 8, 1953): 670.

[22]F. A. Livingston, "Among the Colored Brethren," *Gospel Advocate* 95 (October 29, 1953): 727-728.

[23]Hughes, *Reviving the Ancient Faith*, 50-52. Walter Scott, based on his study of Acts 2:38, concluded that a person had to believe in Christ, repent of sins, and be baptized; in response to these human deeds, God would provide forgiveness of sins, the gift of the Holy Spirit, and eternal life. By combining the last two gifts, these six steps to salvation were reduced to the "five finger

exercise." See Mark G. Toulouse, "Walter Scott," in *The Encyclopedia of the Stone–Campbell Movement*, eds. Douglas A. Foster and others (Grand Rapids: Eerdmans, 2004): 675. The five-step plan of salvation that Scott developed stressed human response to God's work; in the second half of the nineteenth century, preachers in the Stone–Campbell Movement such as Moses Lard accentuated human work instead of God's work. African American Churches of Christ inherited Lard's version, not Scott's. See Gary Holloway and Douglas A. Foster, *Renewing God's People: A Concise History of Churches of Christ* (Abilene, Tex.: Abilene Christian University Press, 2006 [2001]), 64.

[24]Ethel Miller, "Among the Colored Brethren," *Gospel Advocate* 95 (October 29, 1953): 728.

[25]F. A. Livingston, "Among the Colored Brethren," *Gospel Advocate* 96 (April 15, 1954): 303.

[26]F. A. Livingston, "Among the Colored Brethren," *Gospel Advocate* 101 (November 26, 1959): 766.

[27]F. A. Livingston, "Among the Colored Brethren," *Gospel Advocate* 102 (January 14, 1960): 31.

[28]There are, however, a few noteworthy examples of black preachers in Churches of Christ, such Samuel Robert Cassius, Fred Gray, Franklin Florence Sr., and Floyd Rose, who stepped beyond the pulpit to challenge the racial status of Jim Crow America. See Edward J. Robinson, *To Save My Race from Abuse: The Life of Samuel Robert Cassius* (Tuscaloosa: University of Alabama Press, 2007); Edward J. Robinson, *Show Us How You Do It: Marshall Keeble and the Rise of Black Churches of Christ in the United States* (Tuscaloosa: University of Alabama Press, 2008); and Hughes, *Reviving the Ancient Faith*, 270-306.

Chapter 7

[1]Even though Bowser launched the *Christian Echo* in Tennessee, the journal exerted tremendous influence on African American Churches of Christ in Texas and was published there in the late 1940s as its editor's health declined. For the influence of journals on the shaping of various groups within the Stone–Campbell Movement, see James Brooks Major, "The Role of Periodicals in the Development of the Disciples of Christ, 1850–1910" (Ph. D. dissertation, Vanderbilt University, 1966); Richard T. Hughes, Howard Short, and Henry Webb, *The Power of the Press: Studies of the "Gospel Advocate," the "Christian Standard," and the "Christian Evangelist"* (Nashville: Disciples of Christ Historical Society, 1987).

[2]Nell Irvin Painter, *Exodusters: Black Migration to Kansas after Reconstruction* (New York: Alfred A. Knopf, 1977); Eric Foner, *Reconstruction: America's Unfinished Revolution* (New York: Harper & Row, 1988).

[3]R. Vernon Boyd, *Undying Dedication: The Story of G. P. Bowser* (Nashville: Gospel Advocate, 1985).

[4]G. P. Bowser, "As Ye Find Christ, Walk in Him," *Gospel Advocate* 46 (March 24, 1904): 190.

[5]Ibid.

[6]J. P. Lowery, "News and Notes," *Gospel Advocate* 75 (February 2, 1933): 118.

[7]Alexander Campbell, "Among the Colored People," *Gospel Advocate* 56 (April 9, 1914): 414. See also Edward J. Robinson, "'The Two Old Heroes': Samuel W. Womack, Alexander Campbell, and the Origins of Black Churches of Christ in the United States," *Discipliana* 65 (Spring 2005): 3-20.

[8]"A Paper for the Colored Brethren," *Gospel Advocate* 44 (February 6, 1902): 92. Bowser's *Christian Echo* was not the first journal to be established by a black preacher in Churches of Christ. In 1897 Samuel Robert Cassius, an African American minister and educator in Oklahoma, began publishing and circulating his periodical, the *Industrial Christian*, to solicit funds for his Tohee Industrial School in Tohee, Oklahoma. See Edward J. Robinson, *To Save My Race from Abuse: The Life of Samuel Robert Cassius* (Tuscaloosa: University of Alabama Press, 2007).

[9]For Bowser's reference to the NAACP, see G. P. Bowser, "Questions," *Christian Echo* 40 (October 20, 1945): 3.

[10]G. P. Bowser, "Field Notes," *Christian Echo* 11 (November 1915): 3.

[11]Ibid.

[12]Marshall Keeble, "Among the Colored Folks," *Gospel Advocate* 63 (July 14, 1921): 679.

[13]T. P. Burt, "Field Reports," *Gospel Advocate* 64 (December 14, 1922): 1207.

[14]Marshall Keeble, "From the Brethren," *Gospel Advocate* 67 (March 5, 1925): 233.

[15]Marshall Keeble, "Our Messages," *Gospel Advocate* 69 (April 21, 1927): 368.

[16]Marshall Keeble, "Our Messages," *Gospel Advocate* 69 (June 2, 1927): 524.

[17]G. P. Bowser, "Work on the Pacific Coast," *Gospel Advocate* 70 (March 28, 1929): 306.

[18]R. L. Colley, "News and Notes," *Gospel Advocate* 76 (July 19, 1934): 697.

[19]Amos Lincoln Cassius, "News and Notes," *Gospel Advocate* 76 (September 6, 1934): 864.

[20]Amos Lincoln Cassius, "News and Notes," *Gospel Advocate* 79 (June 10, 1937): 545.

[21]Amos Lincoln Cassius, "Colored Work at Hobbs, New Mexico," *Christian Leader* 51 (August 3, 1937): 15.

[22]James L. Lovell, "Hogan Converts Many," *Gospel Advocate* 80 (September 22, 1938): 901.

[23]Amos Lincoln Cassius, "Field Reports," *Christian Leader* 52 (September 27, 1938): 11.

[24]E. W. Anderson, "News and Notes," *Gospel Advocate* 80 (November 24, 1938): 1105.

[25]F. B. Shepherd, "News and Notes," *Gospel Advocate* 81 (August 31, 1939): 828.

[26]Thomas K. Rouse and G. P. Bowser, "The Use of Instrumental Music in the Worship of God: A Review (No. 1)," *Christian Echo* 34 (July 5, 1939): 4. Annie C. Tuggle, in *Another World Wonder* (n.p., n.d.), 86-87, described T. K. Rouse as a "fine young man" who was "very intelligent" and "very religious."

[27] G. P. Bowser, "The Use of Instrumental Music in the Worship of God: A Review (No. 1)," *Christian Echo* 34 (July 5, 1939): 4. See Michael W. Casey, *The Battle over Hermeneutics in the Stone–Campbell Movement, 1800–1870* (Lewiston, N.Y.: Edwin Mellen Press, 1998), 241-247.

[28]T. K. Rouse, "The Use of Instrumental Music in the Worship of God: A Review (No. 2)," *Christian Echo* 34 (July 20, 1939): 7.

[29]G. P. Bowser, "The Use of Instrumental Music in the Worship of God: A Review (No. 2)," *Christian Echo* 34 (July 20, 1939): 7.

[30]T. K. Rouse, "The Use of Instrumental Music in the Worship of God: A Review (No. 3)," *Christian Echo* 34 (August 5, 1939): 5. William T. Ellis, *"Billy" Sunday: The Man and His Message* (Philadelphia: Universal Book and Bible House, 1914), 262.

[31]G. P. Bowser, "The Use of Instrumental Music in the Worship of God: A Review (No. 3)," *Christian Echo* 34 (August 5, 1939): 5.

[32]Rouse and Bowser, "The Use of Instrumental Music in the Worship of God: A Review (No. 3)," *Christian Echo* 34 (August 5, 1939): 5.

[33]Franklin D. Roosevelt's statement, "There, my friends, is a 96-inch dog being wagged by a four-inch tail," was made on January 8, 1938, during a Jackson Day dinner in Washington, D.C. See E. Taylor Parks and Lois F. Parks, *Memorable Quotations of Franklin D. Roosevelt* (New York: Thomas Y. Crowell, 1965), 113. See also G. P. Bowser, "A Correction," *Christian Echo* 34 (August 5, 1939): 8. Leroy Garrett, *The Stone–Campbell Movement: An Anecdotal History of Three Churches* (Joplin, Mo.: College Press, 1981), 468-479.

For an example of John W. McGarvey's opposition to instrumental music in worship, see M. C. Kurfees, *Instrumental Music in the Worship or the Greek Verb Psallo, Philologically and Historically Examined together with a Full Discussion of Kindred Matters Relating to Music in Christian Worship* (Nashville: Gospel Advocate, 1922), 235-236.

For the Alexander Campbell quote, see Robert Richardson, *The Memoirs of Alexander Campbell: Embracing a View of the Origin, Progress and Principles of the Reformation Which He Advocated* (Nashville: Gospel Advocate, 1956 [1868–1869]), 2:366.

[34]T. K. Rouse, "Instrumental Music in the Worship: A Review of T. K. Rouse Tract (No. 4)," *Christian Echo* 34 (August 20, 1939): 5.

[35]Ibid.

[36]T. K. Rouse, "The Use of Instrumental Music in the Worship of God: A Review (No. 6)," *Christian Echo* 34 (September 20, 1939): 7.

[37]G. P. Bowser, "The Use of Instrumental Music in the Worship of God: A Review (No. 6)," *Christian Echo* 34 (September 20, 1939): 7.

[38]T. K. Rouse, "The Use of Instrumental Music in the Worship," *Christian Echo* 34 (November 20, 1939): 7.

[39]G. P. Bowser, "The Use of Instrumental Music in the Worship," *Christian Echo* 34 (November 20, 1939): 7.

[40]T. K. Rouse, "Friendly Criticism," *Christian Echo* 36 (June 20, 1941): 4.

[41]Ibid.

[42]G. P. Bowser, "Editor's Reply," *Christian Echo* 36 (June 20, 1941): 4. See also David Edwin Harrell Jr., *Sources of Division in the Disciples of Christ, 1865–1900: A Social History of the Disciples of Christ* (Tuscaloosa: University of Alabama Press, 2003[1973]), 193-195.

[43] G. P. Bowser, "Questions," *Christian Echo* 36 (June 20, 1941): 7.

[44] G. P. Bowser, "Questions," *Christian Echo* 37 (May 5, 1942): 3.

[45]Earl I. West, *The Search for the Ancient Order: A History of the Restoration Movement* (Indianapolis: Religious Book Service, 1950), 2:81.

[46] G. P. Bowser, "Questions," *Christian Echo* 37 (September 5, 1942): 3; G. P. Bowser, "Questions," *Christian Echo* 37 (November 5, 1942): 7.

[47]"The Outlook," *Christian Echo* 39 (September 5, 1944): 4.

[48]G. P. Bowser, "Questions," *Christian Echo* 40 (August 5, 1945): 7.

[49]G. P. Bowser, "Questions," *Christian Echo* 42 (April 20, 1947): 9. See also G. P. Bowser, "Should Those Coming from the Christian Church Be Baptized?" *Christian Echo* 42 (August 20, 1947): 4-5.

[50]G. P. Bowser, "Questions," *Christian Echo* 45 (November 5, 1949): 5.

[51]James M. Butler, "Meet Our Ministers," *Christian Echo* 36 (December 5, 1941): 3.

[52]Annie C. Tuggle, *Our Ministers and Songleaders* (Detroit: Annie C. Tuggle, 1945), 130.

[53]Sylvia Rose has composed more than two hundred songs, including "Call Him Up," "Holy Spirit," "Restore My Soul," "All My Trials," "Until My Journey's End," and "A Mansion, Robe, and Crown." See her *Songs of Faith* (Detroit: Srose Publishing Company, 1985). For more information on the significance of Sylvia Rose in the history of black Churches of Christ, see chapter 11 of this book.

Chapter 8

[1]This biographical information about J. S. Winston (1906–1997) was extracted from Annie C. Tuggle, *Our Ministers and Song Leaders of the Churches of Christ* (Detroit: Annie C. Tuggle, 1945), 158, and Carl E. Gaines and John C. Whitley, *Black Preachers of Today: Churches of Christ* (n.p., 1974), 76.

[2]David Edwin Harrell Jr., *The Churches of Christ in the Twentieth Century: Homer Hailey's Personal Journey of Faith* (Tuscaloosa: University of Alabama Press, 2000), 225.

[3]J. S. Winston, "Southwestern Christian College Student Accepted by Terre Haute, Ind. Church," *Christian Echo* 50 (October 1954): 8. For a reference to Mizetta Winston's obituary, see Claudia Washington, "Women at Work," *Christian Echo* 84 (February 1986): 6; Tuggle, *Our Ministers and Song Leaders*,

158; and R. Vernon Boyd, *Undying Dedication: The Story of G. P. Bowser* (Nashville: Gospel Advocate, 1985), 78-79.

[4]Boyd, *Undying Dedication*, 79.

[5]J. S. Winston, "Sherman, Texas," *Christian Echo* 34 (June 5, 1939): 2-3. For a reference to the murder of George Hughes, see "Martial Law for Sherman Declared at Report That More Mob Rule Is Feared," *Dallas Morning News* (May 11, 1930): 14, and Alwyn Barr, *Black Texans: A History of African Americans in Texas, 1528–1995*, 2nd ed. (Norman: University of Oklahoma Press, 1973), 137.

[6]Winston, "Sherman, Texas," 2-3.

[7]Booker T. Washington, *Up from Slavery* (New York: Oxford University Press, 1995 [1901]), 34.

[8]Winston, "Sherman, Texas," 3.

[9]Ruby Mae Potts, "The Outlook," *Christian Echo* 36 (October 5, 1941): 5.

[10]L. M. Wright, "The Outlook," *Christian Echo* 36 (November 5, 1941): 5.

[11]Annette Cash, "The Outlook," *Christian Echo* 37 (May 5, 1942): 4.

[12]C. E. Shaw, "A History of the Grand Avenue Church of Christ" (August 2001), 2 [in author's possession].

[13]The testimony of Ardelia Griffin shows that J. S. Winston relocated from Sherman to Fort Worth, Texas, on January 10, 1943. See Griffin, "The Outlook," *Christian Echo* 38 (January 20, 1943): 4.

[14]Annette Cash, "The Outlook," *Christian Echo* 37 (September 20, 1942): 5.

[15]Earthy Miller, "The Outlook," *Christian Echo* 38 (July 20, 1943): 4.

[16]J. S. Winston, "The Outlook," *Christian Echo* 38 (June 20, 1943): 5.

[17]Ardelia Griffin, "The Outlook," *Christian Echo* 38 (July 5, 1943): 1; and Ezekiel Z. Webster, "The Outlook," *Christian Echo* 38 (August 20, 1943): 5.

[18]Ardelia Griffin, "The Outlook," *Christian Echo* 38 (August 20, 1943): 4-5.

[19]Juney Luster, "The Outlook," *Christian Echo* 38 (November 20, 1943): 4.

[20]Ardelia Griffin, "The Outlook," *Christian Echo* 39 (January 20, 1944): 4.

[21]Annette Cash, "The Outlook," *Christian Echo* 39 (February 20, 1944): 7.

[22]H. H. Gray, "The Outlook," *Christian Echo* 39 (May 20, 1944): 5.

[23]Marshall Keeble, "The Outlook," *Christian Echo* 39 (August 5, 1944): 6.

[24]J. S. Winston, "A Report and Mission Call of the Marlin Work," *Christian Echo* 41 (March 20, 1946): 1.

[25]G. E. Steward, "G. E. Steward," *Christian Echo* 40 (May 6, 1945): 1.

[26]Russell H. Moore, "A Zealous Worker," *Christian Echo* 40 (July 20, 1945): 8.

[27]Before the 1954 *Brown* decision was handed down, Pepperdine College, established in southern California in 1937, was the only Church of Christ-related school to admit African Americans during the era of segregation.

[28]J. S. Winston, "Southern Bible Institute," *Christian Echo* 43 (October 5, 1948): 5.

[29]Ibid., 5-6.

[30]J. S. Winston, "Southern Bible Institute: A Message from the President," *Christian Echo* 43 (October 20, 1948): 7.

[31]J. S. Winston, "Southern Bible Institute," *Christian Echo* 44 (December 5, 20, 1948): 5.

[32]J. S. Winston, "A Greater Southern Bible Institute," *Christian Echo* 45 (February 20, 1949): 7.

[33]Ibid.

[34]G. P. Bowser, "An Expression of Profound Gratitude," *Christian Echo* 45 (April 15, 1949): 7.

[35]Lelia Brigham, "The Outlook," *Christian Echo* 45 (August 5, 1949): 7.

[36]J. S. Winston, "Hindering Causes," *Christian Echo* 50 (April 1954): 3. For an insightful overview of Winston's life, see R. N. Hogan, "Tribute to a Great Minister," *Christian Echo* (October 1986): 3.

[37]J. S. Winston, "The Need of Leadership," *Christian Echo* 51 (March 1955): 6.

[38]J. S. Winston, "Hindering Causes: Eldership—'The Churches Need,'" *Christian Echo* 51 (May 1955): 4.

[39]Willie Tucker, "The Miracle at Minda Street," *Christian Echo* (February 1992): 10.

[40]Tony Roach, "A Brief History of the Minda Street Congregation," *26th Anniversary Program* (October 29, 2006). See also Anthony Roach Sr., "A Biblical Program for Building New Self-Love in African American Males and Females" (Doctor of Ministry Thesis, Abilene Christian University, 1992).

[41]J. S. Winston, "Why Are There Not More Churches with Elders among the Black as among the White Brethren of the Church of Christ?" *Christian Echo* 71 (July 1973): 3.

[42]J. S. Winston, "Elders: The Problem of Ordination," *Christian Echo* 71 (November-December 1973): 1, 8.

[43]J. S. Winston, "Work among the Colored People in the U. S.," in *The Harvest Field*, eds. Howard L. Schug and Jesse P. Sewell (Athens, Ala.: Bible School Bookstore, 1947), 72-73.

[44]Ibid., 75.

[45]J. S. Winston, "History of Black Members of the Church of Christ," *Christian Echo* 78 (November-December 1978): 2; and J. S. Winston, "History of Black Members of the Church of Christ," *Christian Echo* 79 (August 1980): 4.

[46]J. S. Winston, "Beginning of Choral Groups among Churches of Christ," *Christian Echo* 83 (January 1985): 2, 4.

Chapter 9

[1]G. P. Bowser, "A Tribute to the Worth of R. N. Hogan," *Christian Echo* 39 (August 20, 1944): 3.

[2]R. N. Hogan, *Sermons by Hogan* (Austin, Tex.: Firm Foundation, 1940), vii. Additional useful biographical information on Hogan can be found in

Calvin H. Bowers, "A Rhetorical Analysis of the Preaching of R. N. Hogan" (Master's thesis, Pepperdine University, 1972), 9-19.

[3]Hogan, *Sermons*, viii.

[4]Ibid., viii-ix.

[5]James L. Lovell to the Church of Christ in Stanford, Kentucky (March 19, 1938) (in the Center for Restoration Studies at Abilene Christian University, Abilene, Texas).

[6]For a good study of R. N. Hogan and the emergence of African American Churches of Christ in Southern California, see Calvin H. Bowers, *Realizing the California Dream: The Story of Black Churches of Christ in Los Angeles* (Calvin H. Bowers, 2001).

[7]Richard N. Hogan, "Another Christian Church Captured," *Firm Foundation* 53 (April 21, 1936): 8. While there are many reports in Church of Christ journals announcing that members of the Christian Church (or Disciples of Christ) came over to Churches of Christ, it is also true that some members of Churches of Christ went over to the Christian Church. For example, A. F. Thurman, a mayor and preacher in Chillicothe, Texas, severed ties with the Church of Christ and aligned himself with the Christian Church. See Charles A. Chasteen, "A Good Man Come to Us from the Church of Christ," *Christian Courier* 44 (December 17, 1931): 8.

[8]R. N. Hogan, "News and Notes," *Gospel Advocate* 78 (September 17, 1936): 905.

[9]R. N. Hogan, "News and Notes," *Gospel Advocate* 78 (October 8, 1936): 978.

[10]R. N. Hogan, "News and Notes," *Gospel Advocate* 78 (August 20, 1936): 809.

[11]J. S. Winston, "Sherman, Texas," *Christian Echo* 34 (June 5, 1939): 2-3.

[12]R. N. Hogan, "The Outlook," *Christian Echo* 36 (December 5, 1941): 4.

[13]"Historical Sketch of the Fifth Ward Church of Christ" [in author's possession].

[14]R. N. Hogan, "A Gospel Blitzkrieg," *Christian Echo* 36 (April 20, 1941): 1.

[15]Ibid.

[16]Carroll Pitts Jr., "A Critical Study of Civil Rights Practices, Attitudes and Responsibilities in Churches of Christ" (Master's thesis, Pepperdine College, 1969), 86.

[17]R. N. Hogan, "Southwestern Is Producing," *Christian Echo* 51 (November 1955): 2; and Marion V. Holt, "What Are They Doing Now?," *Christian Echo* 51 (November 1955): 3-4. See also Jack Evans, "The History of Southwestern Christian College, Terrell, Texas" (Master's thesis, University of Texas, El Paso, 1963).

[18]Theodore G. Bilbo, *Take Your Choice: Separation or Mongrelization* (Poplarville, Miss.: Dream House Publishing, 1947), 65.

[19]Margaret Halsey, *Color Blind: A White Woman Looks at the Negro* (New York: Simon and Schuster, 1946), 101, 117.

[20]Pete Daniel, *Lost Revolutions: The South in the 1950s* (Chapel Hill: University of North Carolina Press, 2000), 189-190, 274. In his biography of football sensation Jim Brown, columnist Mike Freeman has observed that many whites feared black athletes freely interacting with white women. See Mike Freeman, *Jim Brown: The Fierce Life of an American Hero* (New York: HarperCollins Publishers, 2006), 4.

[21]Numan V. Bartley, *The Rise of Massive Resistance: Race and Politics in the South During the 1950s* (Baton Rouge: Louisiana State University Press, 1969), 97-98.

[22]David Edwin Harrell Jr., *White Sects and Black Men in the Recent South* (Nashville: Vanderbilt University Press, 1971), 62.

[23]Clenora Hudson-Weems, *Emmett Till: The Sacrificial Lamb of the Civil Rights Movement* (Troy, Mich.: Bedford Publishers, 1994).

[24]Craig R. Anderson, "Before Little Rock: The Desegregation Crises at Mansfield, Texas, and Clinton, Tennessee" (Master's thesis, Utah State University, 1995), 37, 38, 43. Alwyn Barr, *Black Texans: A History of African Americans in Texas, 1528-1995* (Norman: University of Oklahoma Press, 1995 [1973]), 216, observes that whites successfully prevented blacks from enrolling at Texarkana Junior College in 1955. Bartley, *The Rise of Massive Resistance*, 241, notes that white southerners in the 1950s built their racial ideology on the plank of "interposition." "They made state sovereignty, carried to the point of interposition, the foundation for their program of massive resistance."

[25]R. Vernon Boyd, *Undying Dedication: The Story of G. P. Bowser* (Nashville: Gospel Advocate, 1985).

[26]For reference to R. N. Hogan's assessment of A. M. Burton, see Bowers, *Realizing the California Dream*, 277, and G. P. Holt, "Cool Summers on a Hot Eternity," *Christian Echo* 63 (November 1968): 1, 7.

[27]R. N. Hogan to Jimmy L. Lovell, April 18, 1941 (in the Center for Restoration Studies, Abilene Christian University, Abilene, Texas).

[28]Ira Y. Rice Jr., *Singapore—Far East Newsletter* (March 9, 1964): 16. See also Don Haymes, "Ira Y. Rice in 1964," Memorial University, www.mun.ca/rels/restmov/texts/race/haymes38.html (accessed February 6, 2008). For a more detailed account of the Rice–Wallace squabble, see Ira Y. Rice Jr., *Pressing toward the Mark: An Autobiography by Ira Y. Rice, Jr.* (Dallas: G. T. Press, 1998), 157-165.

[29]Rice, *Singapore*, 16-17.

[30]R. N. Hogan, "The Sin of Being a Respecter of Persons," *Christian Echo* (June 1959): 2.

[31]Ibid. See also Carl Spain, "Modern Challenges to Christian Morals," in *Christian Faith in the Modern World: The Abilene Christian College Annual Bible Lectures, 1960* (Abilene, Tex.: Abilene Christian College, 1960), 217.

[32]Hogan, "The Sin of Being a Respecter of Persons," 2.

[33]Ibid., 5.

[34]Ibid. Some white southerners did indeed give their monetary support to black schools to avoid complying with the *Brown* decision. White legislators in South Carolina, for example, increased funding for black schools in the 1940s and 1950s "hoping desperately to ward off court-ordered desegregation." See Philip G. Grose, *South Carolina at the Brink: Robert McNair and the Politics of Civil Rights* (Columbia, S.C.: University of South Carolina Press, 2006), 69.

[35]Rice, *Singapore*, 16.

[36]Leon C. Burns, "Why Desegregation Will Fail," (March 24, 1957), 4, 6, 7 (in the Center for Restoration Studies, Abilene Christian University, Abilene, Texas).

[37]R. N. Hogan, "Brother C. A. Cannon of Saratoga, Ark., Replies to My Articles on Segregation in the Lord's Church?" *Christian Echo* (January 1960): 2.

[38]R. N. Hogan, "Brother David Lipscomb Stood with God on Race Prejudice in the Church of Christ," *Christian Echo* (June 1960): 2.

[39]Spain, "Modern Challenges to Christian Morals," 217-218.

[40]Roosevelt Sams, *My Experience Relevant to My Work at Southwestern Christian College, Terrell, Texas* (n.p., 1989), 13 [in author's possession]; Rice Jr., *Singapore*, 16-20.

[41]R. N. Hogan, "Is It the Law or Down-Right Prejudice?" *Christian Echo* (June 1963): 3.

[42]Ron Goodman, "Afterthoughts on Neglecting the Weightier Matters?" *Firm Foundation* 85 (July 9, 1968): 437.

[43]R. N. Hogan, "A Lecture on the Church and Integration," *Christian Echo* (October 1987): 4, 6.

[44]Jack Evans, *The Curing of Ham* (De Queen, Ark.: Harrywell Printers, 1976), 104.

[45]Jimmy L. Lovell to the Church of Christ in Stanford, Kentucky (March 19, 1938) (in the Center for Restoration Studies at Abilene Christian University, Abilene, Texas).

Chapter 10

[1]Jarvis Christian Institute did not become Jarvis Christian College until 1927; therefore, I will use Jarvis Christian Institute throughout most of this chapter. See Clifford H. Taylor Jr., "Jarvis Christian College: Its History and Present Standing in Relationship to the Standards of the Texas State Department of Education and the Southern Association of Colleges and Secondary Schools" (Bachelor of Divinity Thesis, Texas Christian University, 1948), 20-21.

[2]David Edwin Harrell Jr., *The Social Sources of Division in the Disciples of Christ, 1865–1900* (Tuscaloosa: University of Alabama Press, 2003 [1973]), 2:179, has given good examples of whites in the Stone–Campbell Movement who were fond of Booker T. Washington and his work as an educator. In 1899

whites in the Stone–Campbell Movement christened Samuel Robert Cassius as the "Booker T. Washington of Oklahoma" because of his effort to launch the Tohee Industrial School in the Oklahoma Territory. See Edward J. Robinson, *To Save My Race from Abuse: The Life of Samuel Robert Cassius* (Tuscaloosa: University of Alabama Press, 2007), 95-110.

[3]W. M. Williams, "Duty of Disciples to the Brother in Black," *Christian Courier* 33 (July 1, 1920): 4.

[4]W. M. Williams, "Disciples' Debt to Negro and Mexican," *Christian Courier* 33 (August 5, 1920): 5.

[5]Ibid.

[6]John B. Lehman, "Lehman's Letter on Lynch Law," *Christian Courier* 33 (March 4, 1920): 12.

[7]John B. Lehman, "Jarvis Christian Institute," *Christian Courier* 36 (March 22, 1923): 3.

[8]George M. Frederickson, *The Black Image in the White Mind: The Debate on Afro-American Character and Destiny, 1817–1914* (New York: Harper & Row, 1971).

[9]Lehman, "Jarvis Christian Institute," 3.

[10]Colby D. Hall, *Texas Disciples* (Fort Worth: Texas Christian University Press, 1953), 247-258.

[11]Ida V. Jarvis, "Daughter of the Old South Writes about the Negro Question," *Christian Courier* 34 (August 31, 1922): 2.

[12]Composed in the context of the Spanish–American War, Rudyard Kipling's poem, "The White Man's Burden," captured the essence of the spreading of so-called superior white culture to supposedly inferior brown and black culture. The 1899 poem reflected the racist thinking of white Americans who felt obligated to uplift so-called inferior black people. See *Rudyard Kipling's Verse* (New York: Doubleday, Doran and Co., 1945), 321-323.

[13]Ida V. Jarvis, "Jarvis Christian Institute," *Christian Courier* 36 (March 13, 1924): 7.

[14]Charles R. Wilson, *Baptized in Blood: The Religion of the Lost Cause, 1865–1920* (Athens: University of Georgia Press, 1980).

[15]Jarvis, "Jarvis Christian Institute," 7.

[16]Hall, *Texas Disciples*, 336; and E. B. Bynum, *These Carried the Torch* (Dallas: Walter F. Clark Company, 1946), 22-24. See also Ida V. Jarvis, "Why We Gave the Land," *Missionary Tidings* (April 1913): 464-466.

[17]Jarvis, "Jarvis Christian Institute," 7. See also Taylor, "Jarvis Christian College," 7-9.

[18]Bynum, *These Carried the Torch*, 25.

[19]This biographical sketch was compiled from the following: "J. N. Ervin, Jarvis Leader, Passes On," *Christian Evangelist* 76 (August 25, 1938): 925; Bynum, *These Carried the Torch*, 39; Hall, *Texas Disciples*, 337.

[20]Leon F. Litwack, *Trouble in Mind: Black Southerners in the Age of Jim Crow* (New York: Vintage Books, 1998).

[21]J. L. Clark, "The Disciples and the Negro Problem," *Christian Courier* 33 (April 7, 1921): 4.

[22]W. W. Phares, "A Visit to Jarvis Institute," *Christian Courier* 38 (June 10,1926): 2.

[23]Henry Dorsey, "Dorsey Does Good Deed," *Christian Courier* 34 (May 4, 1922): 12.

[24]James D. Anderson, *The Education of Blacks in the South, 1860–1935* (Chapel Hill: University of North Carolina Press, 1988), 33-78.

[25]"Commencement at Jarvis Christian Institute: Negro Among World's Great Scientist," *Christian Courier* 34 (June 1, 1922): 7.

[26]"The Negro and Race Hatred," *Christian Courier* 34 (July 27, 1922): 5.

[27]Ibid.

[28]Jarvis, "Daughter of the Old South," 2.

[29]Ibid.

[30]"Dr. Carver Visits Texas," *Christian Courier* 35 (January 18, 1923): 11.

[31]J. N. Ervin, "Southern Anglo-Saxon Has Great Opportunity for Good Service," *Christian Courier* 36 (February 28, 1924): 4. See also Taylor, *Texas Disciples*, 13.

[32]W. A. Brooks, Emily McK. Reagin, and Geo. Riter, "Prominent Church Women Commend Colored School," *Christian Courier* 32 (March 20, 1920): 11.

[33]W. W. Phares, "Jarvis Commencement," *Christian Courier* 33 (May 19, 1921): 12.

[34]The Baldwin quote appears in Anderson, *The Education of Blacks in the South*, 101. *Survey of Service: Organizations Represented in the International Convention of Disciples of Christ* (St. Louis: Christian Board of Publication, 1928), 157. See also Louis Harlan, *Booker T. Washington: The Making of a Black Leader, 1856–1901* (New York: Oxford University Press, 1972).

[35]W. W. Phares, "Jarvis Commencement," *Christian Courier* 33 (May 19, 1921): 12.

[36]J. B. Holmes, "Commending Negro School," *Christian Courier* 34 (November 23, 1922): 7.

[37]W. M. Williams, "Negro School Sends Editor Farm Products," *Christian Courier* 35 (July 19, 1923): 14.

[38]Leon Williams, "In the Field," *Christian Courier* 36 (March 27, 1924): 12-13.

[39]W. M. Williams, "Negroes at the State Fair," *Christian Courier* 39 (October 20, 1927): 4.

[40]"Jarvis Jubilee Singers," *Christian Courier* 35 (July 19, 1923): 4. The Jarvis Jubilee Singers made their first national appearance around 1918. See Taylor, *Texas Disciples*, 15-16, and Andrew Ward, *Dark Midnight When I Rise: The Story of the Jubilee Singers Who Introduced the World to the Music of Black America* (New York: Farrar, Straus and Giroux, 2000).

[41]"Jarvis Jubilee Decided Success," *Christian Courier* 35 (August 2, 1923): 14.

[42]"Negro Singers in Denison," *Christian Courier* 35 (September 6, 1923): 15.

[43]"Jarvis Christian Institute Well Represented at the Convention," *Christian Courier* 35 (October 15, 1925): 10.

[44]Mineola Klan No. 96., "K.K.K. Support for Jarvis Jubilee Singers," *Christian Courier* 35 (July 26, 1923): 5.

[45]"Ku Klux Klan," *Christian Courier* 33 (May 26, 1921): 4. Indeed the second Klan, unlike the Klan of Reconstruction, which sought to overthrow the political program of radical Republicans and to suppress black civil rights, was born in 1915 in Stone Mountain, Georgia, was anti-black, anti-Catholic, and anti-Jewish as well as a reform movement. It was also designed to maintain social order in the United States, and it was comprised of ministers, doctors, and politicians. See Nancy Maclean, *Behind the Mask of Chivalry: The Making of the Second Ku Klux Klan* (New York: Oxford University Press, 1994).

[46]W. M. Williams, "A Day at Jarvis Christian Institute," *Christian Courier* 36 (May 29, 1924): 4-5.

[47]"Preacher Praises Ku Klux Klan," *Christian Courier* 34 (February 16, 1922): 11.

[48]"Leak Discusses Klan," *Christian Courier* 34 (July 6, 1922): 14.

[49]W. M. Williams, "The Cyclops and His Service," *Christian Courier* 34 (July 27, 1922): 13. By 1924, Alexander Campbell Parker had apparently resigned his post as a leader of the Ku Klux Klan. See "Southern Anglo-Saxon Has Great Opportunity for Good Service," *Christian Courier* 36 (February 28, 1924): 4.

[50]Vance Smith, "Facing Up: Are the Disciples of Christ Presenting an Adequate Program of Education of Negroes?" *World Call* (September 1926): 9-10. Smith's assertions merely reflected the on-going conflict and debate among African-American leaders and educators who championed giving black students a liberal arts education (W. E. B. Du Bois) as opposed to a manual and industrial education (Booker T. Washington). See Anderson, *The Education of Blacks in the South*, 238-278.

[51]"Terrible Tragedy Accompanies Burning of Jarvis," *Christian Evangelist* 68 (June 11, 1931): 794.

[52]J. N. Ervin, "President Ervin Is Grateful," *Christian Courier* 43 (June 11, 1931): 3.

[54]"J. N. Ervin Is Ill," *Christian Evangelist* 76 (May 12, 1938): 549; and "J. N. Ervin Passes On," *Christian Evangelist* 76 (August 25, 1938): 925.

[55]Carl E. Gaines and John C. Whitley, eds., *Black Preachers of Today: Churches of Christ* (n.p., 1974), 76.

Chapter 11

[1]Eugene Lawton, "Saluting Dr. Jack Evans—SWCC's President," *Christian Echo* 74 (August 1975): 6. This chapter does not purport to be a full-length study of Southwestern Christian College. Furthermore, it is impossible to list all of the preachers and leaders who have emerged from the college since its

beginning in Terrell. For an incomplete list of preachers who attended or graduated from SWCC, see Appendix II.

[2]Lawton, "Saluting Dr. Jack Evans," 6.

[3]Jack Evans Sr., "Biography," JackEvansonline.com, http://www.jackevansonline.com/DrEvansBio.htm, (accessed February 6, 2008); Pepperdine University in Malibu, California, established in 1937, admitted African Americans from its inception; and in 1971 the Southern California school bestowed on Evans an honorary doctorate. White Church of Christ schools such as Abilene Christian University in Texas and Harding University in Arkansas, which once denied black applicants from their campus, also bestowed honorary doctoral degrees on Evans.

[4]This biographical sketch of Roosevelt Sams was compiled from his book, *My Experience Relevant to My Work at Southwestern Christian College, Terrell, Texas* (n.p., 1989), 7.

[5]Taylor Branch, *Parting the Waters: America in the King Years, 1954–1963* (New York: Simon & Schuster, 1988).

[6]Sams, *My Experience*, 7, 12.

[7]Ibid., 16-17.

[8]Ibid., 26-27. Jack Evans recalled Isbell using the derogatory term "nigra" when referring to African American students at SWCC. "Interview with Jack Evans" (October 25, 2007).

[9]Molefi Kete Asante, *The Afrocentric Idea* (Philadelphia, Penn.: Temple University Press, 1987).

[10]Sams, *My Experience*, 34-35.

[11]Ibid., 18. Anthea D. Butler notes that Jim Crow laws in Memphis, Tennessee, forced black members attending the Church of God in Christ convocation there to house black visitors. See Butler, *Women in the Church of God in Christ: Making a Sanctified World* (Chapel Hill: University of North Carolina Press, 2007), 46.

[12]Sams, *My Experience*, 36-37.

[13]Ibid., 10.

[14]"SWCC Receives Accreditation," *Christian Echo* 72 (January 1974): 1, 2. E. W. McMillan was SWCC's first president from 1950 to 1953; H. L. Barber served from 1953 to 1956; and A. V. Isbell worked from 1956 to 1967.

[15]James Maxwell, "SWCC Approved to Offer Bachelors Degree," *Christian Echo* 80 (April 1982): 6; Evans, "SWCC's New Bible Program: Help!," *Christian Echo* 80 (August 1982): 1.

[16]This biographical information was taken from James Maxwell's book, *The Tangled Web of Deceit: Lessons on Doctrines Including Two Religious Discussions* (Wichita Falls, Tex.: Western Christian Foundation, 1980), i-ii.

[17]Ibid.

[18]Eugene Lawton noted of both Dr. and Mrs. Evans: "For his many sacrifices made during the difficult days of his administration, we salute Dr. and Mrs. Evans and their three children." Lawton, "Saluting Dr. Jack Evans," 6. See

also "Mrs. Evans Honored," *Christian Echo* 73 (October 1974): 5. Jack Evans and SWCC have been assisted by many leaders, including Ben Foster, James Maxwell, Gerald Lee, Rick Hunter, Jack Evans Jr., Herb Evans, G. P. Holt, R. N. Hogan, Clyde Muse, Thelma Holt, Reginald Dulin, Douglass Howie, Gus Farmer, J. C. Davis, Eugene Lawton, R. C. Wells, and many others.

[19]www.jackevansonline.com.

[20]This discussion is delineated in Jack Evans, *The Curing of Ham* (De Queen, Ark.: Harrywell Printers, 1976).

[21]Evans provides a written account of this 1977 debate in his *The Cross or the Crescent?: An Expose of Islam* (Wichita Falls, Tex.: Western Christian Foundation, 1977).

[22]James Maxwell, "Review of the Evans–Rose Dialogue," *Christian Echo* 82 (July 1984): 2.

[23]Evans, *The Curing of Ham*, 18, 22.

[24]Ibid., 25.

[25]Ibid., 26.

[26]Ibid.

[27]Ibid., 27.

[28]Ibid.

[29]Ibid.

[30]Ibid., 29.

[31]Ibid., 31.

[32]Ibid.

[33]Ibid., 33.

[34]Ibid., 34.

[35]Ibid., 37.

[36]Ibid., 36.

[37]Ibild., 40.

[38]Ibid., 42.

[39]Ibid., 41.

[40]Ibid.

[41]Ibid., 78.

[42]C. Myer Phillips, "A Historical Study of the Attitude of the Churches of Christ toward Other Denominations" (Ph. D. dissertation, Baylor University, 1983), 47-83. Radical exclusivists maintained that those who received baptism without understanding that it was "for the remission of sins" were not Christians and in need of re-immersion.

[43]Evans, *The Curing of Ham*, 79.

[44]Ibid., 13.

[45]Ibid., 55.

[46]Ibid., 76.

[47]Ibid., 116.

[48]Ibid., 117.

[49]In some respects, many white and black preachers in Churches of Christ perpetuated the debating tradition of Alexander Campbell, who held five major debates. In 1820 he debated Presbyterian minister John Walker; in 1823 he debated Presbyterian clergyman William Maccalla; in 1829 skeptic Robert Owen; in 1837 Catholic bishop John B. Purcell; and in 1843 Presbyterian leader Nathaniel Rice. See Bill Humble, *Campbell and Controversy: The Story of Alexander Campbell's Five Great Debates with Skepticism, Catholicism, and Presbyterianism* (Joplin, Mo.: College Press, 1986); and Rick Cherok, *Debating for God: Alexander Campbell's Challenge to Skepticism in Antebellum America* (Abilene, Tex.: Abilene Christian University Press, 2008).

[50] "Dr. Frederick Aquino," Abilene Christian University, http://www.acu.edu/academics/cbs/programs/gst/faculty/aquino.html (accessed February 6, 2008).

[51]Derryl B. Bowdre, "Meet Our Minister," The Church of Christ at South Central, http://www.southcentralonline.org (accessed February 6, 2008).

[52]"Two Board Members Honored," *Communique* 35 (April-June): 1, 3.

[53]"A Historical Sketch of the Greenville Avenue Church of Christ, Richardson, Texas" (in author's possession).

[54]Kenneth Greene, "Dallas Conference Seeks to Offer African-American Families Hope, Solutions," *Christian Echo* 84 (January 1991): 3.

[55]www.lightoftheworldchurchofchrist.org.

[56]Jerry A. Taylor, "History of the New Wineskins Retreat" (in author's possession).

[57]Other outstanding SWCC chorus directors include: A. Hugh Graham, Veronica Williams, and Amy Johnson.

[58]Sylvia Rose, *Rise Up: A Call to Leadership for African American Women* (Downers Grove, Ill.: Inter Varsity Press, 2004).

Epilogue

[1]Jerry A. Taylor, "History of the New Wineskins Retreat" (in author's possession).

[2]Jack Evans Sr., "'Undoing Racism' A Doctrinal Change-Agent Ploy," JackEvansonline.com, http://www.jackevansonline.com/Undoing%20Racism.htm (accessed February 6, 2008). In 2004, Evans railed against Rick Atchley after he announced his intent to collaborate with black preachers in Churches of Christ in planting grace-filled and freedom-filled churches in North America.

[3]Kenneth R. Greene, "What African-American Families Need to Hear," in *Unfinished Reconciliation: Justice, Racism, and Churches of Christ*, eds. Gary Holloway and John York (Abilene, Tex.: Abilene Christian University Press, 2003), 166, 174.

[4]Ibid., 182-185.

[5]Ibid., 204, 206.

BIBLIOGRAPHY

Newspapers

Christian Courier (Dallas, Texas), 1919-1938.
Christian Echo (Fort Smith, Arkansas; Fort Worth, Texas, and Los Angeles), 1915-2000.
Dallas Morning News (Texas), 1930.
Firm Foundation (Austin, Texas), 1925-1965.
Gospel Advocate (Nashville, Tennessee), 1866-1968.
Missionary Tidings (Indianapolis, Indiana), 1913.
Singapore—Far East Newsletter (Singapore), 1964.
World Call (Cincinnati, Ohio), 1926.

Articles and Books

Allen, C. Leonard. and Richard T. Hughes. *Discovering Our Roots: The Ancestry of Churches of Christ.* Abilene, Tex.: Abilene Christian University Press, 1988.

Anderson, Craig R. "Before Little Rock: The Desegregation Crises at Mansfield, Texas, and Clinton, Tennessee." Masters Thesis, Utah State University, 1995.

Anderson, James D. *The Education of Blacks in the South.* Chapel Hill: University of North Carolina Press, 1988.

Asante, Molefi Kete. *The Afrocentric Idea.* Philadelphia: Temple University Press, 1987.

Baccus, Carl C. *I Can Tell the World about This.* Los Angeles: Baccus Publications, 1982.

Bailey, Declara Nixon. *From Whence We Came: The History of the Antioch Church of Christ, Midway, Texas.* MTR & Company, 1992.

Barr, Alwyn. *Black Texans: A History of African Americans in Texas, 1528-1995.* Norman: University of Oklahoma Press, 1995 [1973].

Bartley, Numan V. *The Rise of Massive Resistance: Race and Politics in the South During the 1950s.* Baton Rouge: Louisiana State University Press, 1969.

Bernstein, Patricia. *The First Waco Horror: The Lynching of Jesse Washington and the Rise of the NAACP.* College Station: Texas A & M University Press, 2005.

Bilbo, Theodore G. *Take Your Choice: Separation or Mongrelization.* Popularville, Miss.: Dream House Publishing, 1947.

Bowers, Calvin H. *Realizing the California Dream: The Story of Black Churches of Christ in California.* Calvin H. Bowers, 2001.

_____."A Rhetorical Analysis of the Preaching of R. N. Hogan." Masters thesis, Pepperdine University, 1972.

Boyd, R. Vernon. *Undying Dedication: The Story of G. P. Bowser.* Nashville: Gospel Advocate, 1985.

Brown, Norman D. *Hood, Bonnet, and Little Brown Jug: Texas Politics, 1921-1928.* College Station: Texas A & M University Press, 1984.

Burns, Leon C. "Why Desegregation Will Fail." March 24, 1957, in the Center for Restoration Studies, Abilene Christian University, Abilene, Texas.

Bynum, E. B. *These Carried the Torch.* Dallas: Walter F. Clark Company, 1946.

Campbell, Randolph B. *An Empire for Slavery: The Peculiar Institution in Texas,1865-1865.* Baton Rouge: Louisiana State University Press, 1989.

Casey, Michael W. *Saddlebags, City Streets, and Cyberspace: A History of Preaching in the Churches of Christ.* Abilene, Tex.: Abilene Christian University Press, 1995.

_____. *The Battle over Hermeneutics in the Stone-Campbell Movement, 1800-1870.* Lewiston, New York: Edwin Mellen Press, 1998.

Chambers, Bill. "The History of the Texas Negro and His Development Since 1900." Masters thesis, Texas State Teachers College, 1940.

Choate, J. E. *Roll Jordan Roll: A Biography of Marshall Keeble.* Nashville: Gospel Advocate, 1974.

Christian, Garna L. *Black Soldiers in Jim Crow Texas, 1899-1917.* College Station: Texas A & M University Press, 1995.

Crouch, Barry A. *The Freedmen's Bureau and Black Texas.* Austin: University of Texas Press, 1992.

Daniel, Pete. *Lost Revolutions: The South in the 1950s.* Chapel Hill: University of North Carolina Press, 2000.

Eckstein, Jr. Stephen D. *History of the Churches of Christ in Texas, 1824-1950.* Fort Worth: Star Bible Publications, 1992 [1963].

Ellis, William T. *"Billy" Sunday: The Man and His Message.* Philadelphia: Universal Book and Bible House, 1914.

Evans, Jack. *The Curing of Ham.* De Queen, Ark.: Harrywell Printers, 1976.

_____. "The History of Southwestern Christian College, Terrell, Texas." Masters thesis, University of Texas, El Paso, 1963.

First Annual Lectureship Booklet, 1976. n.d., n.p.

Fletcher, David W. ed., *Baptism and the Remission of Sins: A Historical Perspective.* Joplin, Mo.: College Press, 1992 [1990].

Foner, Eric. *Reconstruction: America's Unfinished Revolution.* New York: Harper & Row, 1988.

Foster, Douglas A., Paul M. Blowers, Anthony L. Dunnavant, and D. Newell Williams. *The Encyclopedia of the Stone-Campbell Movement.* Grand Rapids: Eerdmans, 2004.

Frederickson, George M. *The Black Image in the White Mind: The Debate on Afro-American Character and Destiny.* New York: Harper & Row, 1971.

Freeman, Mike. *Jim Brown: The Fierce Life of an American Hero.* New York: HarperCollins, 2006.

Gaines, Carl E., and John C. Whitley. *Black Preachers of Today: Churches of Christ.* n.p., 1974.

Garrett, Leroy. *The Stone-Campbell Movement: An Anecdotal History of Three Churches.* Joplin, Mo.: College Press, 1981.

Goree, Langston James. ed., *The Thomas Jewett Goree Letters: The Civil War Correspondence.* Bryan, Tex.: Family History Foundation, 1981.

Grose, Philip G. *South Carolina at the Brink: Robert McNair and the Politics of Civil Rights.* Columbia: University of South Carolina, 2006.

"A Half Century of Praise! A Historical Sketch of the North Tenneha Church of Christ, 1935-1985." n.p., n.d.

Hall, Colby D. *Texas Disciples: A Story of the Rise and Progress of That Protestant Movement Known as Disciples of Christ or Christian Churches, As It Developed in Texas, Including, through the Nineteenth Century Decades, A Story of the Kindred Movement, the "Churches of Christ."* Fort Worth: Texas Christian University Press, 1953.

Halsey, Margaret. *Color Blind: A White Woman Looks at the Negro.* New York: Simon and Schuster, 1946.

Harlan, Louis. *Booker T. Washington: The Making of a Black Leader, 1856-1901.* New York: Oxford University Press, 1972.

Harrell, Jr. David Edwin. *Quest for a Christian America: The Disciples of Christ and American Society.* Tuscaloosa: University of Alabama Press, 2003 [1966].

_____. *The Social Sources of Division in the Disciples of Christ, 1865-1900.* Tuscaloosa: University of Alabama Press, 2003 [1973].

_____. White *Sects and Black Men in the Recent South.* Nashville: Vanderbilt University Press, 1971.

Haselden, Kyle. *The Racial Problem in Christian Perspective.* New York: Harper & Row, 1959.

Haynes, Robert V. *A Night of Violence: The Houston Riot of 1917.* Baton Rouge: Louisiana State University Press, 1976.

Hazel, Michael V. *Dallas: A History of "Big D."* Austin: Texas State Historical Association, 1997.

"Historical Sketch of the Fifth Ward Church of Christ." N.p., n.d.

A History of Madison County, Texas. Madisonville, Tex.: Madison County Historical Commission, n.d.

Hogan, R. N. *Sermons by Hogan.* Austin: Firm Foundation Publishing House, 1940.

Holloway, Gary, and Douglas A. Foster. *Renewing God's People: A Concise History of Churches of Christ.* Abilene, Tex.: Abilene Christian University Press, 2006 [2001].

Holloway, Gary, and John York. eds., *Unfinished Reconciliation: Justice, Racism, and Churches of Christ.* Abilene, Tex.: Abilene Christian University Press, 2003.

Hudson-Weems, Clenora. *Emmett Till: The Sacrificial Lamb of the Civil Rights Movement.* Troy, Mich.: Bedford Publishers, 1994.

Hughes, Richard T. *Reviving the Ancient Faith: The Story of Churches of Christ in America.* Abilene, Tex.: Abilene Christian University Press, 2008 [1996].

Hughes, Richard T., Howard Short, and Henry Webb. *The Power of the Press: Studies of the "Gospel Advocate," the "Christian Standard," and the "Christian Evangelist."* Nashville: Disciples of Christ Historical Society, 1987.

Humble, Bill. *Campbell and Controversy: The Story of Alexander Campbell's Five Great Debates with Skepticism, Catholicism, and Presbyterianism.* Joplin, Mo.: College Press, 1986.

Johnson, Wiley W. *History of the Antioch and Midway Church of Christ, Midway, Texas.* Wiley Johnson, 1959.

Kurfees, M. C. *Instrumental Music in the Worship or the Greek Verb Psallo, Philologically and Historically Examined together with a Full Discussion of Kindred Matters Relating to Music in Christian Worship.* Nashville: Gospel Advocate, 1922.

Litwack, Leon F. *Trouble in Mind: Black Southerners in the Age of Jim Crow.* New York: Vintage Books, 1998.

Logan, Rayford W. *The Negro in American Life and Thought: The Nadir, 1877-1901.* New York: Dial Press, 1954.

Lynn, Mac. *Churches of Christ in the United States: Inclusive of Her Commonwealth and Territories, 2006 Edition.* Nashville: 21st Century Christian, 2006.

Maclean, Nancy. *Behind the Mask of Chivalry: The Making of the Ku Klux Klan.* New York: Oxford University Press, 1994.

Major, James Brooks. "The Role of Periodicals in the Development of the Disciples of Christ, 1850-1910." Ph.D. dissertation, Vanderbilt University, 1966.

McPherson, Chalmers. *Disciples of Christ in Texas: A Partial History of Disciples of Christ in Texas during the Past Forty-One Years, Together with Personal Remembrances of Both the Living and the Dead, Addresses, Forms, Etc.* Cincinnati: Standard Publishing Company, 1920.

McQueen, Clyde. *Black Churches in Texas: A Guide to Historic Congregations.* College Station: Texas A & M University Press, 2000.

Moneyhon, Carl H. *Texas after the Civil War: The Struggle of Reconstruction.* College Station: Texas A & M University Press, 2004.

Painter, Nell Irvin. *Exodusters: Black Migration to Kansas after Reconstruction.* New York: Alfred A. Knopf, 1977.

Parks, E. Taylor., and Lois F. Parks. *Memorable Quotations of Franklin D. Roosevelt.* New York: Thomas Y. Crowell, 1965.

Phillips, C. Myer. "A Historical Study of the Attitude of the Churches of Christ toward Other Denominations." Ph. D. dissertation, Baylor University, 1983.

Pitts Jr., Carroll. "A Critical Study of Civil Rights Practices, Attitudes and Responsibilities in Churches of Christ." Masters Thesis, Pepperdine College, 1969.

Rawick, George P., ed. *The American Slave: A Composite Autobiography.* Volume 9. Westport, Conn.: Greenwood Press, 1979.

Rice, Jr. Ira Y. *Pressing toward the Mark: An Autobiography by Ira Y. Rice, Jr.* Dallas: G. T. Press, 1998.

Richardson, Robert. *The Memoirs of Alexander Campbell: Embracing a View of the Origin, Progress and Principles of the Reformation Which He Advocated.* Nashville: Gospel Advocate, 1956 [1868-1869].

Roach Sr., Anthony. "A Biblical Program for Building New Self-Love in African American Males and Females." Doctor of Ministry Thesis, Abilene Christian University, 1992.

Roach, Tony. "A Brief History of the Minda Street Congregation." *26th Anniversary Program* (October 29, 2006).

Roberts, Cokie. *Founding Mothers: The Women Who Raised Our Nation.* New York: Harper-Collins, 2004.

Robinson, Edward J. *Show Us How You Do It: Marshall Keeble and the Rise of Black Churches of Christ in the United States.* Tuscaloosa: University of Alabama Press, 2008.

_____. "'The Two Old Heroes': Samuel W. Womack, Alexander Campbell, and the Origins of Black Churches of Christ in the United States." *Discipliana* 65 (Spring 2005): 3-20.

_____. *To Save My Race from Abuse: The Life of Samuel Robert Cassius.* Tuscaloosa: University of Alabama Press, 2007.

Robinson, John L. *David Lipscomb: A Journalist in Texas, 1872.* Wichita Falls, Tex.: Nortex Offset Publications, 1973.

Rose, Sylvia. *Songs of Faith.* Detroit: Srose Publishing Company, 1985.

Sams, Roosevelt. *My Experience Relevant to My Work at Southwestern Christian College.* N.p., 1989.

Spain, Carl. "Modern Challenges to Christian Morals." In *Christian Faith in the Modern World: The Abilene Christian College Annual Bible Lectures, 1960.* Abilene, Tex.: Abilene Christian College, 1960.

Survey of Service: Organizations Represented in the International Convention of Disciples of Christ. St. Louis: Christian Board of Publication, 1928.

Taylor, Jr. Clifford H. "Jarvis Christian College: Its History and Present Standing in Relationship to the Standards of the Texas State Department of Education and the Southern Association of Colleges and Secondary Schools." Texas Christian University, Bachelor of Divinity Thesis, 1948.

Taylor, Quintard. *In Search of the Racial Frontier: African Americans in the American West, 1528-1990.* New York: W. W. Norton, 1998. *Thirty-Fifth Annual West Texas Lectureship Booklet.* n.p., n.d.

Tuggle, Annie C. *Another World Wonder.* Detroit: Annie C. Tuggle, 1945.

Ward, Andrew. *Dark Midnight When I Rise: The Story of the Jubilee Singers Who Introduced the World to the Music of Black America.* New York: Farrar, Straus and Giroux, 2000.

Washington, Booker T. *Up from Slavery*. New York: Oxford University Press, 1995 [1901].

West, Earl I. *The Search for the Ancient Order: A History of the Restoration Movement*.Volume 2. Indianapolis: Religious Book Service, 1950.

Wilson, Charles Reagan. *Baptized in Blood: The Religion of the Lost Cause*. Athens: University of Georgia Press, 1980.

Winston, J. S. "Work among the Colored People in the U.S." In Howard L. Schug and Jesse P. Sewell, eds., *The Harvest Field*. Athens, Ala.: Bible School Bookstore, 1947.

Interviews

"Interview with Cremmon Alexander" (June 25, 2005).

"Interview with Jack Evans" (October 25, 2007).

Internet Sources

www.jackevansonline.com

www.lightoftheworldchurchofchrist.org

www.mun.ca/rels/restmov/texts/race/haymes38.html

www.southcentralonline.org

INDEX

A

Abilene Christian College, 115, 130
Acox, Sarah J., 100
Adams, Abigail, 14, 182n9
Adams, John, 14, 182n9
Adams, W. A., 184n23
Aker, O. L., 54, 58, 59
Alexander, Cremmon, 80, 193n3
Alexander, Harold, 179
Alexander, L. H., 14, 79-83, 173, 178
Alexander, Matilda, 79
Anderson, Elmo W., 59, 60, 84, 94, 102, 110, 153, 178
Aquino, Frederick, 166, 179
Asante, Molefi Kete (Arthur L. Smith), 158, 179
Ashurst, James 24

B

Baccus, Carl C., 24
Baccus, Edna, 23, 24
Bailey, Declara Nixon, 23, 24, 25
Bailey, Jeffery, 21
Bailey, Mack Allen, 21, 184n23
Bailey, Oscar, 184n23
Baldwin, Jr. William H., 145
Barber, H. L., 159
Barr, Vernon L., 134, 161
Barton, Johnny, 179
Bass, W. G., 72
Before the Thicket, 162
Benford, David, 179
Berry, C. A., 141
Bethany College (West Virginia), 115
Beyond the Thicket, 162
Bilbo, Theodore G., 125
Bills, W. D., 58
Birt, Robert, 179
Bob Jones University, 165
Boles, H. Leo, 32
Bouye, Joseph, 179
Bowdre, Jr., Alvertice, 179
Bowdre, Sr., Alvertice, 48, 124
Bowdre, Darryl, 166, 179, 190n37
Bowman, Ryan, 179
Bowser Christian Institute (Fort Smith, Arkansas), 46, 111
Bowser, G. P., 9, 11, 13, 15, 37, 46, 89-103, 106, 110, 112, 113, 117, 119, 120, 121, 126, 127, 156, 164, 171, 173, 174, 177
Brabham, Lewis, 179
Brents, T. W., 106
Brigham, Lelia, 113
Brown, Jim, 201n20
Brown v. Board of Education, 125, 131, 202n34
Brown, Wesley, 179
Brutton, A. J., 58
Bullock, Maggie, 120
Burson, Jesse T., 55
Burt, T. P., 92
Burton, A. M., 52, 98, 117, 127
Busby, Horace W., 36
Busby, T. H., 107, 110, 117
Butler, Annie Mae, 42
Butler, James M., 101, 102, 129
Butler, O. B., 41
Butler, Rose Lee, 80
Butler University, 151
Bynum, D. J., 117

C

Campbell, Alexander (black preacher), 90, 91, 102
Campbell, Alexander (white leader), 11, 19, 96, 98, 115, 117, 165, 181n2
Campbell, Edna, 80
Campbell, Thomas, 181n2
Campbell, W. C., 80
Campbell, W. D., 35, 36
Cannon, C. A., 131
Carnagie, Andrew, 52
Carson, Anthony, 21
Carson, F. F., 21, 22, 23, 25, 102, 153
Carter, Dorothy, 46
Carter, James, 179
Caruthers, Courtney, 179
Caruthers, Jr., Jefferson R., 165, 179
Caruthers, Sr., Jefferson R., 81, 82
Carver, George Washington, 143, 144, 145, 163
Cash, Annette, 109, 110
Casiano, Luis, 179
Cason, Billy, 179
Cassius, Amos Lincoln, 93, 178
Cassius, Samuel Robert, 33-36, 37, 39, 41, 51, 93, 102, 203n2
Cathey, Nathan, 119
Cebrun, Samuel L., 55, 188n12
Childress, William M., 22
Christman, A. C., 124
Christian Counselor, 12, 82, 110
Christian Courier, 138, 143, 144, 145, 148, 149
Christian Echo, 12, 13, 14, 15, 47, 48, 82, 89, 91, 94, 98, 99, 101, 103, 106, 110, 114, 115, 118, 124
Christian Soldier, 127
Christian Standard, 97, 98
Clark, J. L., 143
Clay, John Henry, 74
Cloys, Cecil, 179
Cofield, J. F., 80
Colley, R. L., 55, 56, 93
Collins, E. G., 79
Combe, Frederick J., 28
Cook, Ronnie, 179
Cooper, I. Q., 24, 25
Cottingham, Jr. Norvie, 179
Cottingham, Sr. Norvie, 179
Cox, Frank L., 36
Crayton, C. E., 41
Cross, Allen D., 179
Curl, Billy, 166, 179

D

Daniels, Timothy, 179
David Lipscomb University (Tennessee), 115, 130
Davis, Abraham, 101
Davis, J. C., 207n18
Davis, Samuel, 90
Davis, William M., 91, 92
Davis, Willie, 179
Dean, Wayburn, 170, 171
Dedrick, Issac, 124, 179
Derrick, A. E., 55
Derrick, Eugene, 178
Diggs, Lewis, 80
Dillingham, Mack, 179
Dorris, C. E. W., 126
Doss, Eric, 179
Dorsey, Henry, 143
Draper, Ralph H., 165, 179
Drummer, Harvey, 179
Dulin, Reginald, 179, 207n18
Dulin, Rodney, 179
Duncan, W. Ray, 76

E

Ebony News Journal, 166
Eckstein, Stephen D., 32
Edmerson, John, 179
Eisenhower, Dwight D., 126
Elam, E. A., 31
English, D. M., 102
English, Paul, 178

Enochs, S. A., 35
Errett, Isaac, 97
Ervin, J. N., 137, 141-153
Essien, Ansen A., 158
Evans, Herb, 207n18
Evans, Jr., Jack, 161, 179, 207n18
Evans, Sr., Jack, 128, 134, 155, 156, 159-165, 171, 174, 179, 206n3
Evans, Jacque, 179
Evans, Michael, 179
Evans, Patricia, 160, 161
Every, Fred, 179

F

Fanning, Tolbert, 30
Farmer, Gus, 207n18
Feimster, Michael J., 179
Ferrell, Carrie C., 84
Finley, Cedric, 179
Firm Foundation, 12, 15, 25, 52, 91,
Fisher, Lester David, 179
Fitzgerald, Thomas, 179
Foster, Ben, 179, 207n18
Freed-Hardeman University (Tennessee), 130
Frost, Thomas B., 141
Fryer, Lucy, 28
Fulson, Arthur, 124, 179

G

Gaines, Carl E., 179
Gainey, Barry, 179
Gamble, Dennis, 179
Garnier, Kenneth, 179
Garrison, Jerome, 179
Gaston, Bernard B., 179
Gatlin, Delbert M., 60
Gibbs, Joe, 179
Gibbs I, S. T. W., 177
Gibbs II, S. T. W., 84
Gibbs III, S. T. W., 48, 166, 179, 188n41
Gibbs IV, S. T. W., 179
Gillepsie, J. W., 25
Goodloe, J. E., 30
Goree, Langston James, 20
Goree, Sarah Margaret, 20
Gospel Advocate, 12, 15, 25, 30, 32, 33, 35, 36, 52, 54, 82, 85, 89, 91, 92, 132
Graves, Finos, 24
Graves, W. C., 92
Gray, H. H., 44, 46, 110, 113
Greene, Charles, 179
Greene, Kenneth, 167, 168, 171, 174, 175, 176, 179
Griffin, Ardelia, 109, 110
Grimsley, Columbus, 57, 157, 190n37

H

Hairston, Andrew, 124, 179
Haley, Alex, 118
Hamilton, Harry, 25
Hamilton, Jamal, 165, 179
Hamilton, John, 179
Hann, Arthur, 41
Harding, Warren G., 144
Harper, Eddie, 179
Harper, Robert, 179
Harris, Ivan, 179
Harris, James D., 179
Harris, R. C., 91, 92
Hayes, Hugh L., 20, 21, 177
Hayes, Lovell, 165, 179
Hayes, Patrick H., 20, 21
Haygood, Fate, 166, 179
Herndon, Cecil B., 179, 190n37
Herring, Dennie, 41
Hill, A. V., 192n24
Hill, Willie Ray, 179
Hogan's Helper, 121
Hogan, Emma, 120
Hogan, R. N., 11, 13, 14, 44, 45, 48, 55, 93, 101, 103, 106, 107, 113, 119-134, 161, 173, 177, 207n18
Hogan, Willie, 120
Holmes, J. B., 146

Holt, G. P., 127, 207n18
Holt, Marion V., 124, 125, 179
Holt, Thelma, 207n18
Holton, Verda, 107
Houston, Archester, 179
Houston, Katherin, 46
Howie, Douglass, 179
Howland, John A., 32
Hubbard, Paul, 190n37
Hunter, Rick, 165, 179, 207n18

I

Ibokete, Isong, 23
Isbell, A. V., 157, 159

J

Jackson, John, 124
Jackson, John E., 179
Jackson, Shermond, 41
James, Jr. Ivory, 179
Jarvis Christian College (Hawkins, Texas), 13, 22, 25, 98, 102, 137-153
Jarvis, Ida Van Zandt, 137-141, 144, 145
Jarvis, J. J., 137-141
Johnson, Benjamin F., 184n23
Johnson, David, 184n23
Johnson, George, 179
Johnson, J. M., 184n23
Johnson, L. M., 48
Johnson, Lovette, 46
Johnson, Rufus, 190n37
Johnson, S. C., 76, 77
Johnson, Sutton, 54
Johnson, Thomas H., 179
Johnson, Wesley, 184n23
Johnson, Wiley, 184n23
Johnson, Winter I., 124, 180
Jones, Grady T., 180
Jones, Jr. James, 180
Jones, Mack, 41
Jones, Robert C., 84
Jones, Warrick, 125, 180

K

Keeble, Marshall, 9, 11, 13, 14, 29, 42, 43, 48, 51-65, 67, 68, 69, 77, 80, 83, 84, 86, 92, 93, 101, 102, 107, 110, 117, 126, 134, 156, 161, 164, 171, 173, 174, 177
Kennedy, Levi, 107, 110, 113
King, Dennis, 180
King, Martin Luther, 164
Kipling, Rudyard, 203n12
Kirkpatrick, Foy Lee, 113
Kreigler, Willie, 180
Ku Klux Klan, 25, 28, 29, 149, 150
Kurfees, M. C., 32

L

Lambert, O. C., 57
Lane, David, 180
Lanham, Lewis, 180
Larimore, T. B., 31, 32
Lauderdale, James, 180
Lavera, Hattie, 112
Lawton, Eugene, 155, 180, 207n18
Leak, D. A., 150
Lee, Christopher, 180
Lee, Gerald, 166, 180, 207n18
Lee, Horace, 180, 184n23
Lee, Jessie, 184n23
Lee, Robert, 184n23
Lee, Robert E., 20
Lehman, John B., 138, 139, 141
Lemon, Ernest, 180
Lewis, Jack P., 188n12
Lewis, Vanderbilt, 156
Lippord, W. C., 113
Lipscomb, A. B., 32
Lipscomb, David, 30, 31, 52, 89, 115, 132, 182n7
Livingston, F. A., 14, 61, 79, 83-86, 173
Locke, C. C., 42, 43, 44, 48, 187n20
Lockett, E. S., 45

Lodge, Gary, 180
Lovell, James L., 93, 120, 121, 133, 134
Lowery, J. P., 90
Lowery, Peter, 98
Lynch, Tom, 21

M

Maccalla, John, 208n49
Macon, Jerry, 180
Manning, Karie, 184n23
Martin, Charles, 180
Martin, Jr. Peter, 180
Matthews, Bonnie, 124, 180
Maxwell, Apollos, 180
Maxwell, James O., 159, 160, 180, 207n18
McArthur, Noah, 180
McChristian, Zachary, 180
McClendon, Michael, 180
McCoy, Alvin, 180
McDuffey, Douglass, 180
McFarland, E. T., 138
McGarvey, John W., 96, 98
McGary, Austin 25
McGilbra, W. A., 184
McIntosh, Dollie Mae, 46
McIntyre, Imogene, 46, 112
McMillan, E. W., 159
McPherson, John, 52, 53
McQuiddy, J. C., 32
Melton, Vesta Rea, 12
Merchant, T. H., 36, 37, 39, 51, 117
Michael, John, 180
Miles, Mark, 180
Miles, Matthew, 180
Miles, Luke, 180
Millen, P. G., 68
Miller, Earthy, 109, 110
Miller, Luke, 9, 14, 42, 55, 56, 57, 58, 67-77, 79, 80, 86, 101, 102, 173, 177, 178, 192n24
Mills, Robert, 190n37
Mitchell, Christopher, 180
Mitchell, John, 32
Mitchell, O. Z., 100
Mitchell, Steve, 106
Montgomery, Lewis, 125, 180
Moody, Dan, 106
Moore, Alberta J., 42
Moore, Elbert, 48
Moore, Russell H., 42, 43, 45, 48, 110, 111, 190n37
Moore, William, 39
Morrison, Woodie, 124, 180
Muhammad, Iman Wallace D., 161
Murray, Lawrence, 166, 180
Muse, Clyde, 207n18
My Experience Relevant to My Work at Southwestern Christian College, 156

N

National Association for the Advancement of Colored People (NAACP), 91, 126
Nashville Christian Institute (NCI), 174
Nealy, George, 184n23
Nelson, R. N., 190n37
Nelson, W. H., 30
Nichols, W. S., 71
Nixon, Cornell, 184n23
Nixon, Edward, 23
Nixon, Kermit, 23
Nixon, Lawrence, 29
Nixon, Maceal, 184n23
Nixon, Stephen W., 180
Nixon, Walter, 23
Nixon, Waydell, 9, 24, 180
Norton, Ted, 63
Norwood, Willie, 24

O

Oliphant, W. L., 41
Our Ministers and Our Songleaders, 118
Owen, Robert, 208n49

P
Parker, Alexander Campbell, 150
Patterson, Robert, 125
Pendergrass, George, 169, 170, 180
Penrose, Charles, 27
Pepperdine University (California), 125
Phares, W. W., 143, 145, 146
Phillips, LaBerta D., 112
Pink, Sopha, 80
Pinkerton, L. L., 100
Pitts, Carroll, 124
Pointer, Sr. Russell, 180
Potts, Ruby Mae, 108
Purcell, John B., 208n49

R
Raleigh Morning Post, 145
Rambo, D. B., 117
Ramsey, John T., 11, 15, 25, 29-33, 37, 51
Rawlinson, Harold, 180
Rand, L. R., 44
Reynolds, O. C., 71
Rice, Ira Y., 127, 129, 130, 132
Rice, Nathaniel, 208n49
Richard, Bula, 22
Richards, J. H., 113
Richardson, Laura, 54
Richardson, Lee, 54
Rise Up: A Call to Leadership for African American Women, 170
Roach, Candyce, 115
Roach, Tony E., 115
Robin, George, 43, 178, 190n37
Robinson, Edward J., 180
Robinson, Jesse, 190n37
Rockefeller, John D., 52
Rogers, Nokomis, 180
Roosevelt, Franklin D., 96
Roosevelt, Theodore, 28
Roots, 118
Rose, Alonzo, 102
Rose, Floyd, 102, 180
Rose, Jimmy, 102, 180
Rose, Marshall Keeble, 102, 180
Rose, Richard, 102, 180
Rose, Sylvia, 102, 169, 170
Rosenwald, Julius, 52
Ross, Hobart, 41
Rouse, Thomas, K., 94-99

S
Sampson, Thomas, 180
Sams, Roosevelt, 132, 156-159
Sandles, Charles, 21
Scates, James, 180
Scott, Harvey, 59, 60
Scott, Walter, 181n2, 194n23
Seamster, Ervin, 9, 167, 168, 171, 180
Sells, Timothy, 180
Settles, Paul, 55, 110, 155, 161
Sewell, E. G., 31, 32
Shepherd, F. B., 73, 94
Shield, Jack, 42
Shivers, Allan, 126
Showalter, G. H. P., 35, 71
Simon, Joe C., 124, 180
Slayter, John G., 138
Smith, Arthur L. (Molefi Kete Asante), 157, 179
Smith, C. C., 140
Smith, Charles, 180
Smith, Daniel, 180
Smith, Herman, 180
Smith, Clide, 58
Smith, Eugene, 45
Smith, F. W., 32
Smith, Henry, 27
Smith, John T., 60
Smith, Lonnie, 73
Smith, Mabel M., 112
Smith, Vance, 151
Spain, Carl, 129, 132
Sparks, L. W., 93
Speer, Asa H., 54
Spiller, Charlie, 74

Southern Bible Institute (forerunner of SWCC in Fort Worth, Texas), 105, 111, 112, 113, 118
Southern Christian Institute (Edwards, Mississippi), 138, 151
Southwestern Christian Advocate, 82
Southwestern Christian College (SWCC), 9, 13, 105, 117, 124, 125, 131, 155-171, 173, 174
Srygley, F. B., 79
Stanley, Will, 28
Starks, Eva, 44, 45, 46, 47
Starks, J. H., 41
Steven, Hazel, 46
Steward, G. E., 107, 110, 113
Stewart, James, 180
Stokes, Anthony, 166, 180
Stone, Barton W., 14, 19, 181n2
Stuckey, Ryan, 180
Sunday, Billy, 95, 96

T

Tarpley, Reginald, 180
Taylor, Bob, 141
Taylor, Gerald, 180
Taylor, Jerry, 168, 170, 171, 174, 176, 180
Taylor, John, 180
Taylor, Richard, 80
Terry, Matthew, 180
Thomas, Alvin A., 81, 82, 178
Thomas, J. C., 180
Thomas, Sr. K. C. (father), 23, 37, 46, 48, 51, 178, 186n8
Thomas, Jr. K. C. (son), 46
Thomas, Martin, 180
Thomas, Orlander, 180
Thompson, Joel, 60, 190n37
Thompson, Mark, 180
Thompson, Otis, 184n23
Thompson, Philip, 180
Thompson, Stephen, 180
Thurman, A. F., 200n7
Thurmond, R. B., 47, 178
Till, Emmett, 126
Tillman, John 180
Tinsley, James, 125, 180
Tucker, Willie, 115, 180
Tuggle, Annie C., 118
Tune, M. T., 132
Tune, Tom, 23
Turner, Sonny, 180
Tyner, H. C., 178

U

Underwood, J. W., 150
Unfinished Reconciliation: Justice, Racism, and Churches of Christ, 174, 175
Up from Slavery, 52

W

Waldrum, J. R., 84
Walker, John, 208n49
Walker, P. E., 178
Wallace, Jr. Foy E., 127
Walls, Benny, 180
Wanamaker, John, 76
Ward, Henry, 165
Warrick, Jessie, 22
Washington, Booker T., 52, 108, 137, 138, 143, 145, 153, 163
Washington, Carrie, 44
Washington, Grover C., 112, 113, 156, 187n37
Washington, Jessie, 28, 58
Washington, Jimmy Lacy, 184n23
Washington, Lacy Lee, 184n23
Watson, R. L., 117
Weathers, Walter, 12, 178
Webb, Isaac, 125
Webb, Varner, 180
Webster, Ezekiel Z., 109
Welch, Marcus, 180
Wells, R. C., 180, 207n18
Wesley, Darryl, 180
Wesley, Herman, 180
What Did the Apostles Bind?, 82

Wheaton, Addie, 21
Whitaker, Louise, 76
White, Gary, 180
White, George, 180
White Citizens' Council, 125
Whitley, John C., 180
Willeford, James, 132
Williams, Soul, 20
Williams, W. M., 138, 144, 146, 148, 149, 150
Wilson, David, 180
Wilson, Woodrow (black preacher), 124, 153, 180
Winnrow, Dwayne, 180
Winston, J. S., 11, 14, 23, 103, 105-118, 129, 173, 177, 186n8
Winston, Mizetta, 23, 106
Winston, Roy, 46
Womack, M. F., 89
Womack, Samuel W., 52, 90, 91, 102, 117
Wright, L. M., 42, 43, 108
Wright, Mac, 47
Wright, Ron, 180
Wyrick, Narleski, 180

Y

York, T. H., 54, 117
Young, John G., 113
Young, Jonathan, 180
Young, Paul, 180, 190n37